The College History Series

ALCORN STATE UNIVERSITY

AND THE NATIONAL ALUMNI ASSOCIATION

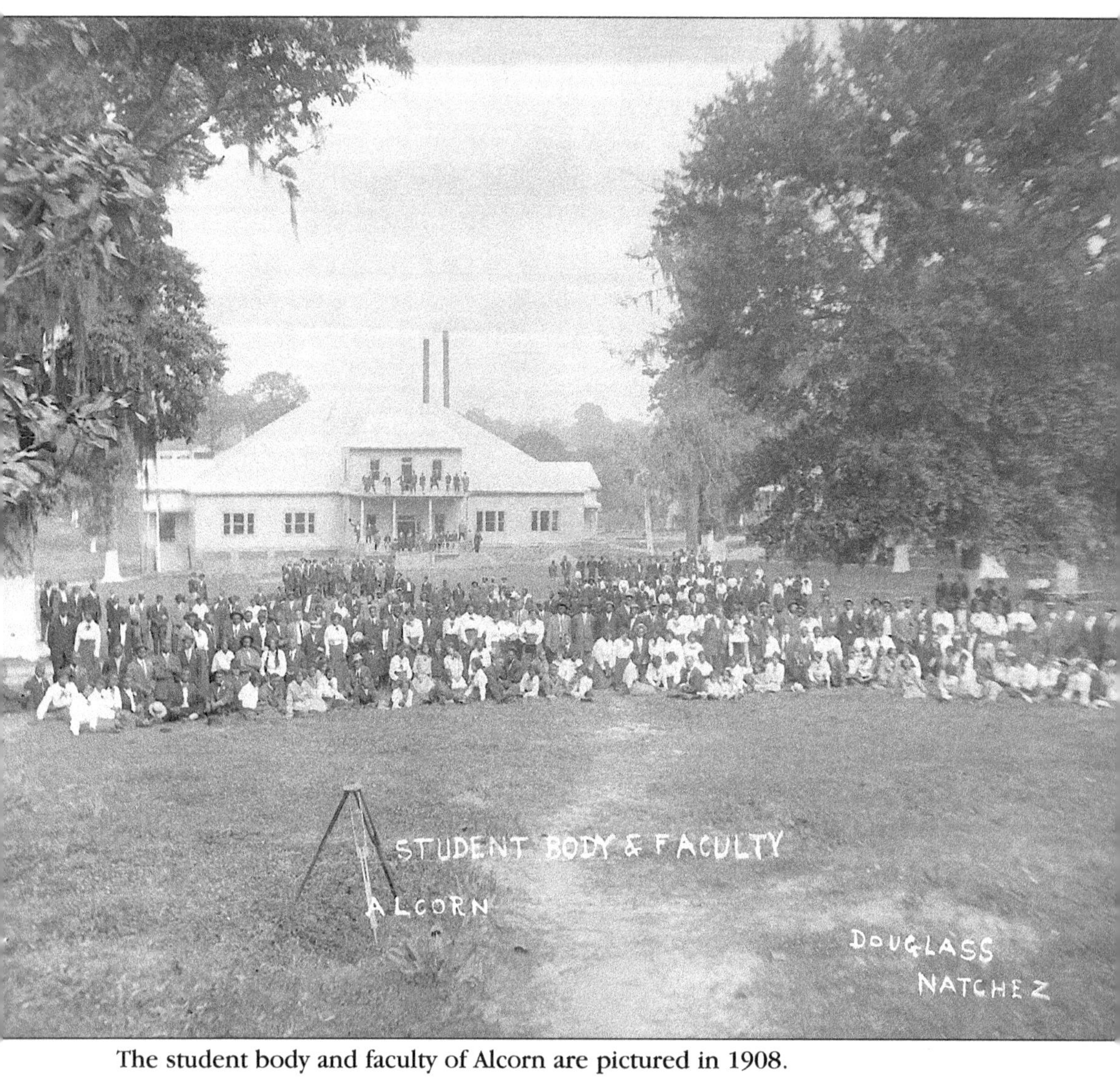

The student body and faculty of Alcorn are pictured in 1908.

The College History Series

ALCORN STATE UNIVERSITY

AND THE NATIONAL ALUMNI ASSOCIATION

JOSEPHINE MCCANN POSEY

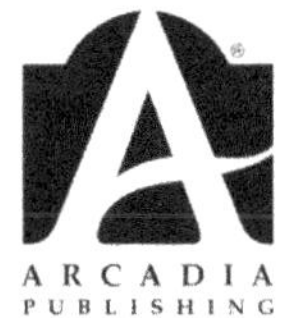

ISBN 978-0-7385-0591-6

Published by Arcadia Publishing
Charleston, South Carolina

Library of Congress Control Number: 00-104313

For all general information, please contact Arcadia Publishing:
Telephone 843-853-2070
Fax 843-853-0044
E-Mail sales@arcadiapublishing.com
For customer service and orders:
Toll-Free 1-888-313-2665

Visit us on the Internet at www.arcadiapublishing.com

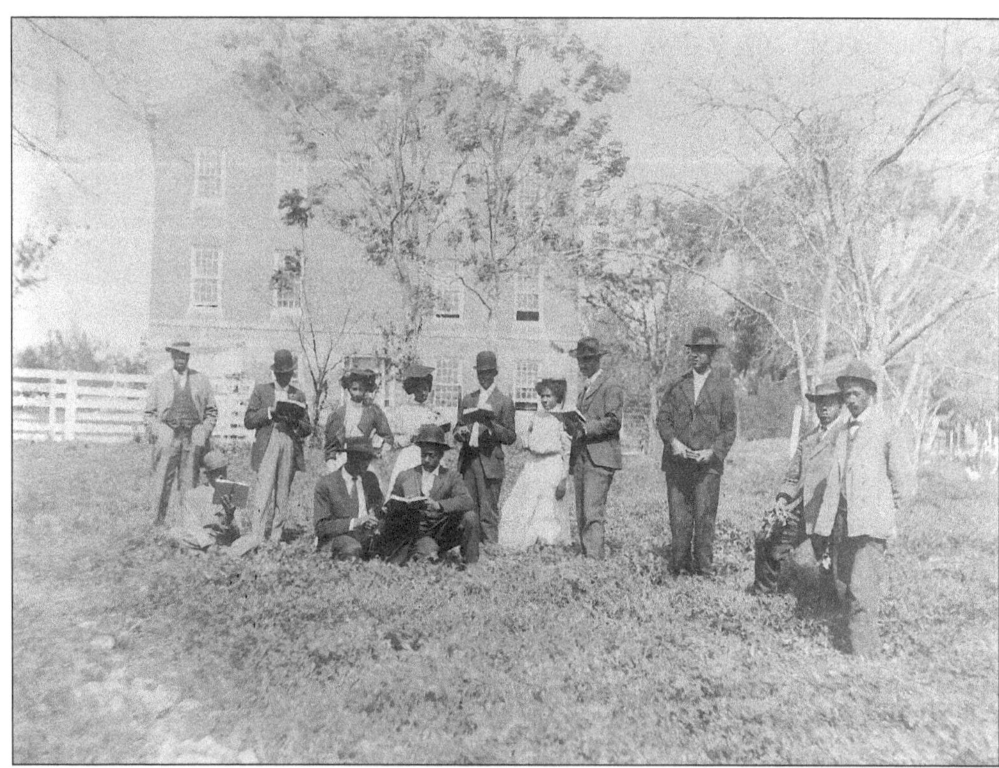

An Alcorn horticulture class is pictured in 1897.

Contents

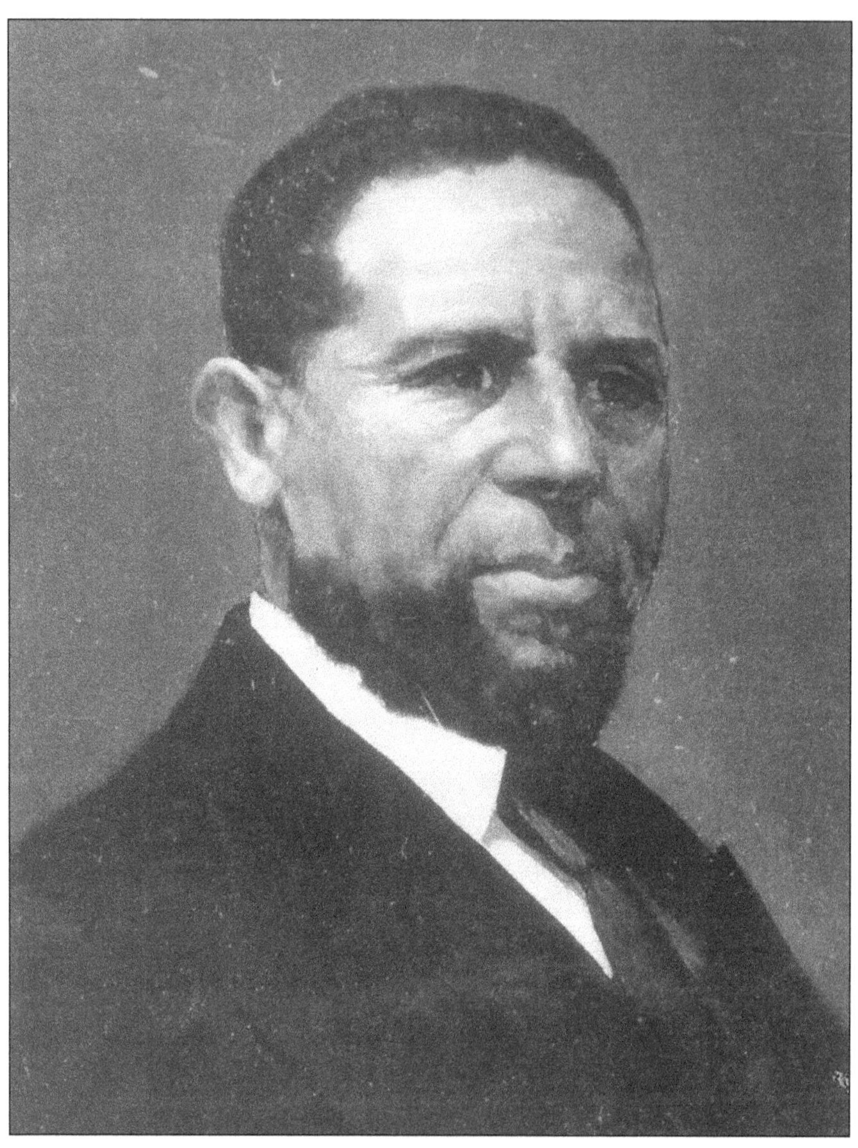

This volume of the College History Series is dedicated to the memory of Senator Hiram R. Revels, the first president of Alcorn, who served from 1871 to 1882. A native of North Carolina and a descendant of free blacks, Revels resigned his seat as the first black United States senator to become president of Alcorn. He was an ordained Methodist minister and once served as pastor of Zion AME Church on Pine Street in Natchez, Mississippi.

Alcorn State University National Alumni Association

1615 Rich Avenue • Gulfport, Mississippi 39501
Dr. Robert W. Bowles, President
(228) 864-3960

Dear Alcornites

Today, I am proud to be an Alcornite and Alcornites have a lot to be proud of. For more than 128 years, Alcorn State University has been a bright light in a dark world, standing watch along the borders of darkness and ignorance, helping young Black men and women conquer those weaknesses of mind and character that so often beset our youth.

For more than 128 years, Alcorn State University has been a symbol of hope, taking the torch of knowledge and lighting little candles of hope in the hearts and minds of our boys and girls.

For more than 128 years, Alcorn State University has empowered young people and old people alike, by giving them something on the inside that no MAN could affect from the outside.

For more than 128 years, Alcorn State University has instilled in its graduates that if we fall, we will work all the harder to get up and get on. If things look bleak, we will not despair but find the inner courage to try all the more. If we find ourselves on the bottom, we will know that the only way we can go is upward, and we will scramble and climb all the harder. If another Alcornite sister or brother should fall, we will be the first to offer a hand to help them up. And, when Alcorn has a financial need, we, not the legislature, not the College Board, will be the first to pick up our checkbook. This is what makes us great. This is what defines us as Alcornites. This is what being an Alcornite and being "family" these past 128 years is all about.

We invite you to relive those glorious 128 years in the pages of this publication as it chronicles, in pictures, the historical development of Alcorn and the National Alumni Association. I am sure that this volume will become a valuable keepsake and a ready reference as it provides a nostoglic link to our rich past and a reminder of our stellar tradition. To that end, you have my very best wishes.

Sincerely,

Robert W. Bowles, Ph.D.
13th President

There's No S__CCESS Without "U"

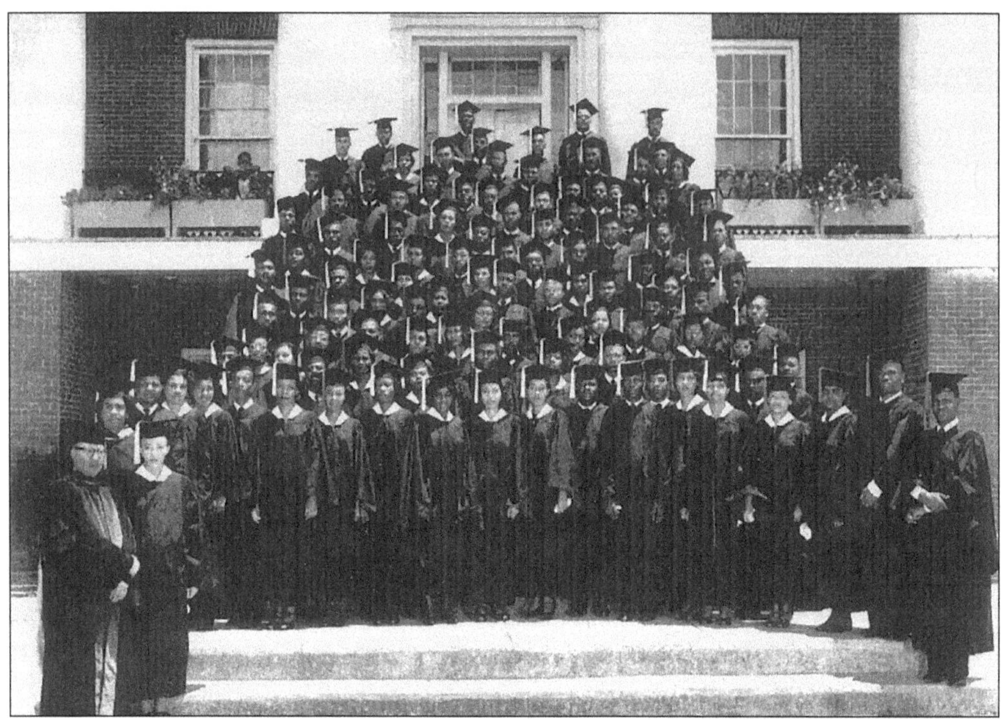

Shown here is the graduating class of 1950.

ACKNOWLEDGMENTS

I am delighted to acknowledge the hard work and cooperative spirit demonstrated by Ms. Artie Smith, Ms. Doreacer Turner, and Dr. Otha Sullivan after regular work hours in assisting with the typing of captions and the formatting of images included in this pictorial history. I am grateful to alumni members who responded to the many requests for pictures to include in this book, as well as those individuals who helped me identify some of the pictures in order to ensure proper descriptions. I would especially like to express my appreciation to the alumni who answered the spur-of-the-moment request for pictures of alumni who fell in love, graduated from Alcorn, and got married—this resulted in a very special section in the book. I would like to acknowledge my husband, Curtis, for his support during the many nights that I stayed away from home to work on this project, and my son Carlos, a 1999 graduate of Alcorn, who expressed his interest and support. I apologize to Cartez and Courtland, my grandsons, for not getting to see them very much during this period of time! A final word of thanks goes to Dr. Robert W. Bowles, for his tireless efforts as president of the National Alumni Association and for writing the introduction to this pictorial history. Dr. Bowles has made limitless contributions to Alcorn and the National Alumni Association. And last but not least, congratulations to the members of the graduating class of 1950 who were part of the first "Golden Class" to graduate during the new millennium.

One

Campus Structures

Alcorn has always been known for its picturesque campus. This chapter features some of the older buildings on the campus as well as those used in present-day operations. Residential housing is also depicted and shows where faculty and staff lived during Alcorn's early years.

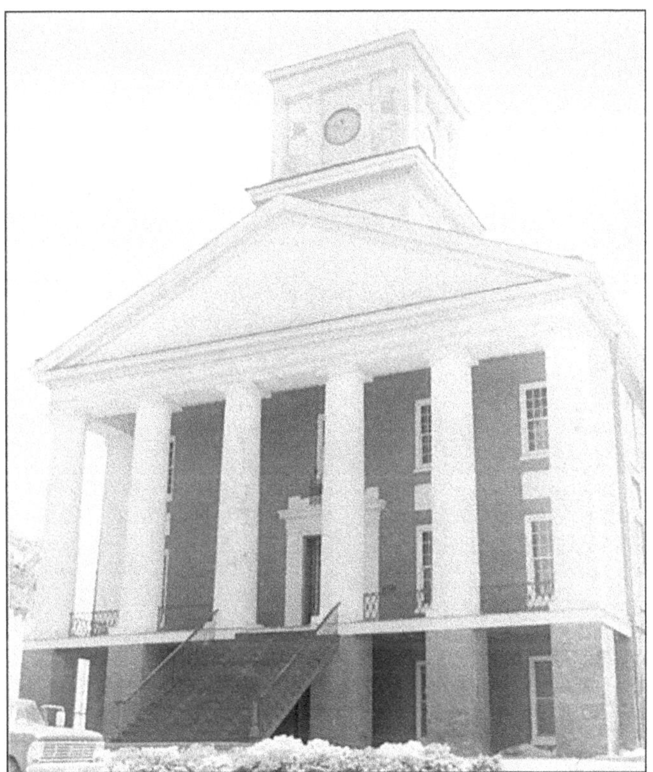

Constructed in 1830, Oakland Memorial Chapel is the oldest building on Alcorn's campus. The first college degree issued by a Mississippi institution was conferred inside this famed landmark.

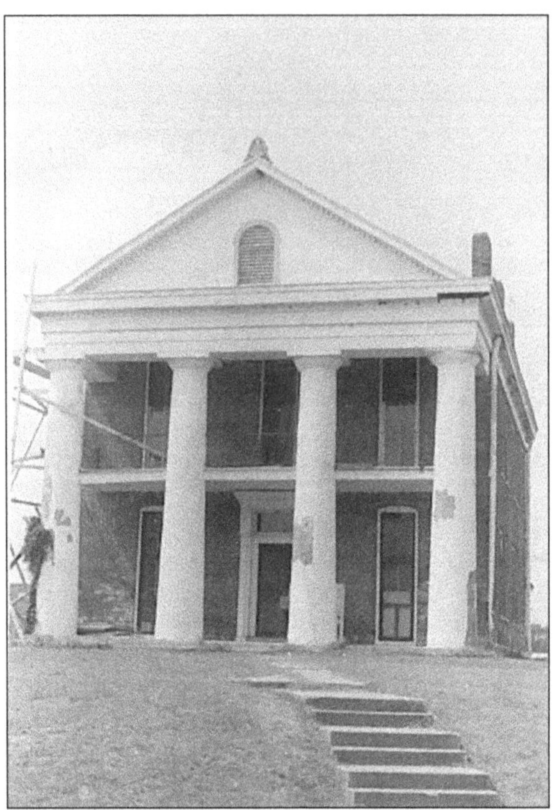

Belle Lettres Hall is a historical landmark and was constructed in 1830. It was later converted to a dormitory for female teachers. Belle Lettres Hall covers 3,861 square feet and cost $15,750 to build. It is presently being renovated.

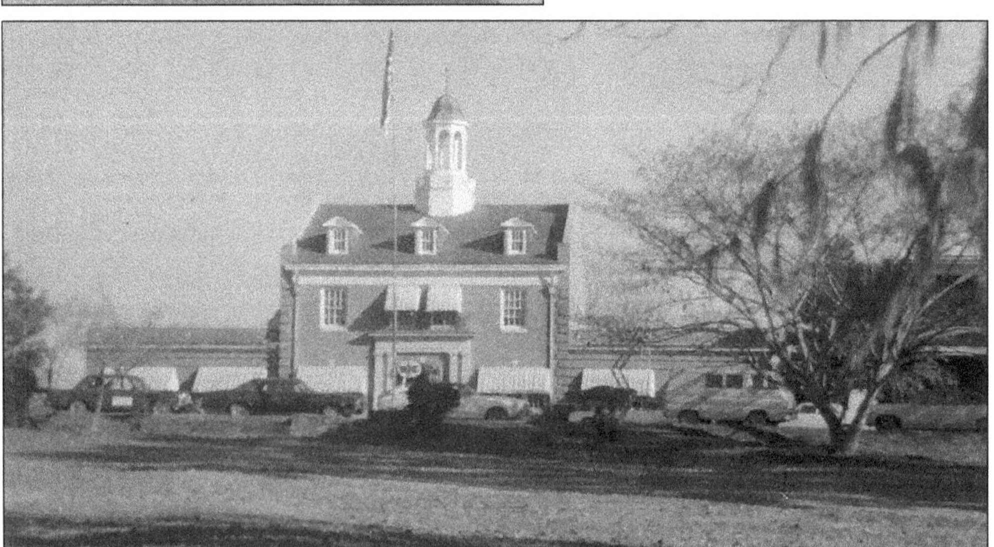

This old administration building housed administrative affairs during the early years at Alcorn, before being replaced by a new facility. The new building was constructed in 1977, at a cost of $3.5 million, and houses administrative offices, faculty and staff offices, classrooms, and other major components of operations at the university. The facility covers 80,001 square feet and is named for President Walter Washington, the 15th president of Alcorn and the longest serving—he was president for 25 years until his retirement in 1994.

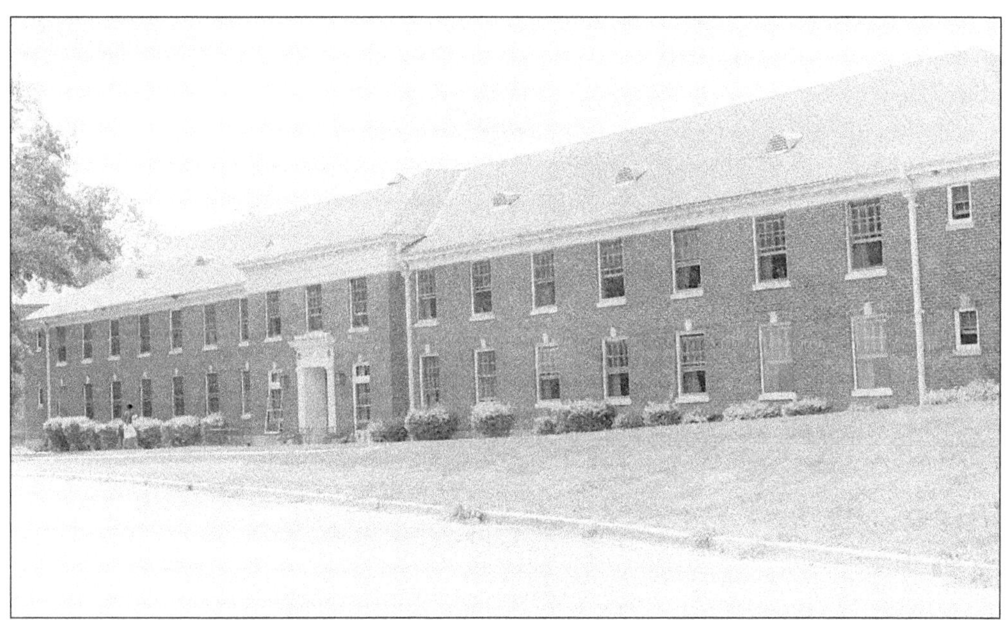

Pictured here is Lanier Hall, a dormitory for female students.

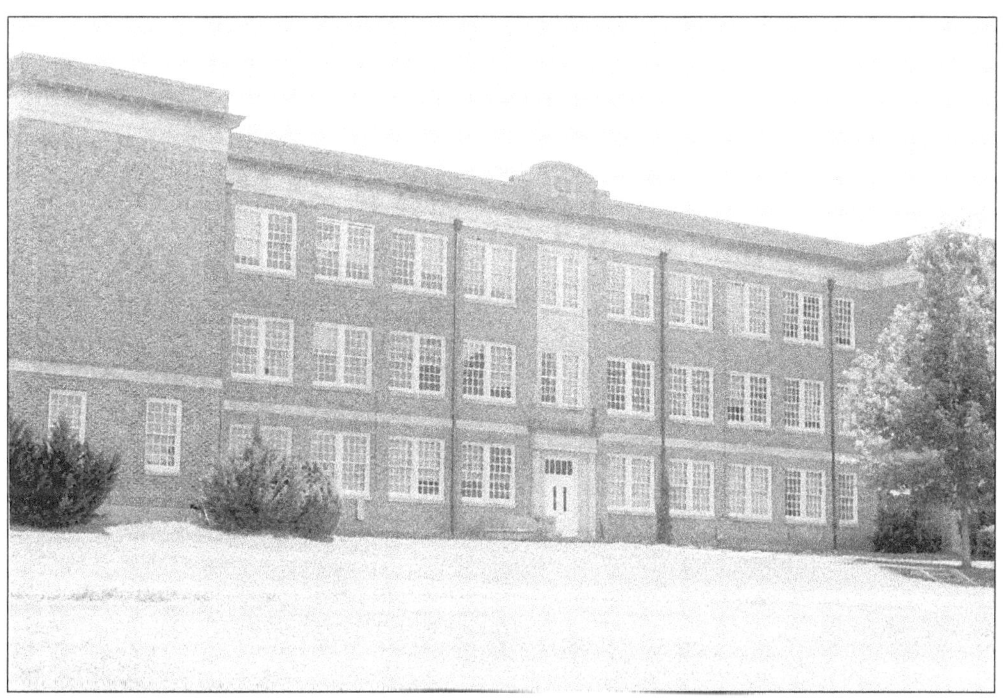

Bowles Hall housed classrooms, laboratories, and offices for academic purposes.

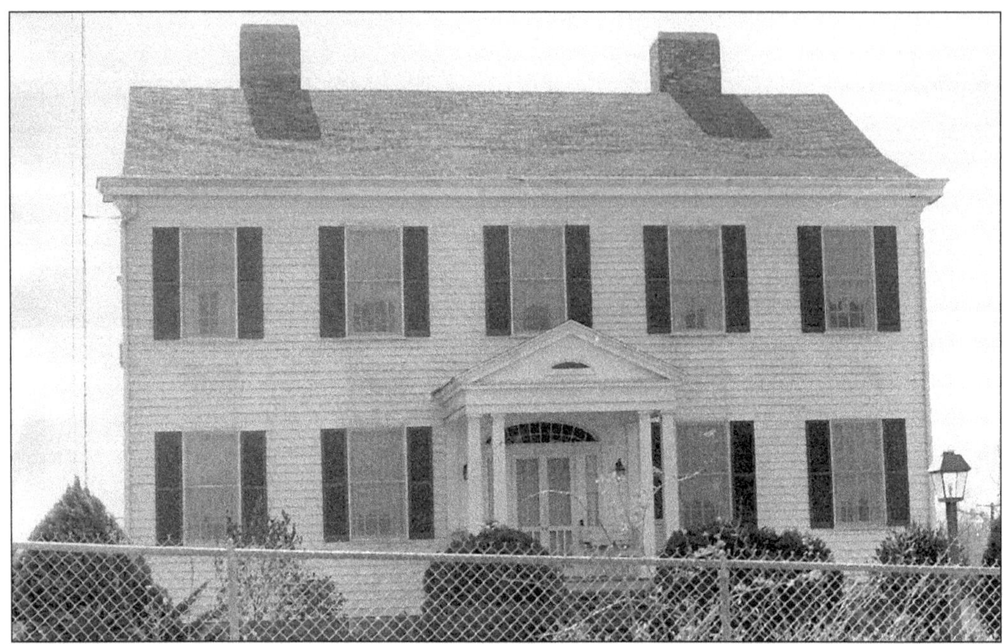

A historical landmark, the president's colonial-style home was constructed in 1830 at a cost of $6,500. It encompasses 6,975 square feet and was restored and redecorated to it original style in 1959.

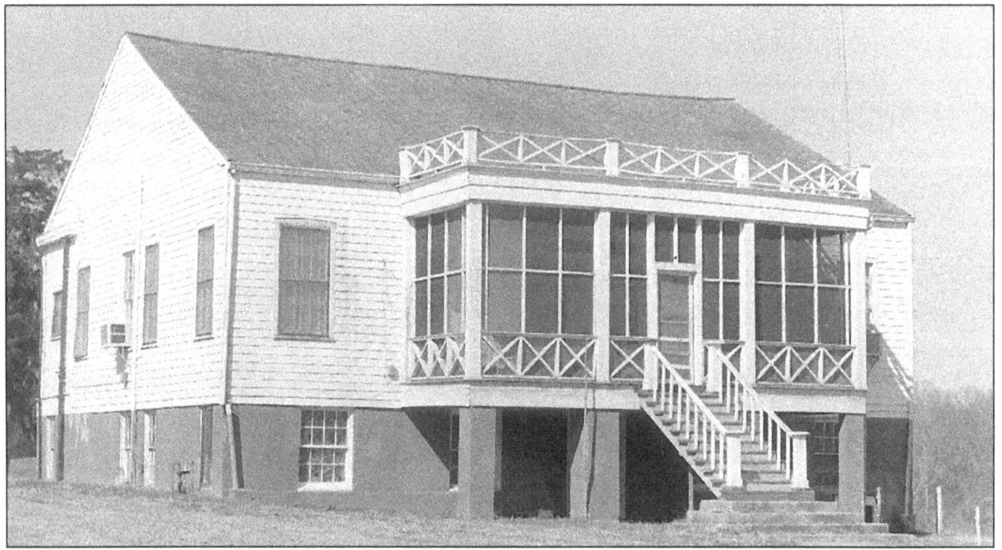

Rowan Model Home was named after President Levi J. Rowan, who served as Alcorn's president from 1905 to 1911 and from 1915 to 1934. His appointment marked the first time an Alcorn alumnus was named to the presidency. Mississippi Hall, a male dormitory, was built during Rowan's first term, and each year of his presidency, Rowan made sure that some type of campus improvement took place. He supervised the construction of buildings such as Academic Hall, a steam laundry, a dining hall, and a trades building for the mechanical arts. Rowan put Alcorn in communication with the outside world through the installation of a telephone line to Port Gibson, Mississippi, one of the towns closest to campus.

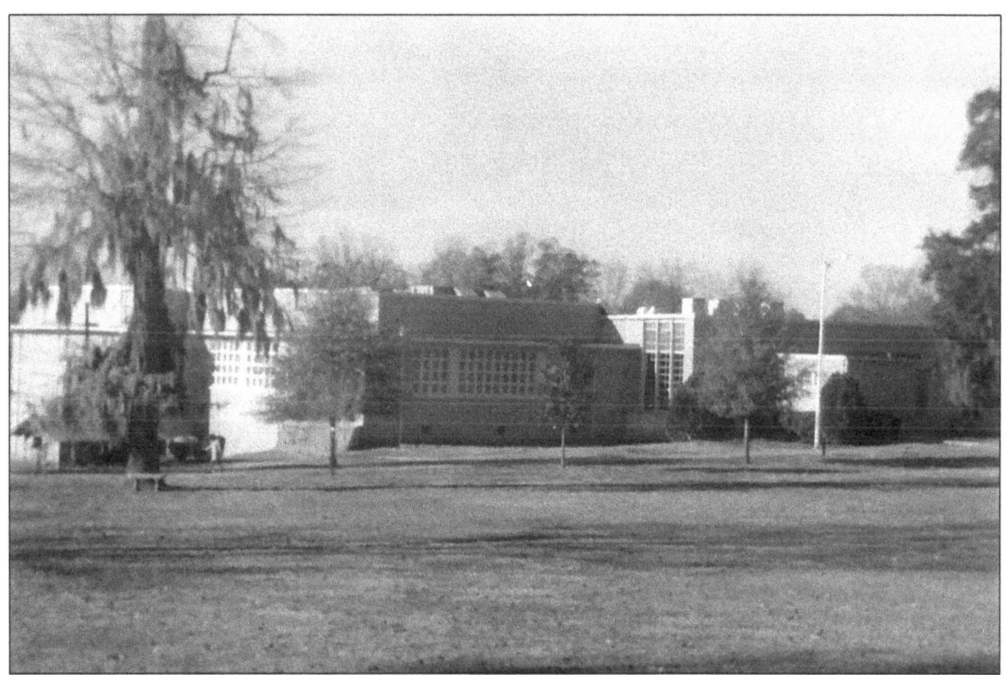

The dining hall was constructed in 1951 and was named in honor of William H. Bell, the president of Alcorn from 1934 to 1944. It was renovated in 1967 and in 1976.

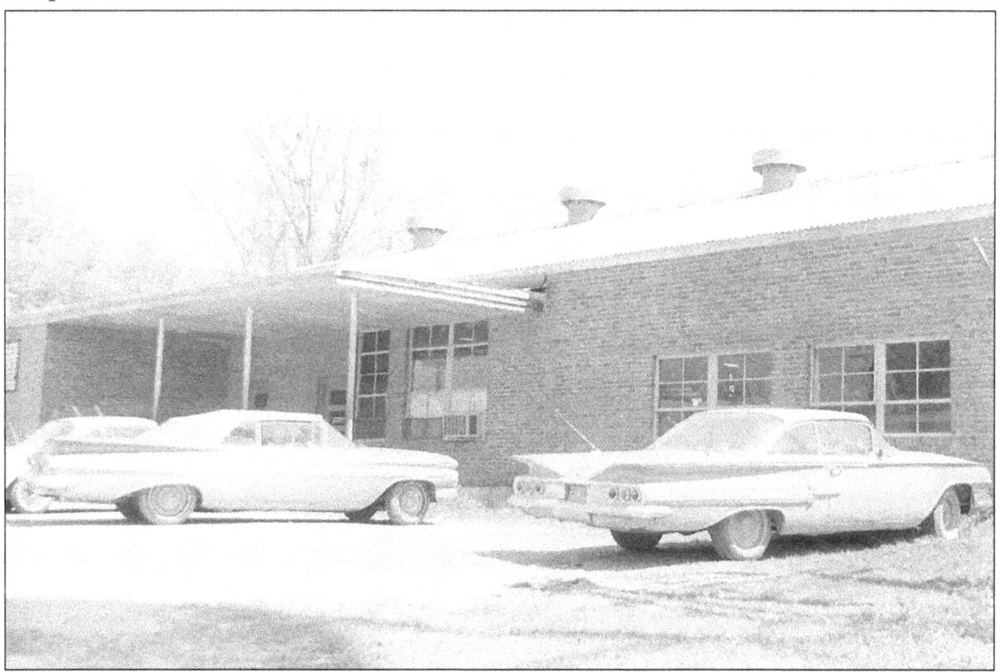

The college laundry was erected in 1951, during the presidency of J.R. Otis, and serves faculty and staff as well as the student body. The architect of the building was Jones and Haas, the general contractor was H.V. Button, the electrical contractor was J.E. Hale Jr., and the mechanical contractor was Prather and Seal Plumbing and Heating Company. The building, which covered 6,500 square feet, cost $50,440.10 to erect.

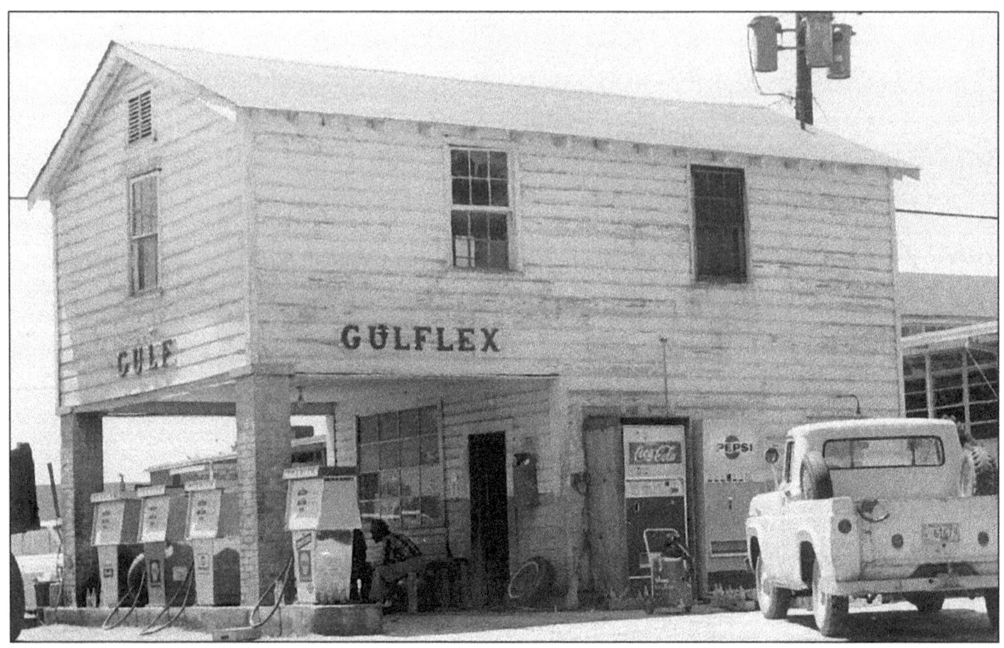

This service station, which serves as a gas station and convenience store and provides services to vehicles on campus and in the general community, fulfills the needs of employees, students, and visitors to the campus. The structure is 981 square feet and cost $7,000 to construct in 1947.

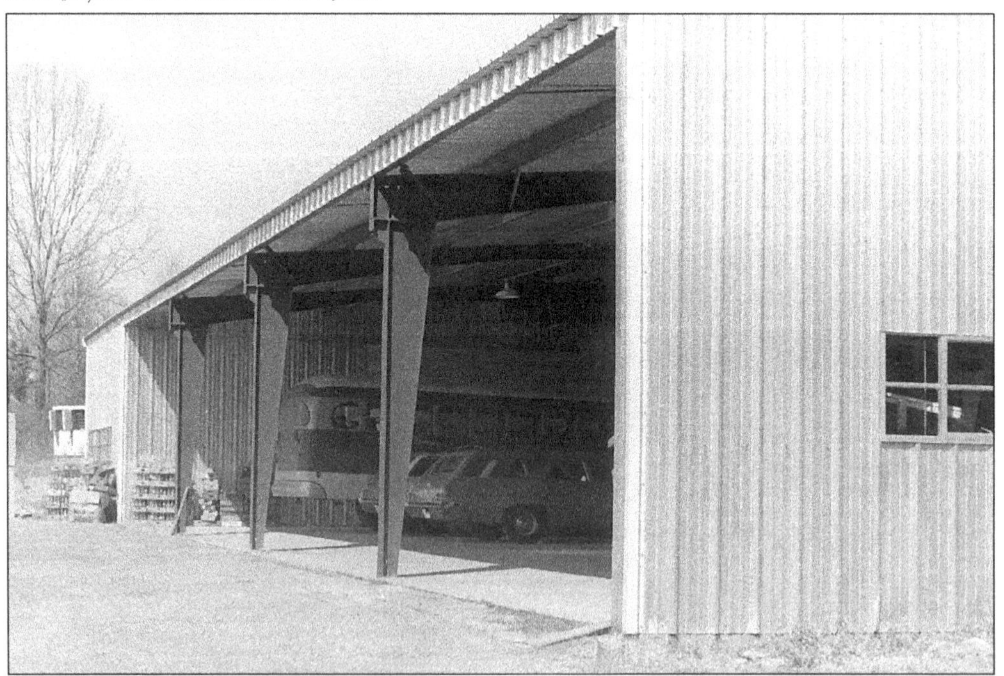

This storage facility, built in 1967 and covering 6,444 square feet, was used to house school-owned vehicles. The architect on the project was Mississippi Pre-Engineered Building Company and the general, mechanical, and electrical contractor was Alcorn College Maintenance Department.

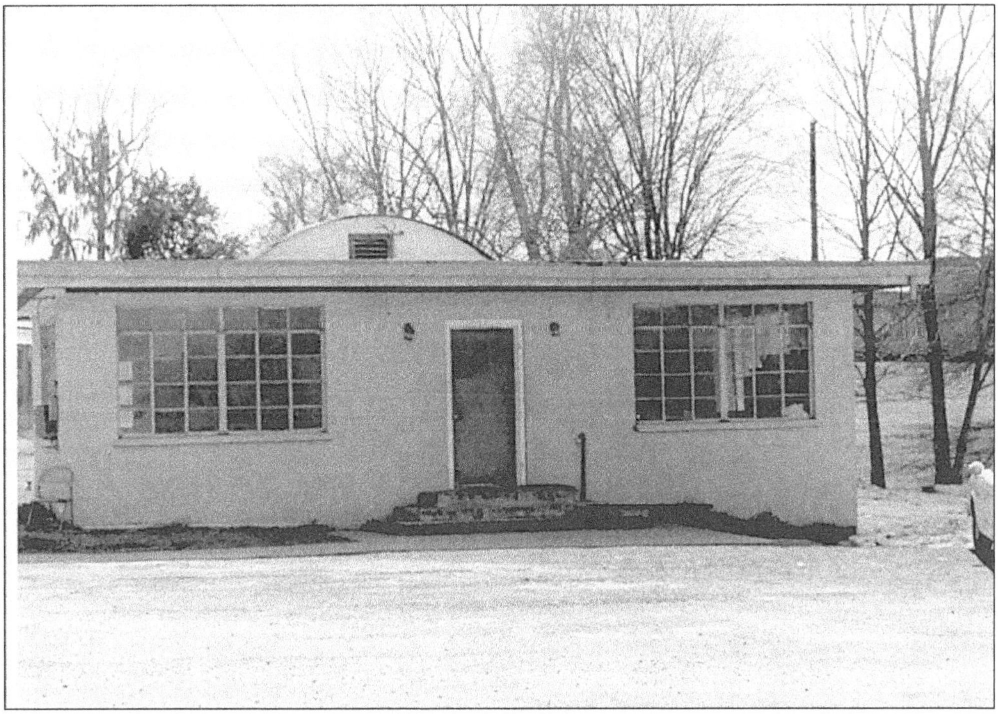

This image shows the buildings and grounds structure, which housed offices and other necessities for successfully administering a safe and comfortable college environment.

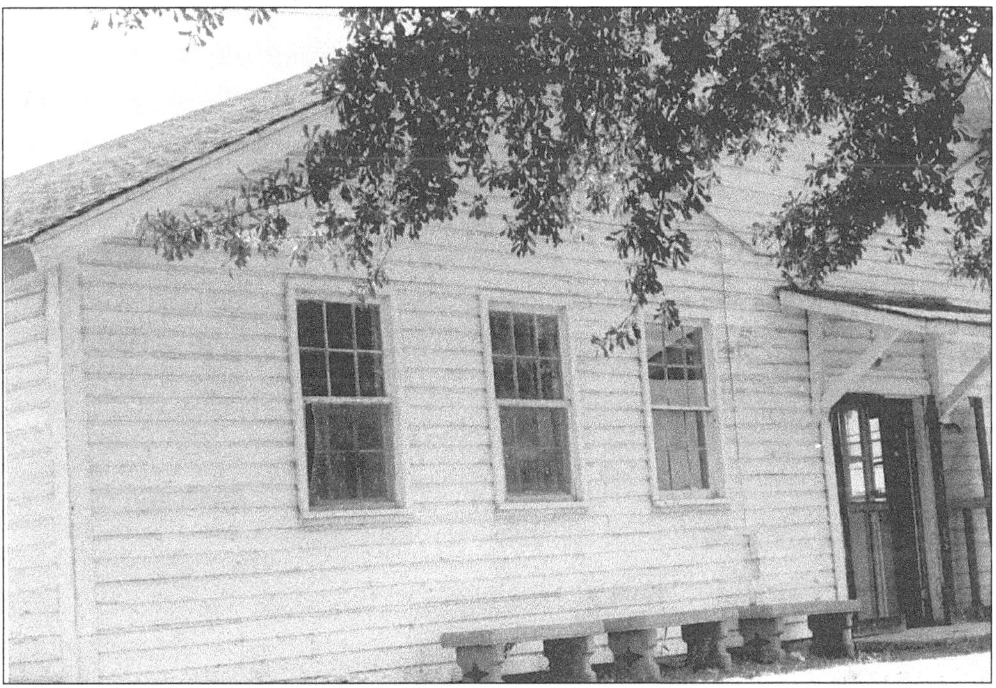

The Engineering Building, or farm shop, was a storage facility for various pieces of farm equipment, parts, and lubricants. The structure was also used for maintaining and repairing tillers and other equipment.

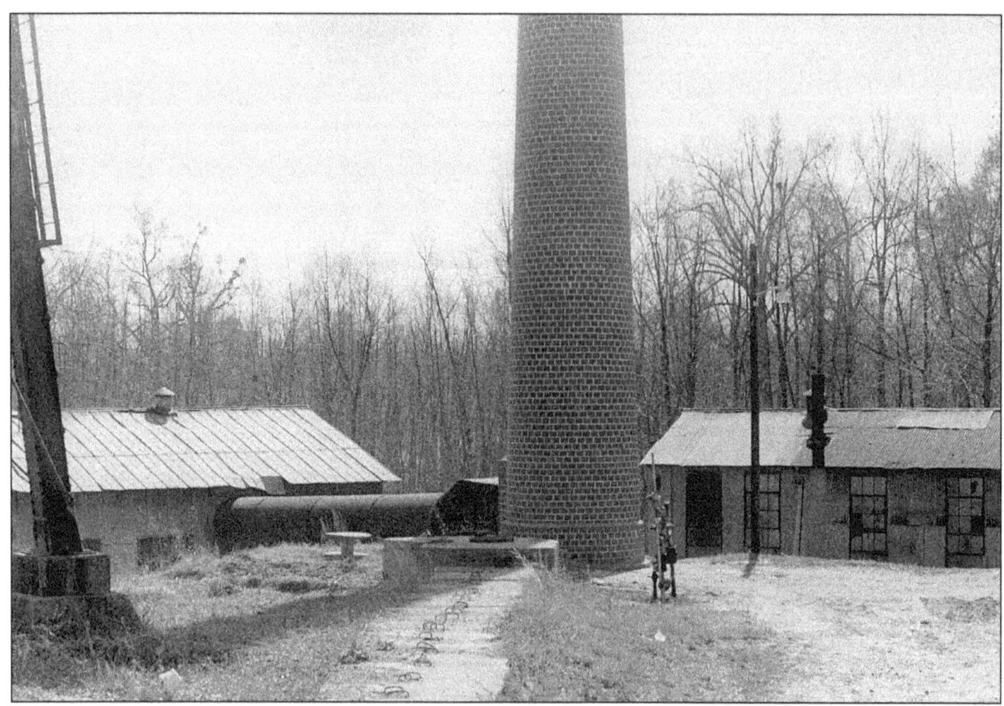

The old boiler room was constructed in 1929 at a cost of $500. The structure covers 1,456 square feet.

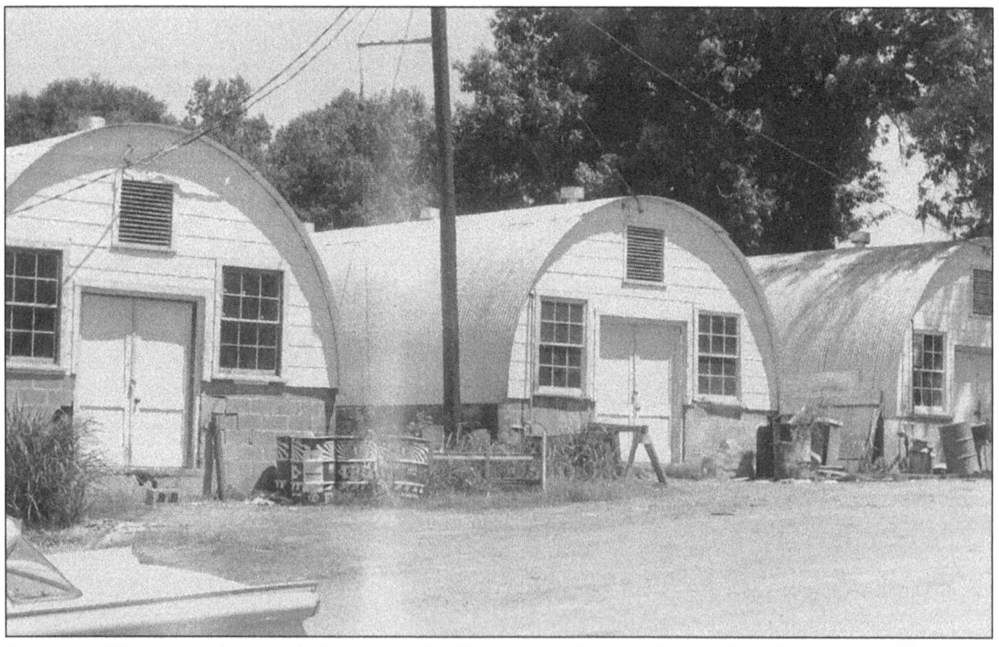

Quonset Hut once housed the union/grill services for students, faculty, and staff. A new student union building was later constructed in 1964, and it not only contained a grill, where patrons could buy sandwiches and snacks, but a bookstore, a post office, barber and beauty shops, music listening rooms, a bowling alley, a game room, meeting rooms, guest rooms, and a student publication office.

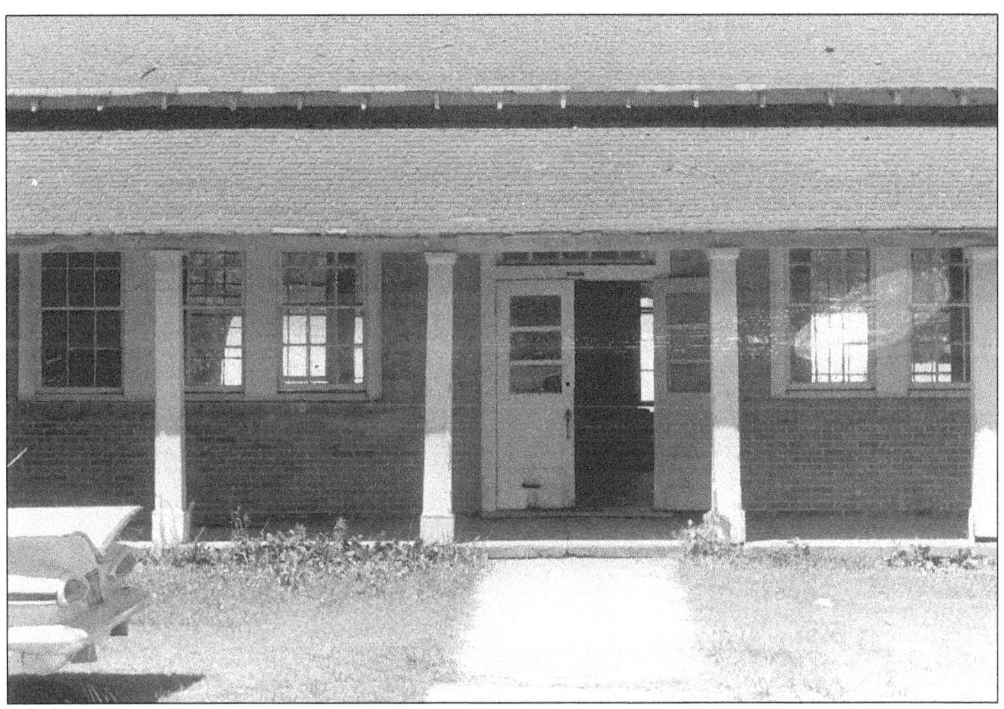

The Practice School was used to train elementary students.

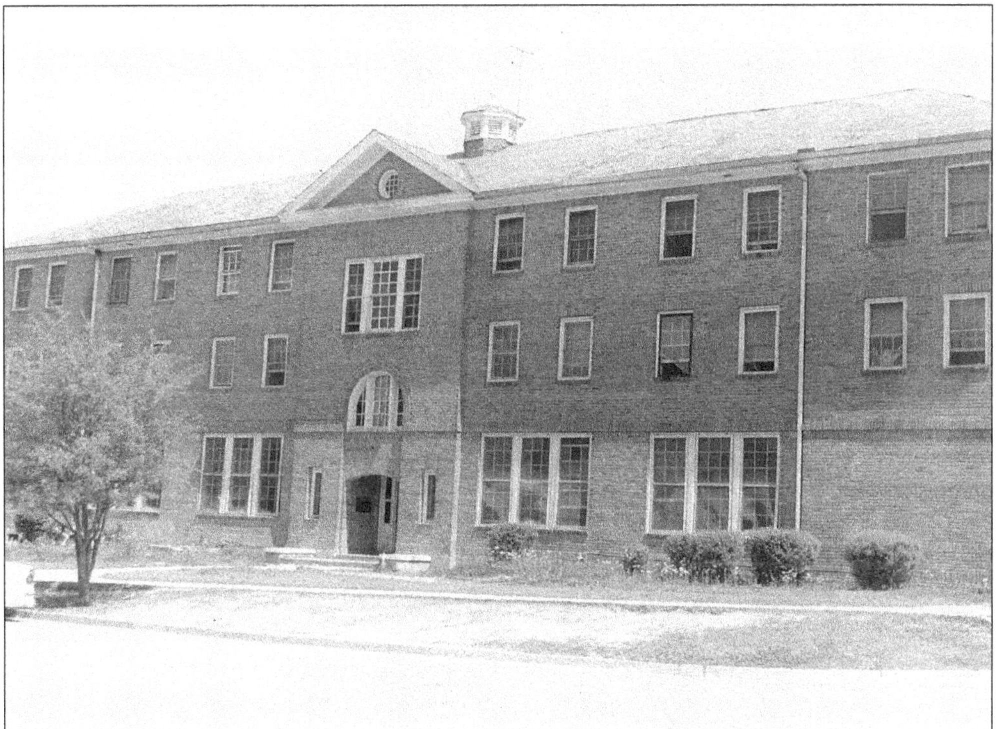

Academic Hall housed classes for secondary school students.

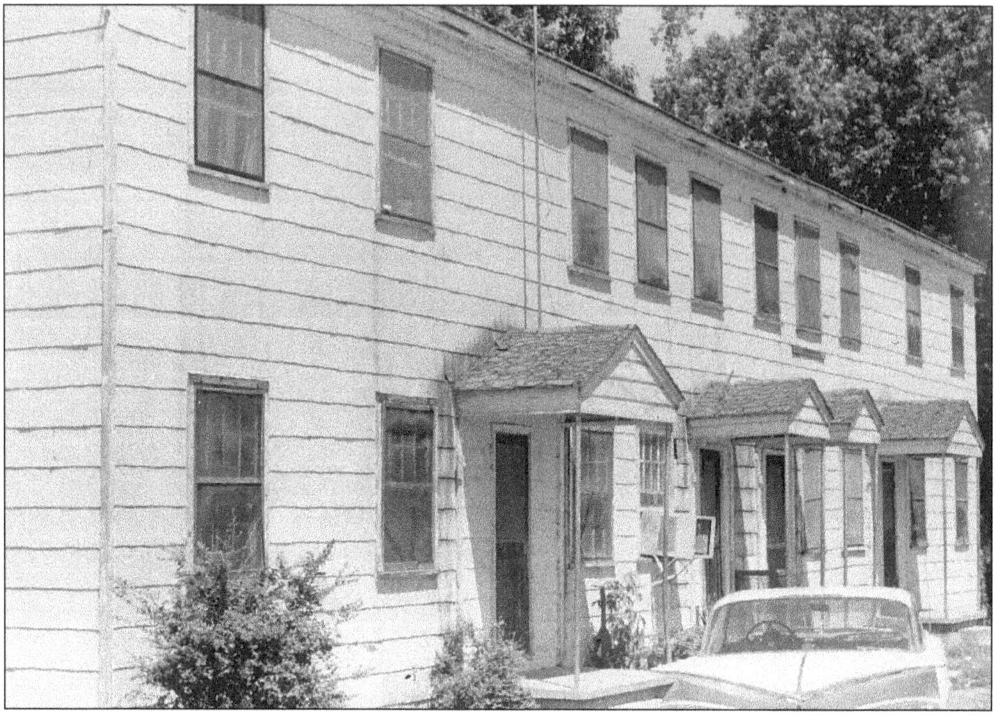

Veterans Apartment V2, a housing complex designated specifically for veterans of war, was also called "Vet City."

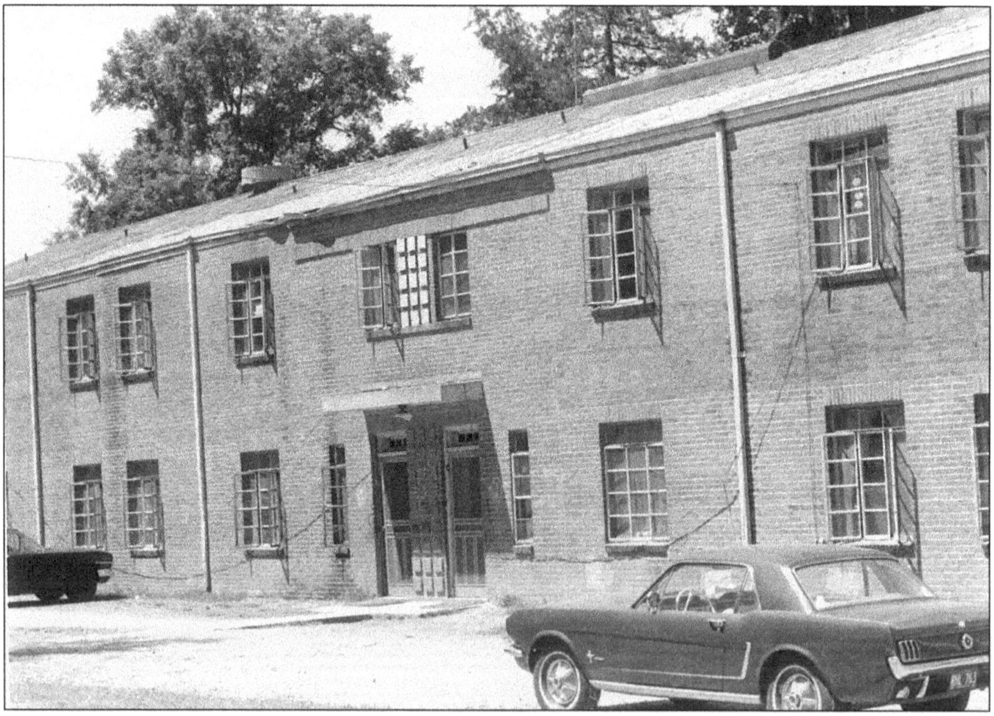

Veterans Dormitory #2-B was also designated for students who were veterans.

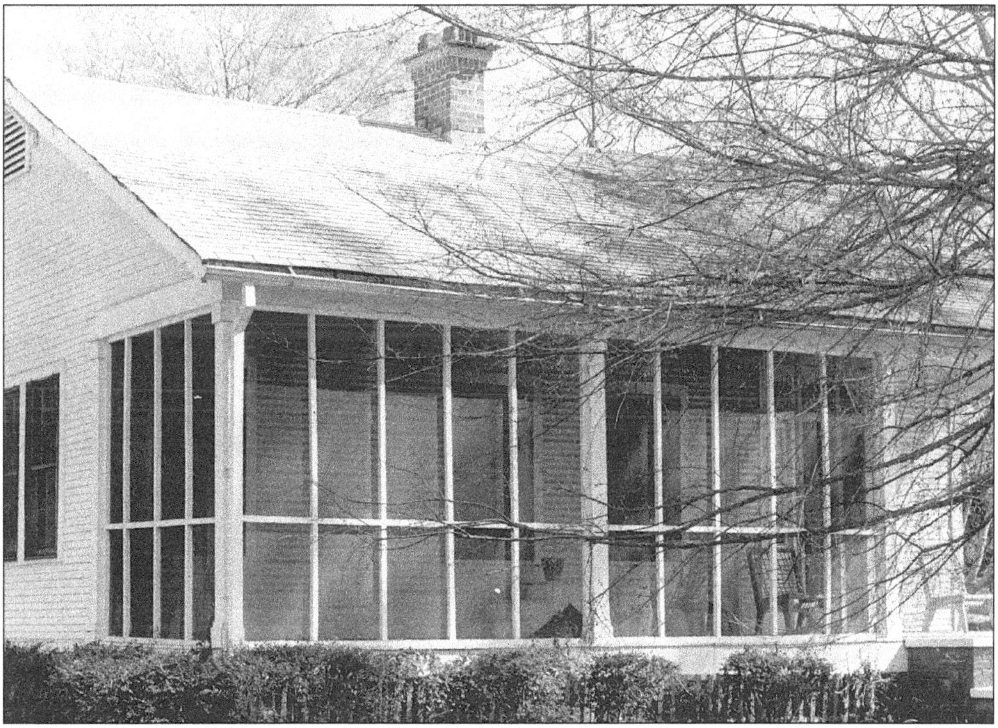

Cottage #9, constructed in 1961 at a cost of $13,154, was one of the houses where faculty and staff members lived while employed on the campus. This home was 1,300 square feet. There were several of these cottages identified by number.

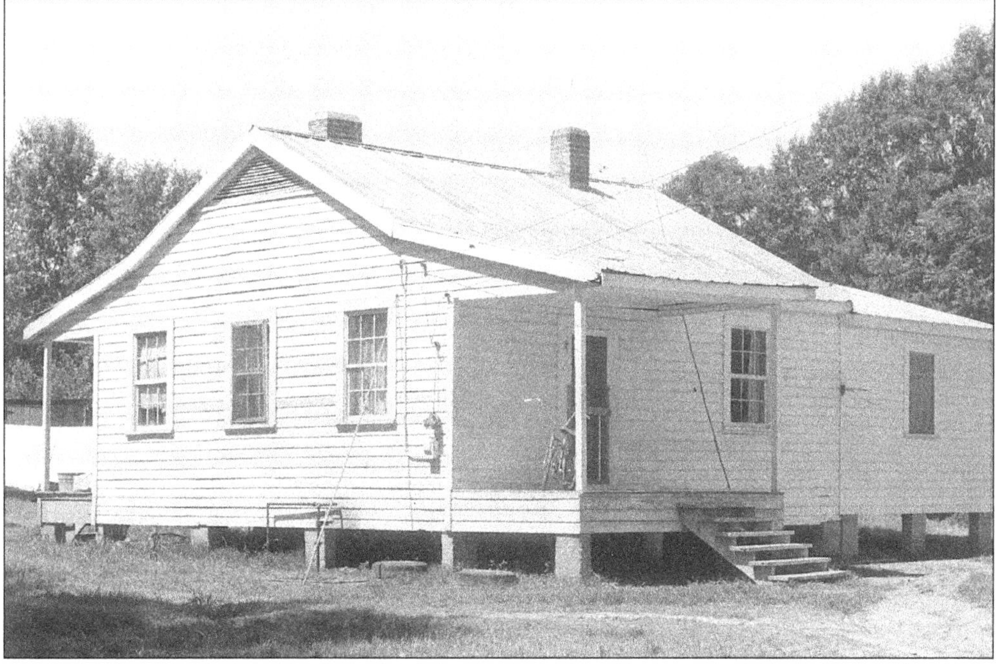

Cottage #23 was another campus residence for faculty and staff members. It was constructed in 1955 at a cost of $14,500 and covered 1,728 square feet.

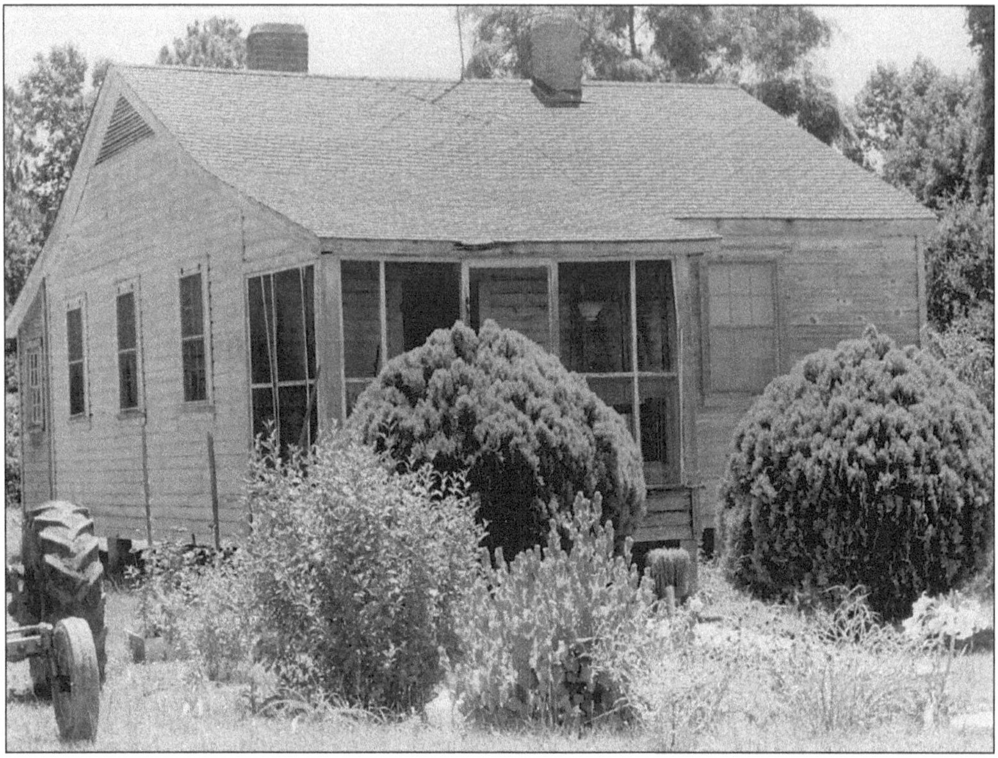

Cottage #18 was constructed in 1965 as a faculty/staff residence at a cost of $14,500. This home covered 1,218 square feet.

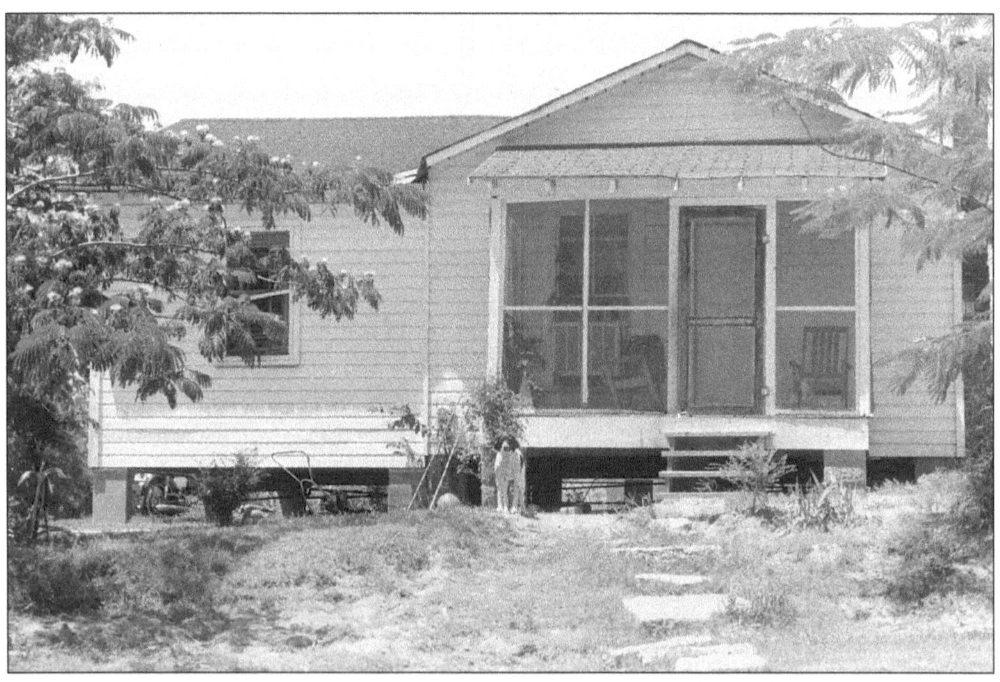

Cottage #19, at 1,300 square feet, was constructed in 1961 for $14,500.

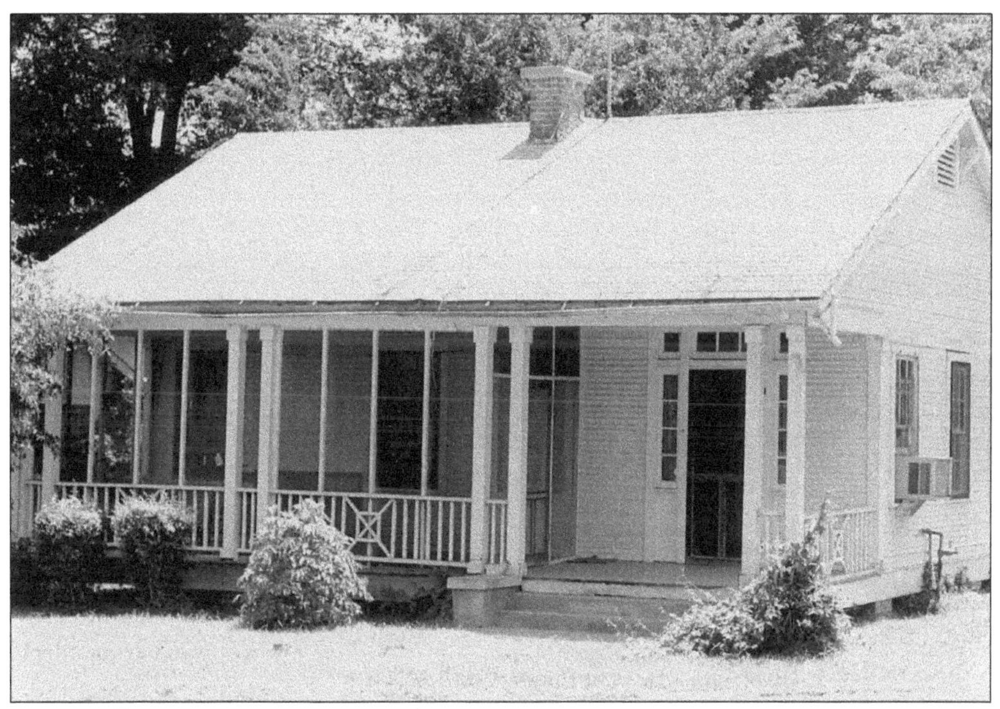

Cottage #5 was constructed in 1961 to house faculty/staff members. The home cost $13,154 and covered 1,300 square feet.

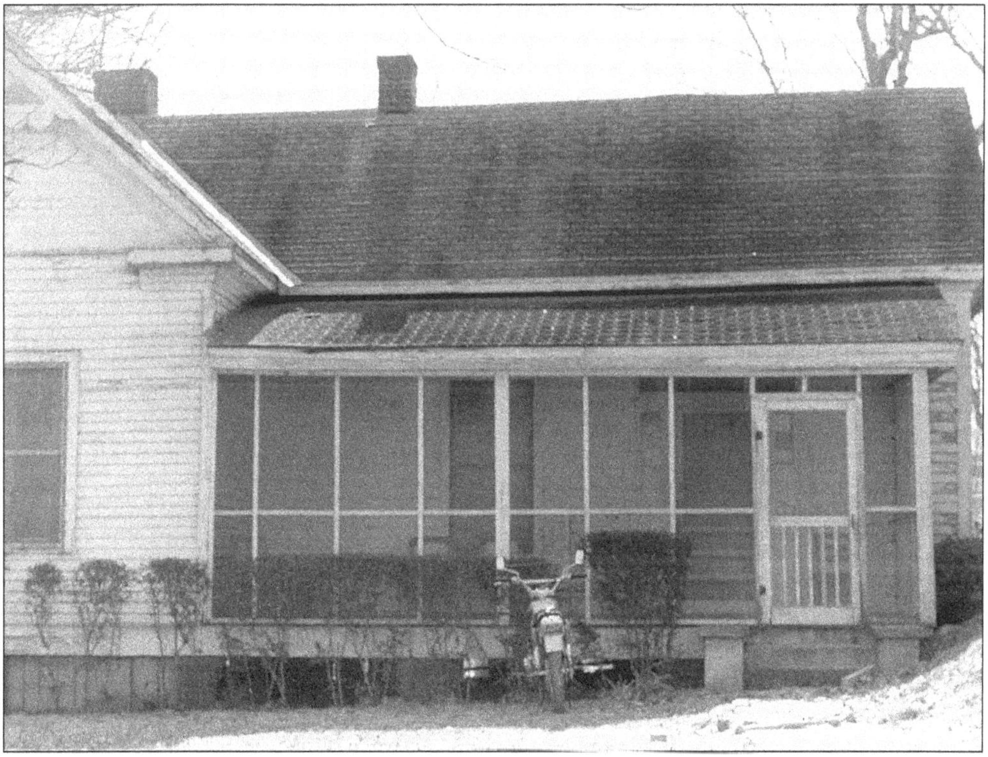

Cottage #14 was a 1,218-square-foot home that was built in 1965 at a cost of $14,500.

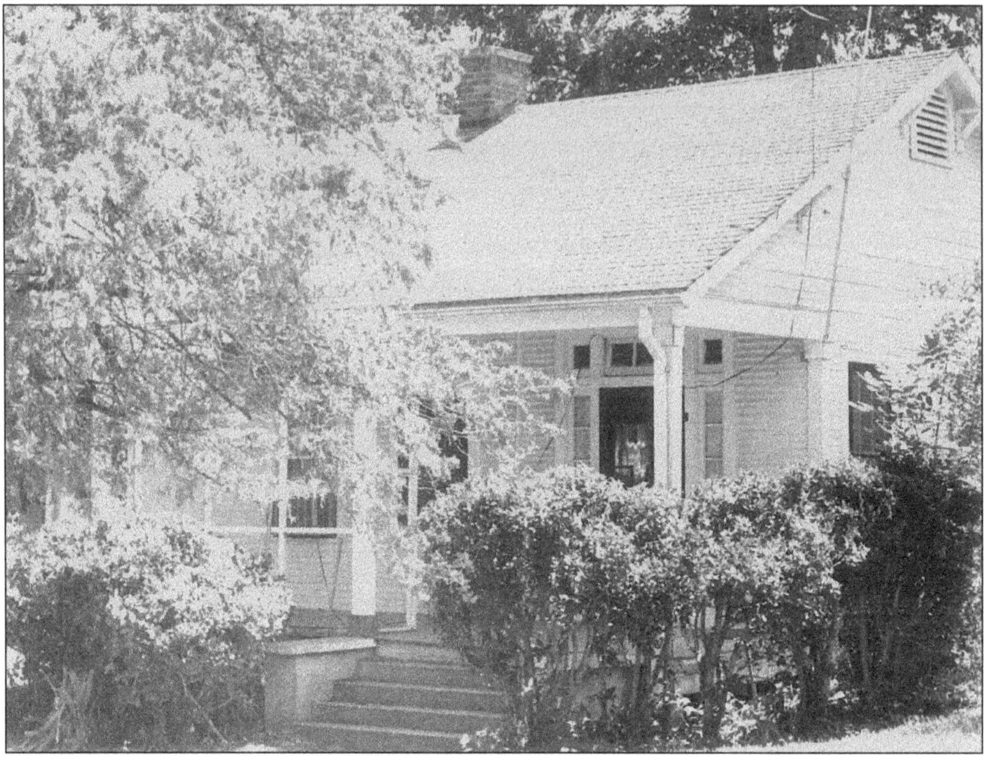

Cottage #6, built in 1961, was a 1,300-square-foot residence for faculty/staff members on campus. The home cost $14,500.

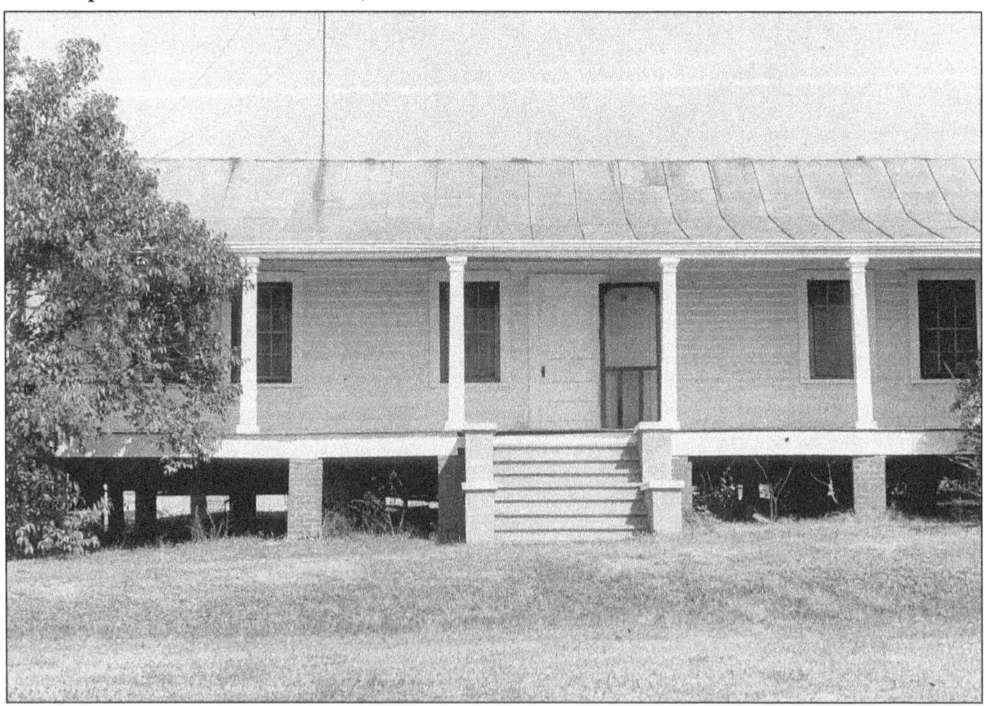

Cottage #2 was built at a cost of $13,154 in 1961. It covered 1,300 square feet.

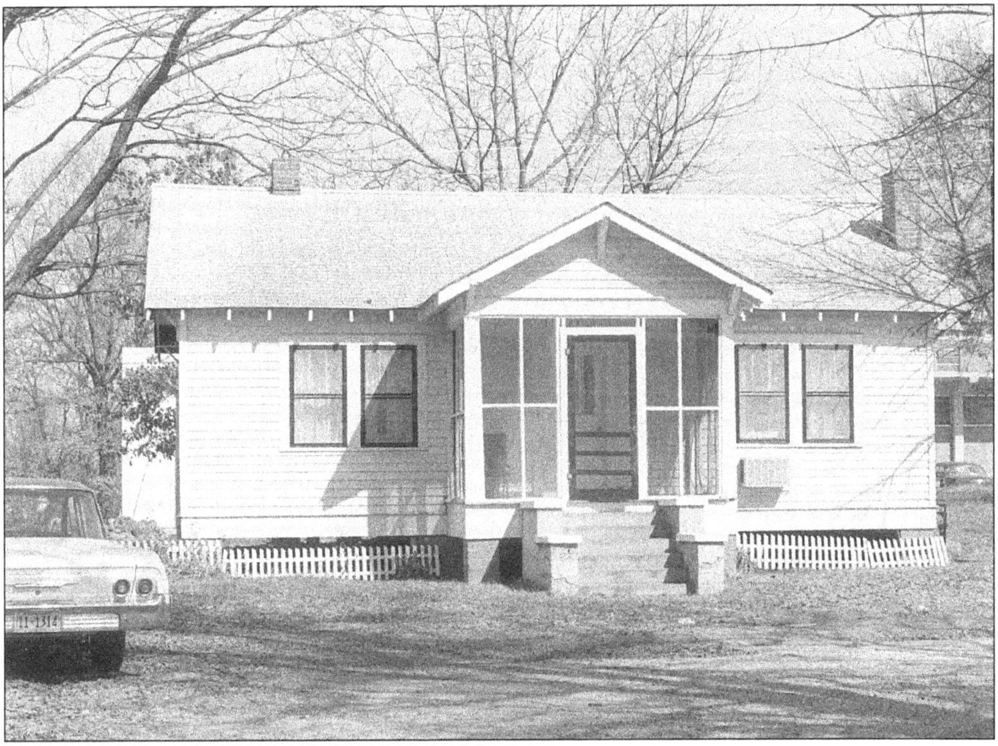

Cottage #4 was constructed in 1961 at a cost of $13,154.

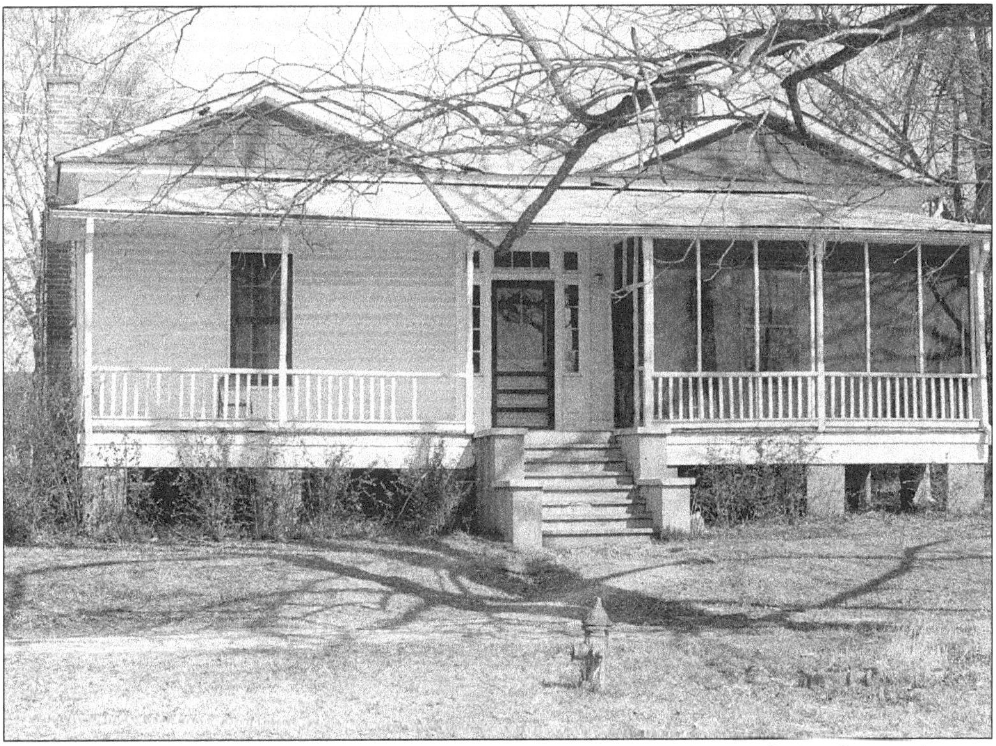

Cottage #3, another faculty/staff residence, was constructed in 1961 for $13,154.

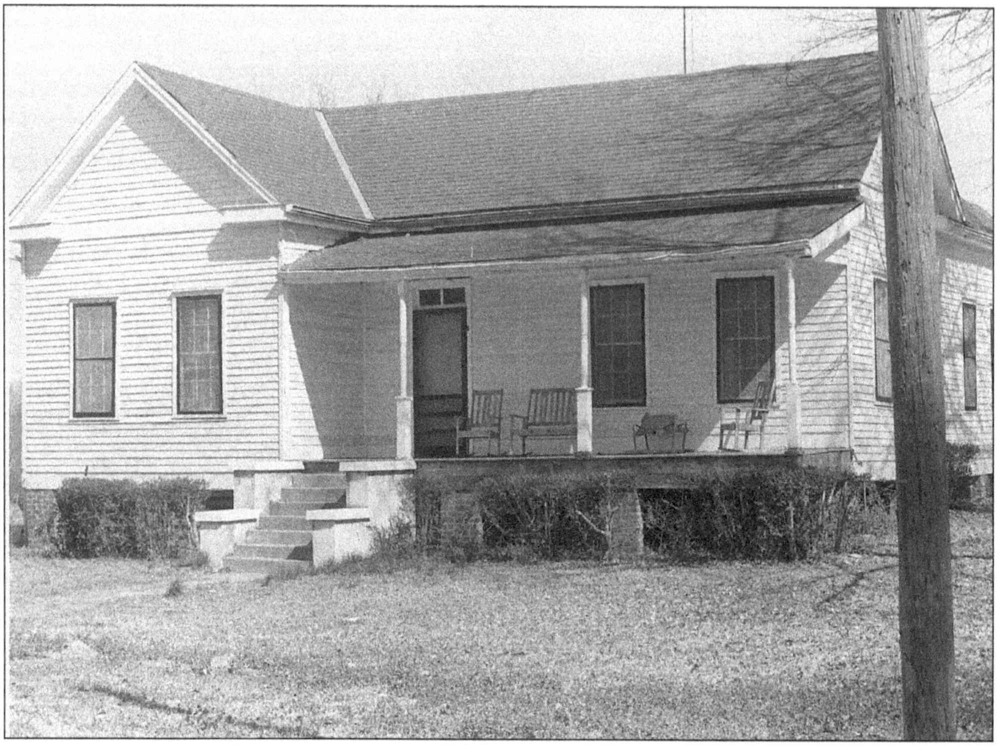

Cottage #10 was also built in 1961 for $13,154. It covered 1,300 square feet.

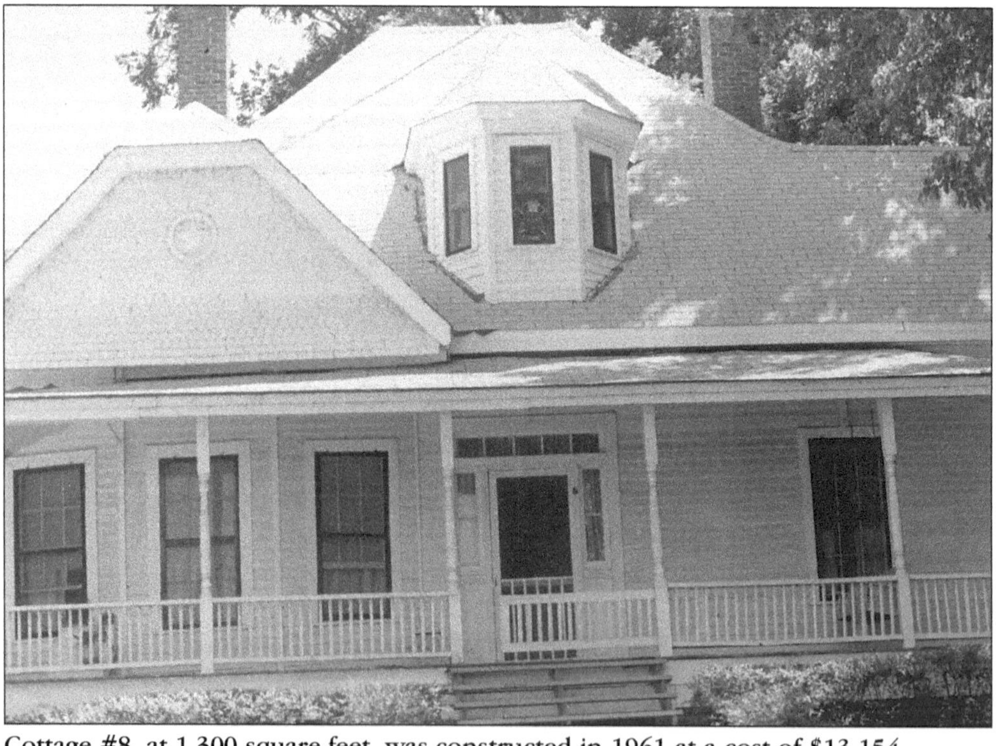

Cottage #8, at 1,300 square feet, was constructed in 1961 at a cost of $13,154.

Two

Campus Life

Campus life at Alcorn creates a bond between its students, faculty, and staff that lasts through the years. The family atmosphere that has always existed at Alcorn continually attracts new students and faculty and draws alumni back year after year.

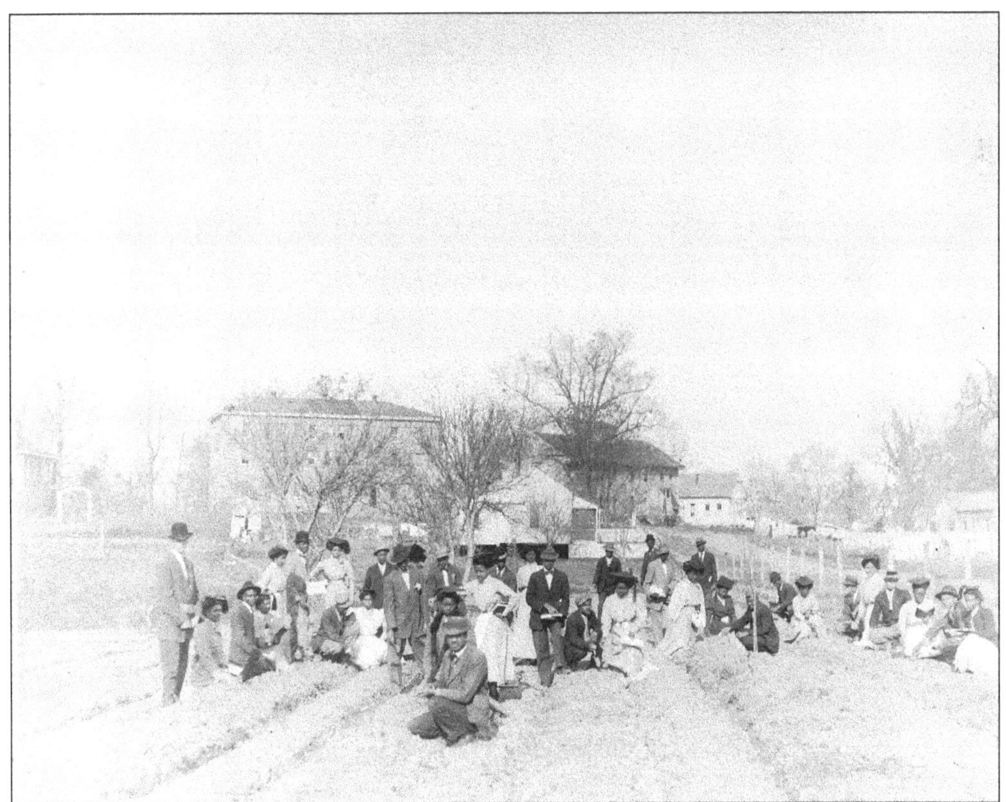

College life for the student body and faculty at Alcorn was full of excitement and an overwhelming commitment to the mission of the college.

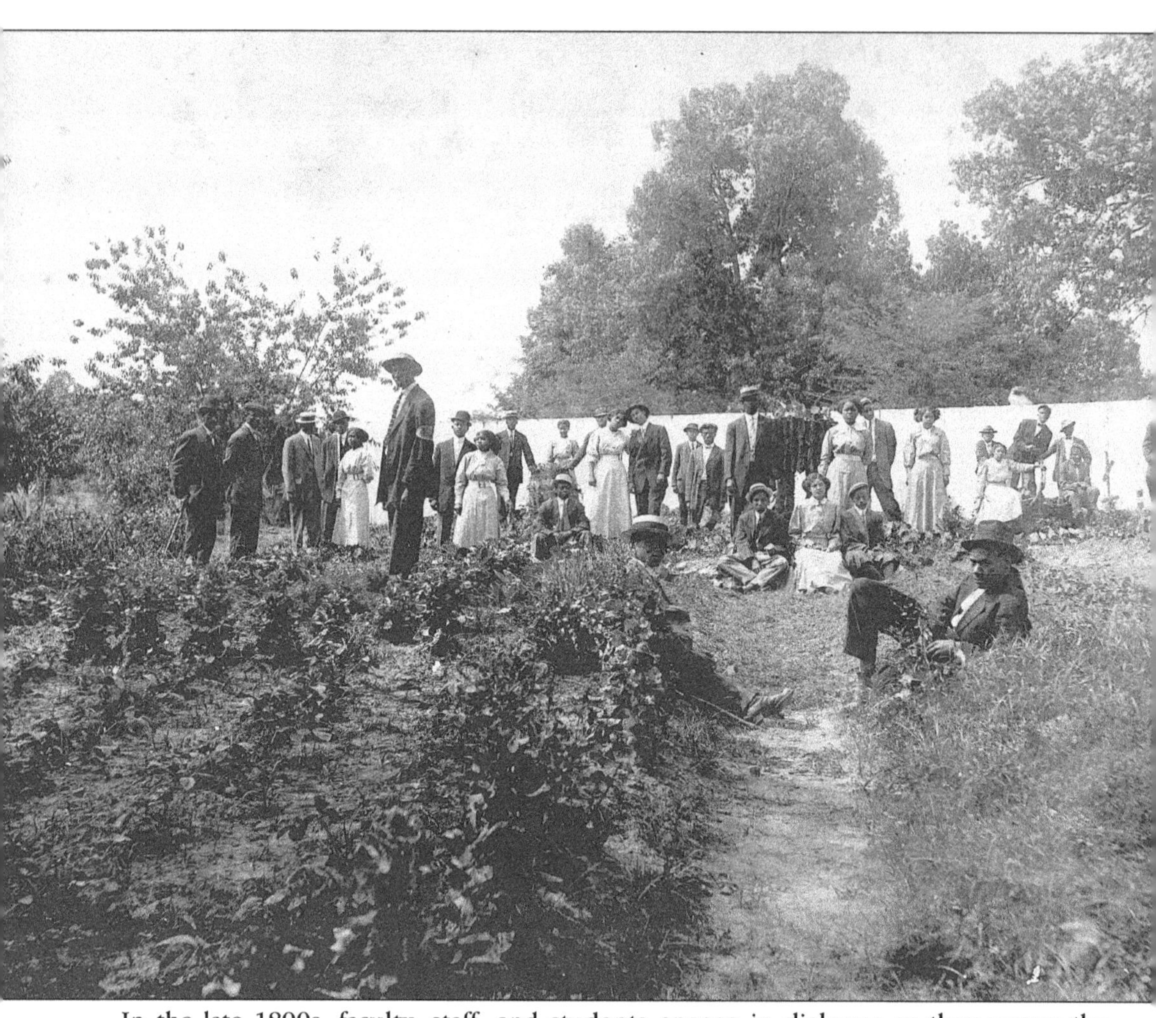

In the late 1800s, faculty, staff, and students engage in dialogue as they survey the outcome of their hard work and continuous study.

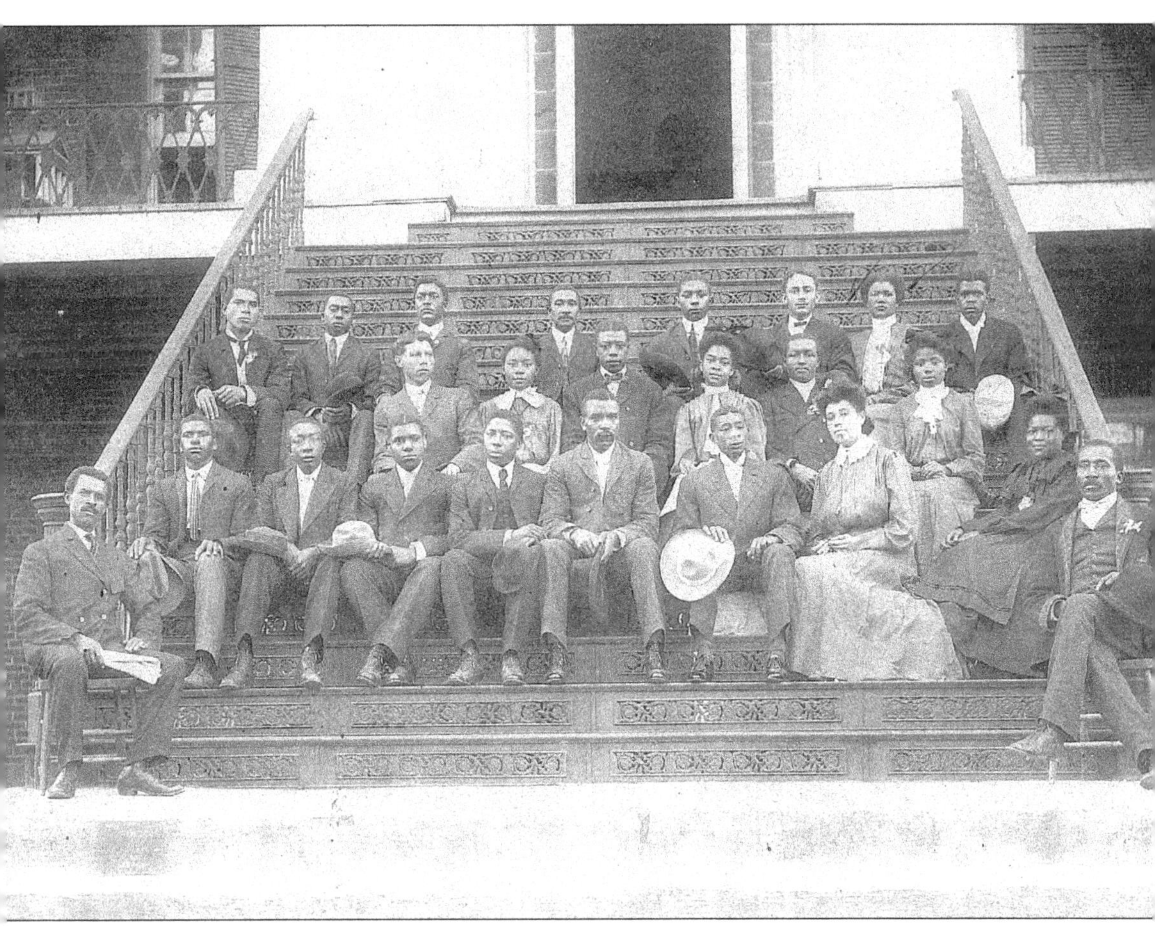

Alcorn's first co-ed graduation took place in the early 1900s. This photograph depicts some of the progress that the college had made since its establishment in 1871.

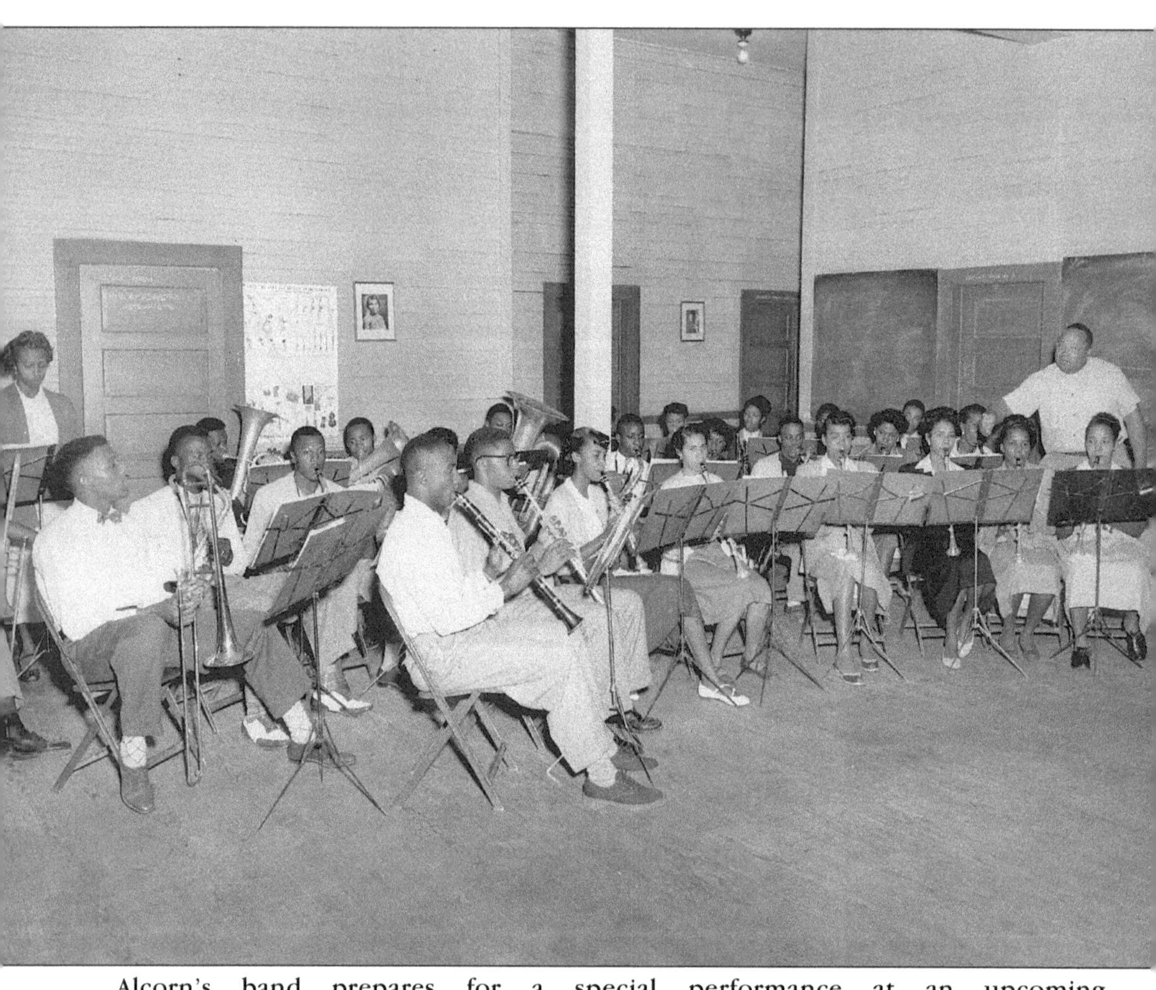

Alcorn's band prepares for a special performance at an upcoming commencement exercise.

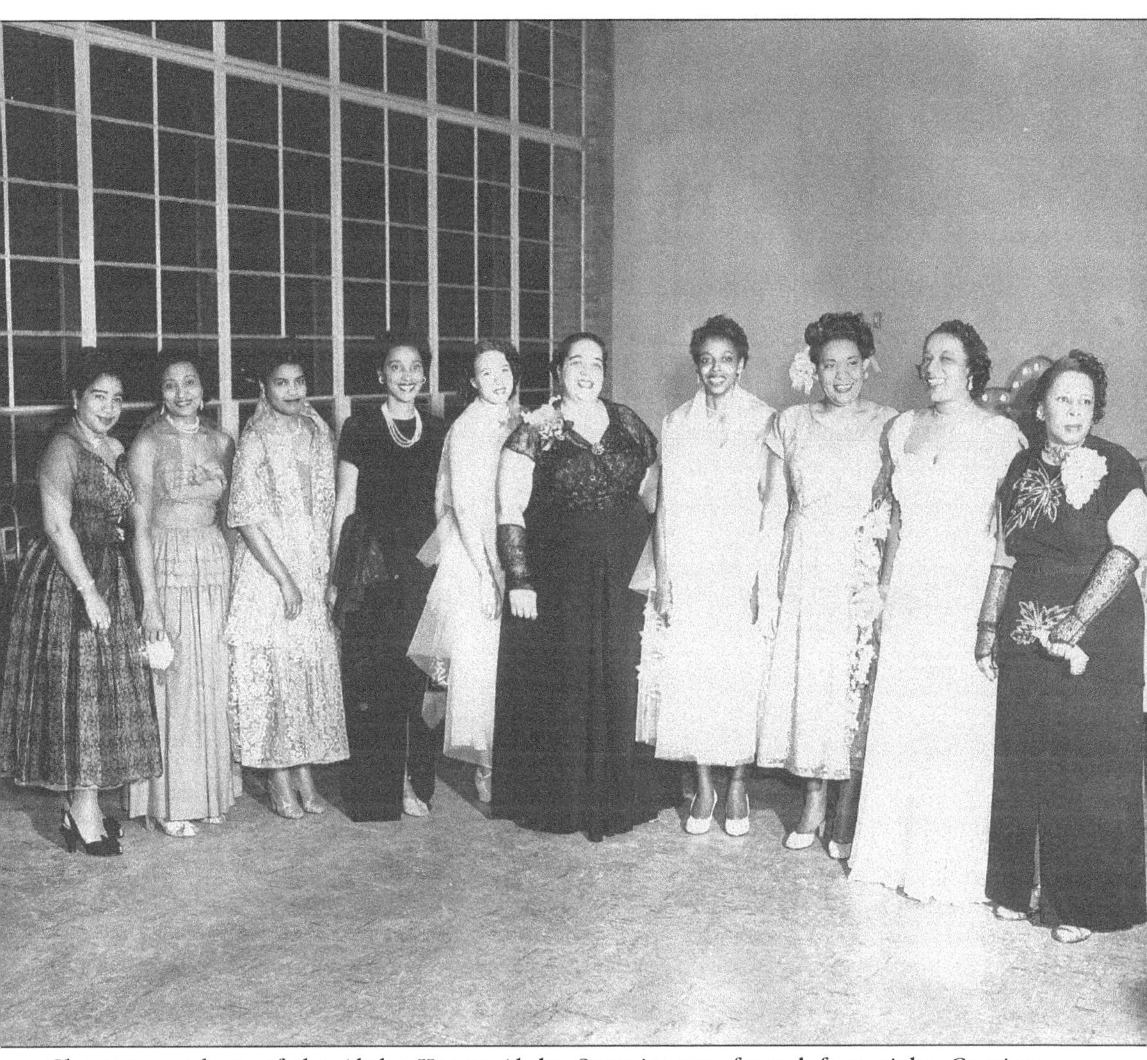

Charter members of the Alpha Kappa Alpha Sorority are, from left to right, Corrine Craddock, Ann Hunter, Hazel McCarter, Sarah Berry, Elizabeth Wilson, Blanche Evans, Doris Garrett, Lillian Whitmore, Dorothy Gordan Gary, and Cornelia Carter.

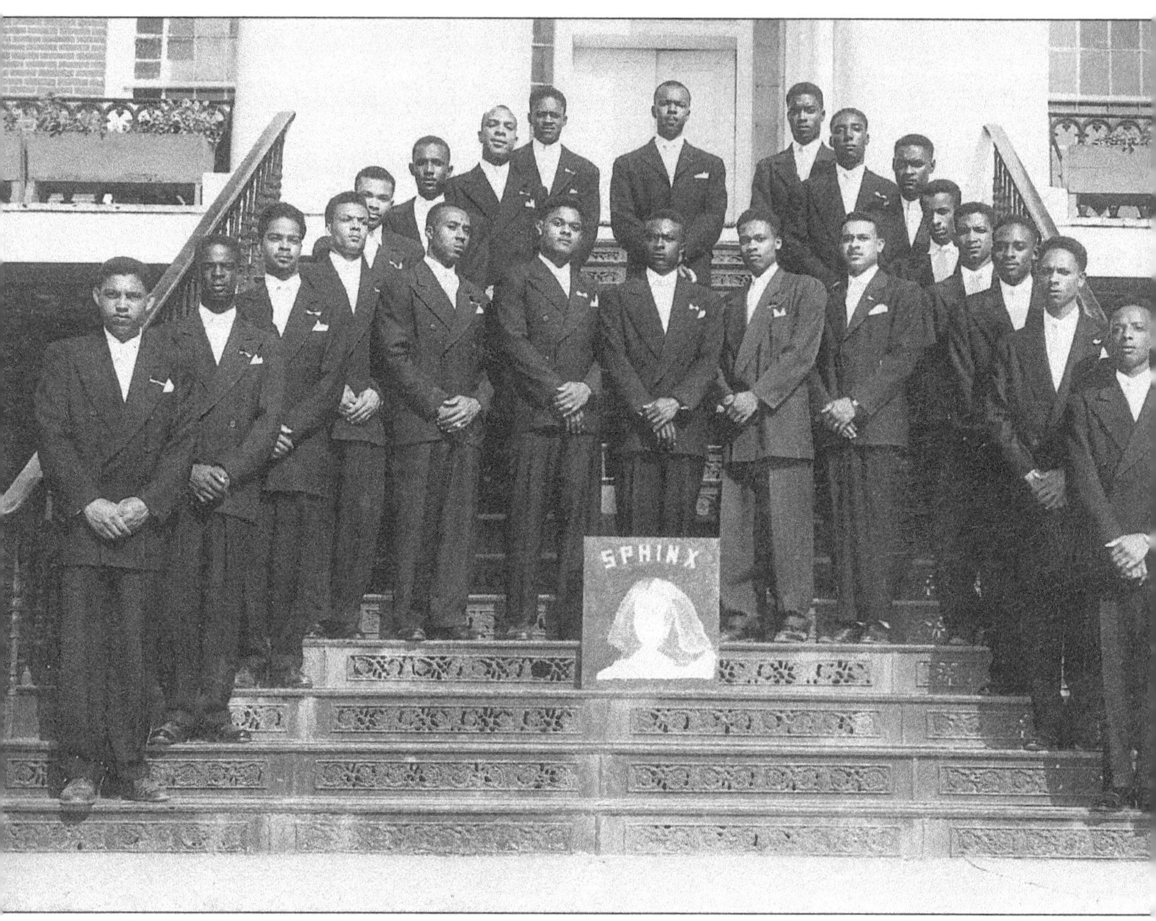

The Sphinx Club of Alpha Phi Alpha Fraternity poses on the steps of Oakland Chapel. Members anxiously await their chance to become a member of the fraternity through hard work and endurance.

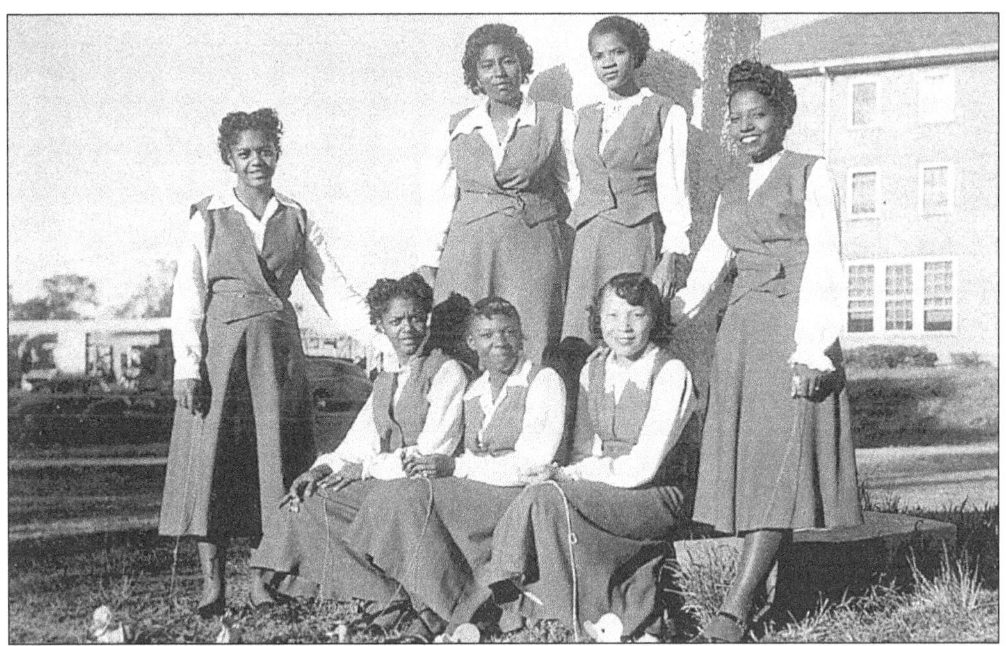

Charter members of the Delta Epsilon Chapter of Delta Sigma Theta Sorority are pictured here in 1949. From left to right are (seated) Bernice Moore Gamblin, Addie Burke, and Etta Cowen; (standing) Eunice Moore, Albertine Davis, unidentified, and Helen Johnson Pointer.

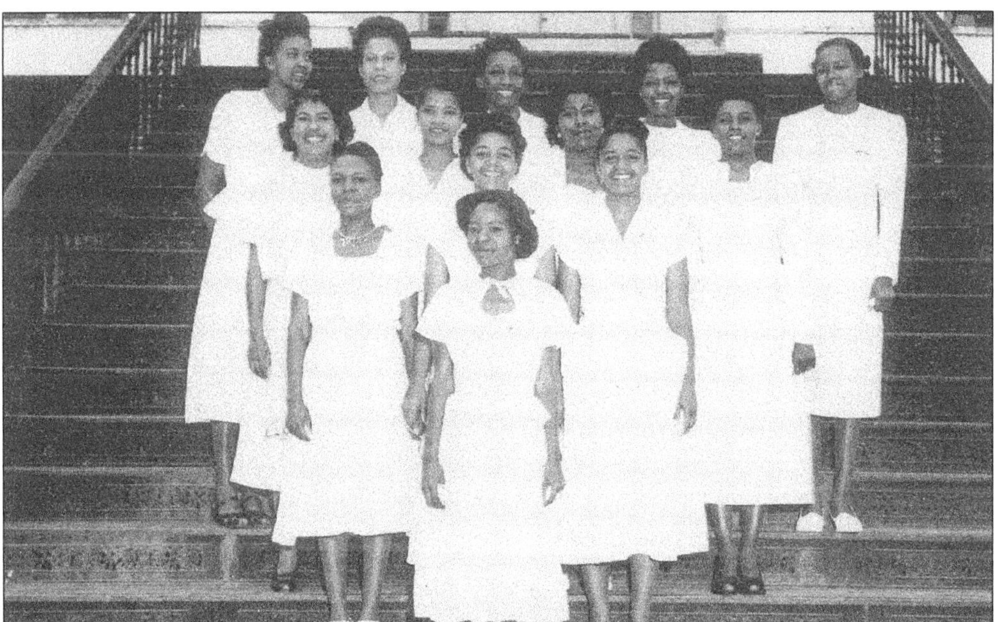

Delta Sigma Theta's First Pyramid Club was started in October 1949. Pictured, from left to right, are (front row) Mildred Grady; (second row) Addie Burke, Eunice Moore, and Bernice Moore; (third row) Armentia Davis, unidentified, unidentified, and unidentified; (back row) Juanita Bishop, Ann Johnson Stepney, Mary Perry, Helen Johnson Pointer, and Adeline Guy Posey.

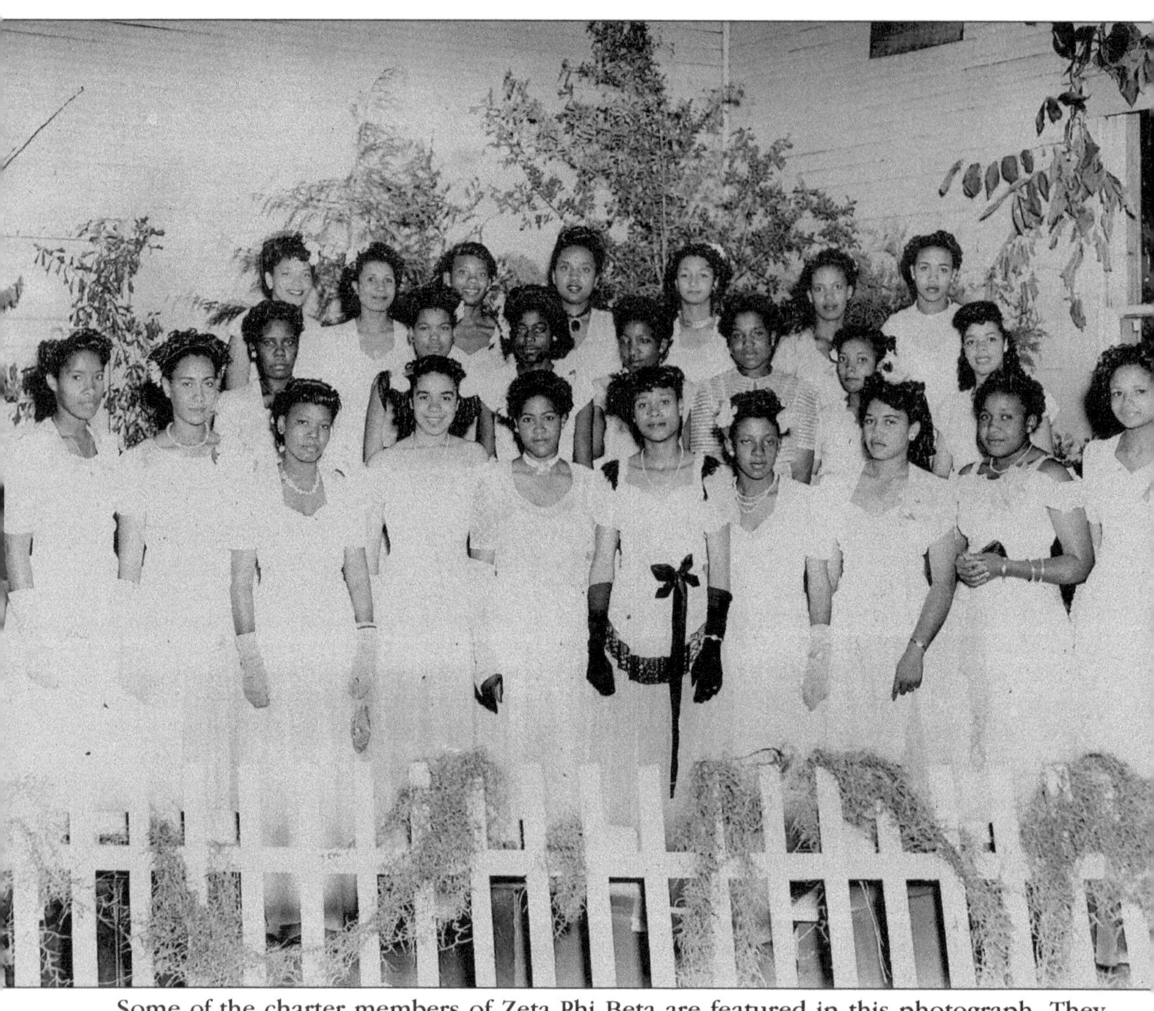

Some of the charter members of Zeta Phi Beta are featured in this photograph. They are, from left to right, (front row) Gertrude Price Peyton, Florence Butler, Lurlean Jones, Ruby Gray Smith, unidentified, unidentified, unidentified, unidentified, Cedonia Cain, and Pauline Gray Jordan; (second row) unidentified, John Ethel Harrel, Essie McCune, unidentified, unidentified, Nannie Aldridge, and Mildred Pierson; (back row) Gertrude Quralls, Essie Ford, unidentified, Annie B. Fairley, Leatrice Collins Buie, and Helen Sansing.

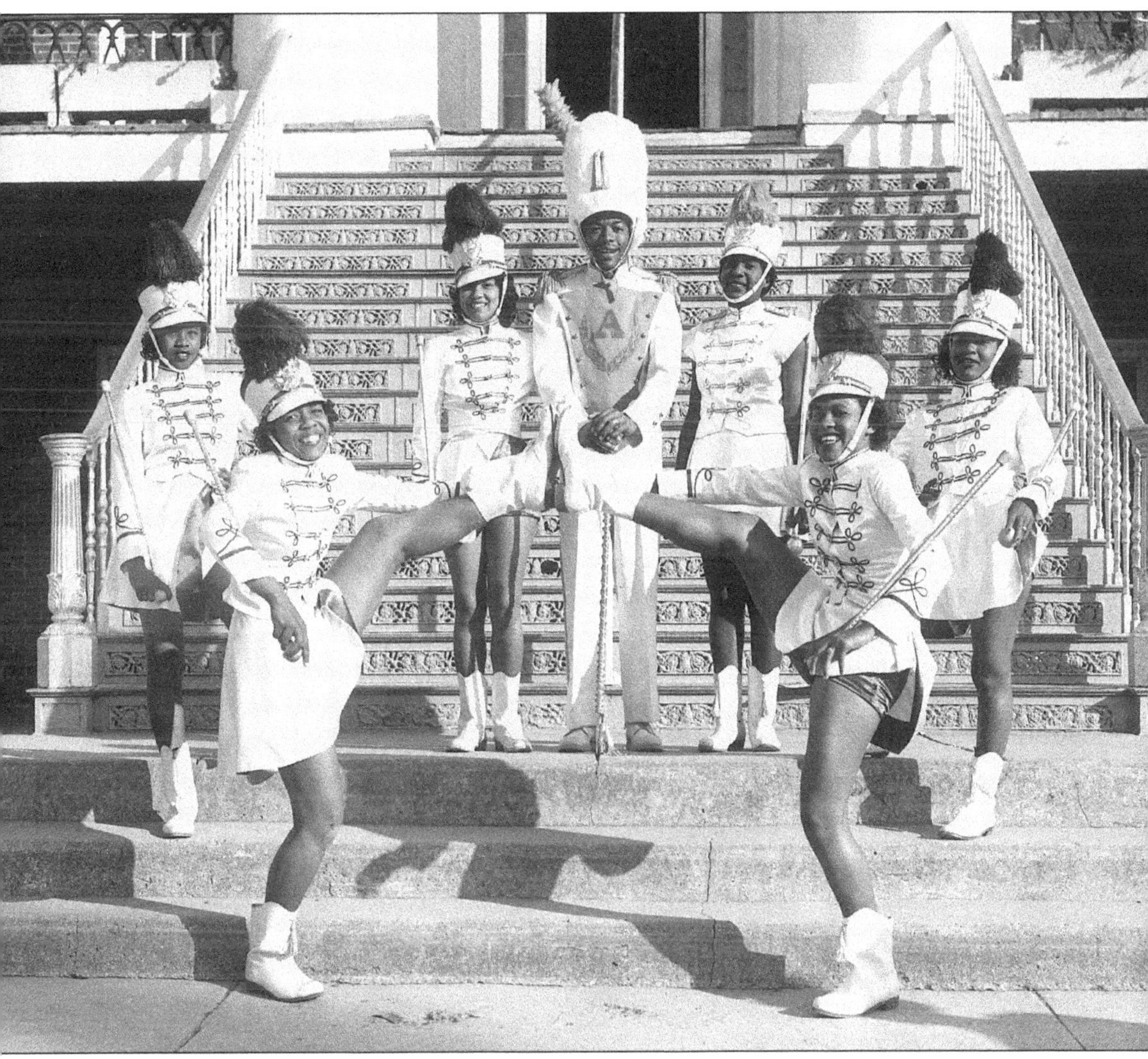

The Majorettes are in action and ready to do their best at any Alcorn function. Here, they prepare for an upcoming homecoming celebration.

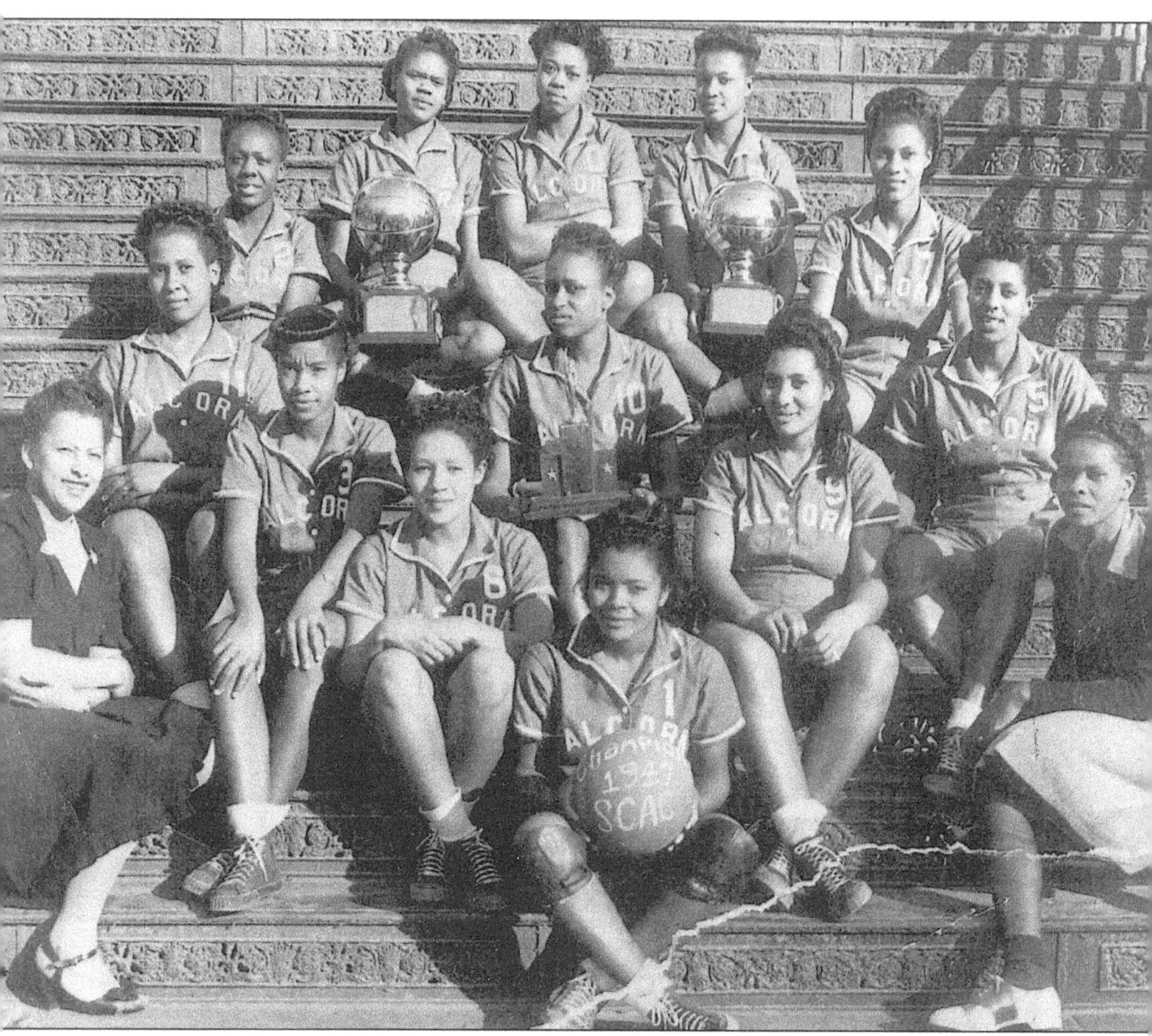

The 1947 South Central Conference women's basketball championship team members are as follows: Mrs. Jewell Allen, coach (lower left in dress); Hazel Watson, trainer (lower right in skirt); Margie Price (Funches), jersey #1; Gertrude Price (Payton), jersey #3; Pearl Smith, jersey #6; Dessie Paige, jersey #9; Juanita Martin, jersey #11; Alma Sutton (Duffy), jersey #10; Beatrice Jordan (Boose), jersey #5; Roxie Thurman, jersey #2; Helen Johnson, jersey #7; Ruby Moore, jersey #4; unidentified; Frankie Baird, jersey #0; and Mary Esther Ward (Johnson), jersey #8.

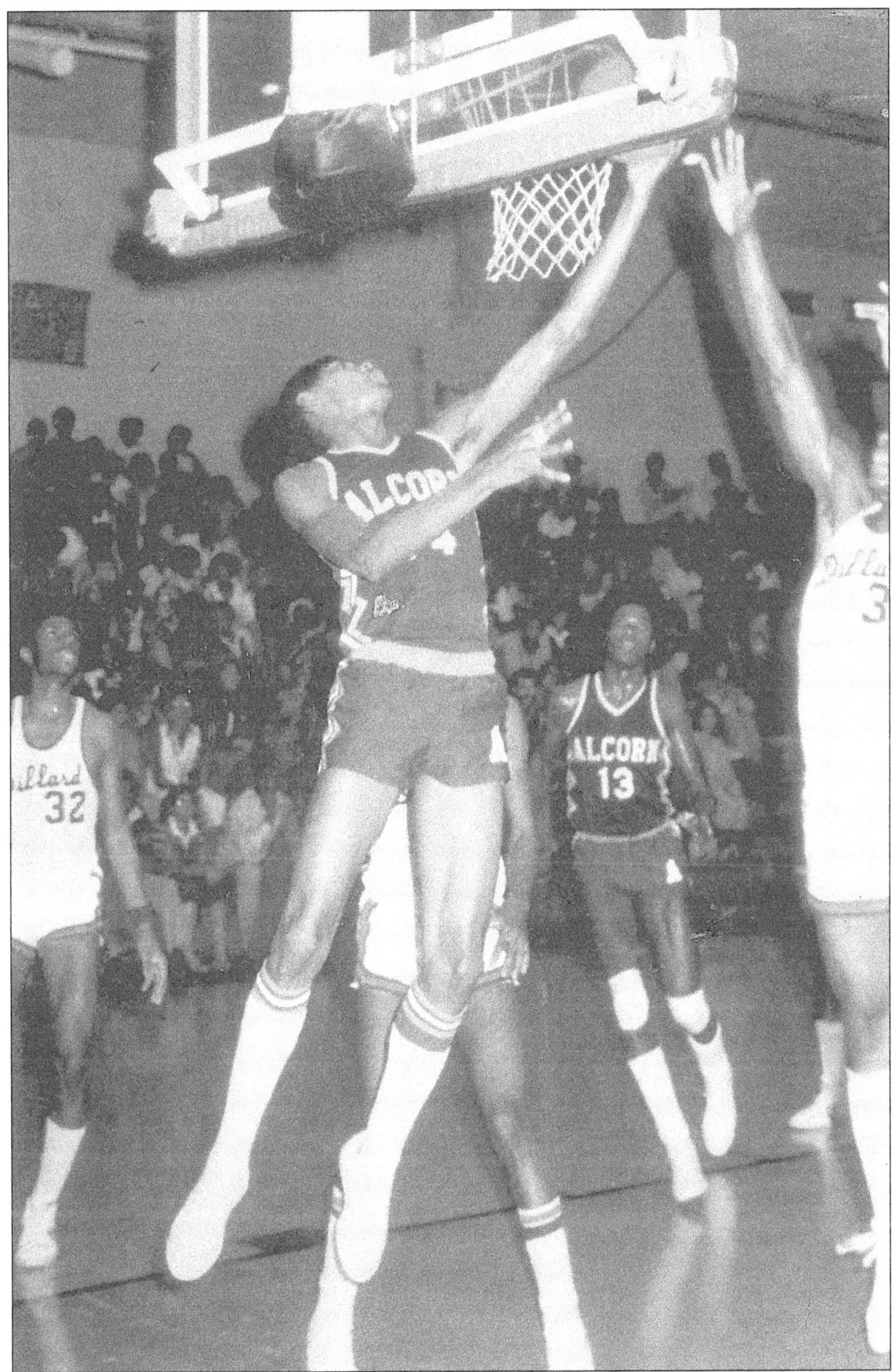

Alcorn's basketball team is seen here playing against Dillard. The year and outcome of the game are not known, but the prediction is that Alcorn was victorious.

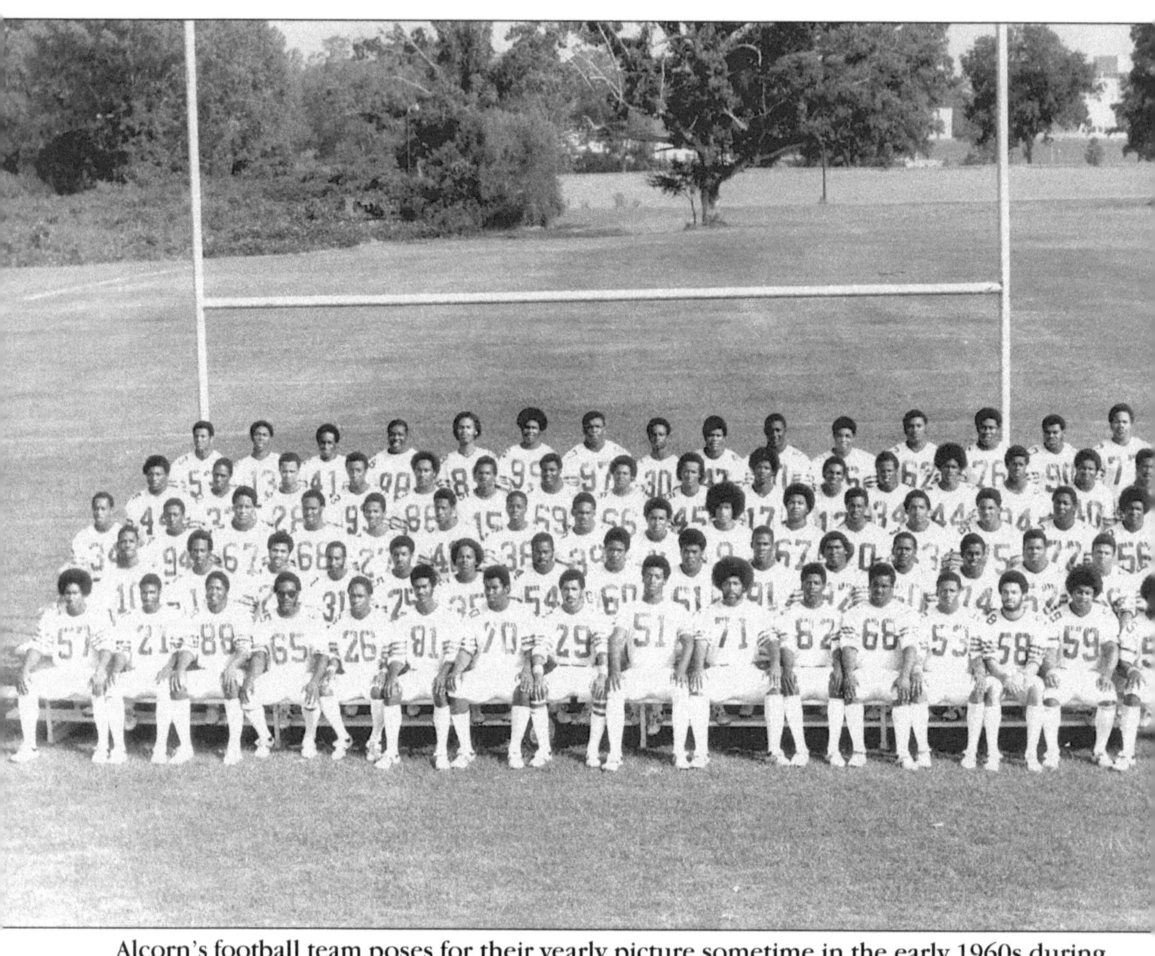

Alcorn's football team poses for their yearly picture sometime in the early 1960s during the administration of Coach Marino Casem.

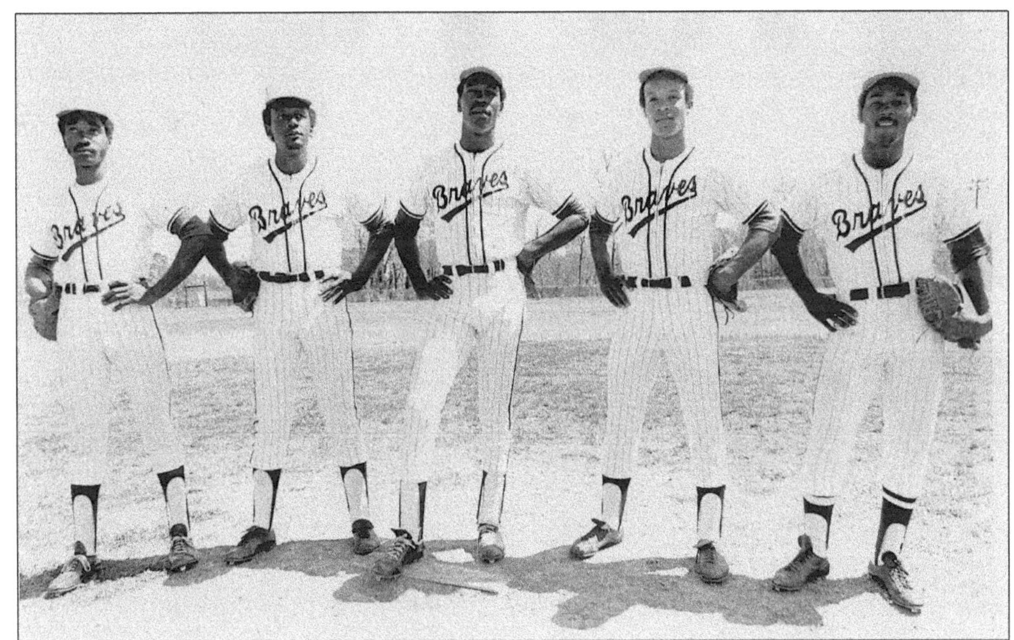

Alcorn's baseball team, poised for a great season, portray a winning attitude in this photograph. Today, Coach Willie McGowan provides leadership to Alcorn's baseball team, and its members still demonstrate that winning spirit.

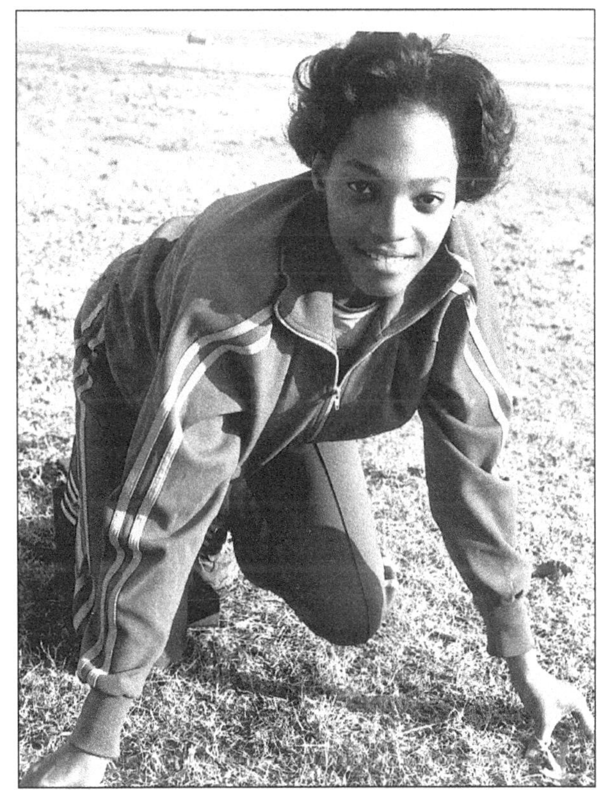

Track has been a highly-recognized sport at Alcorn over the years. In this picture, Gail Hicks gears up for a run.

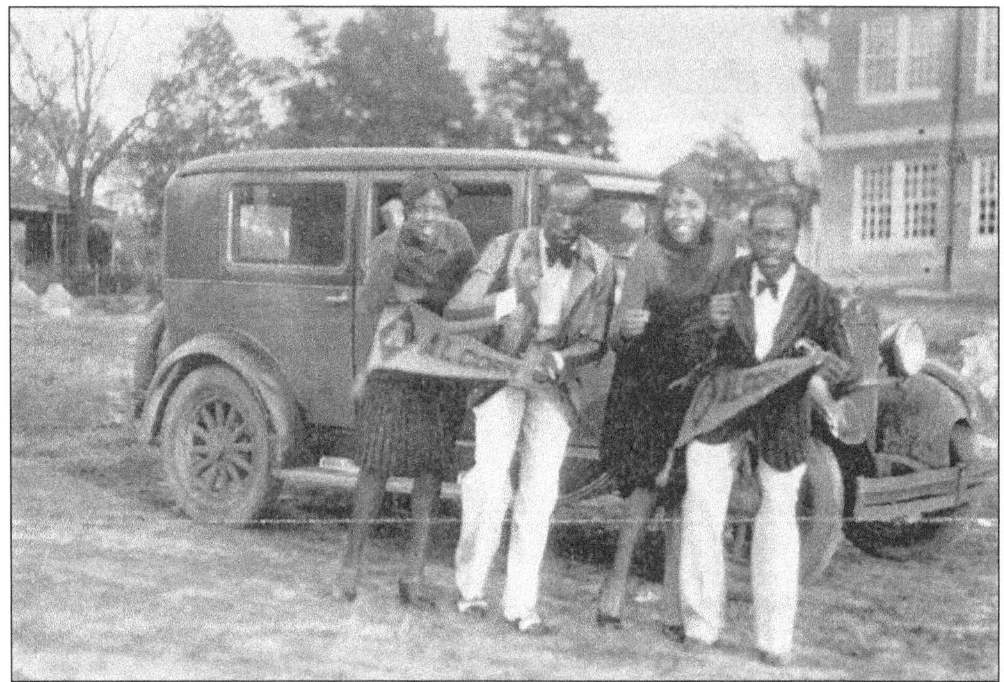

These 1930 cheerleaders were really on the move in an effort to keep the Alcorn spirit alive. "Pep" is the buzz word, and they don't mind letting it show. They cheer the "Purple and Gold" forever.

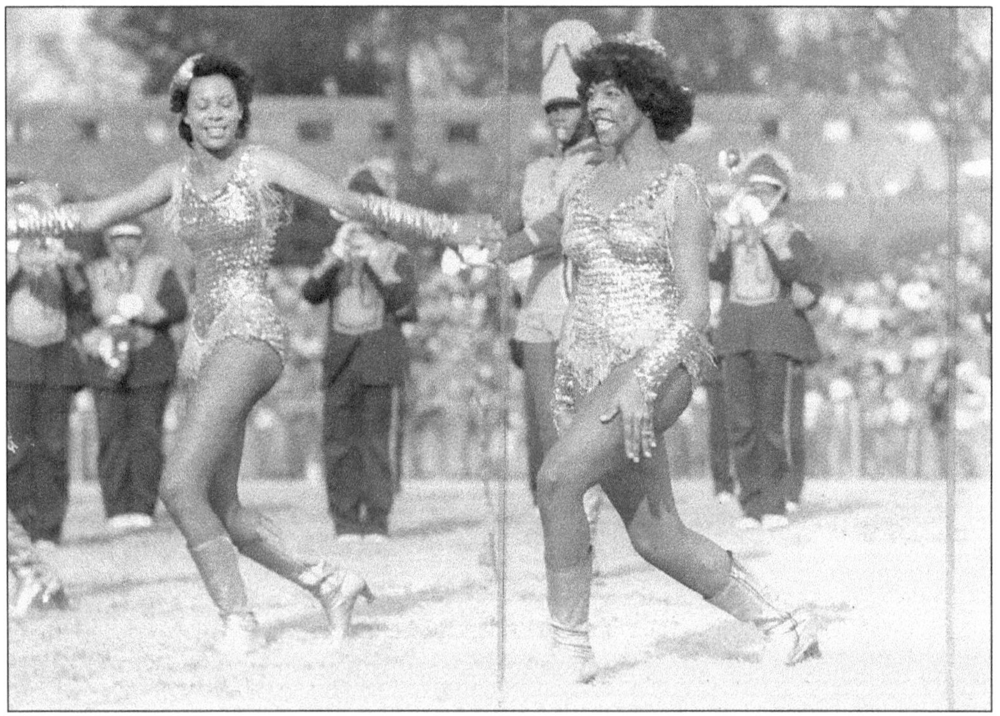

Many alumni return to the games, not only to see the football team in action but to see the golden girls as well. The golden girls perform at halftime during each home game.

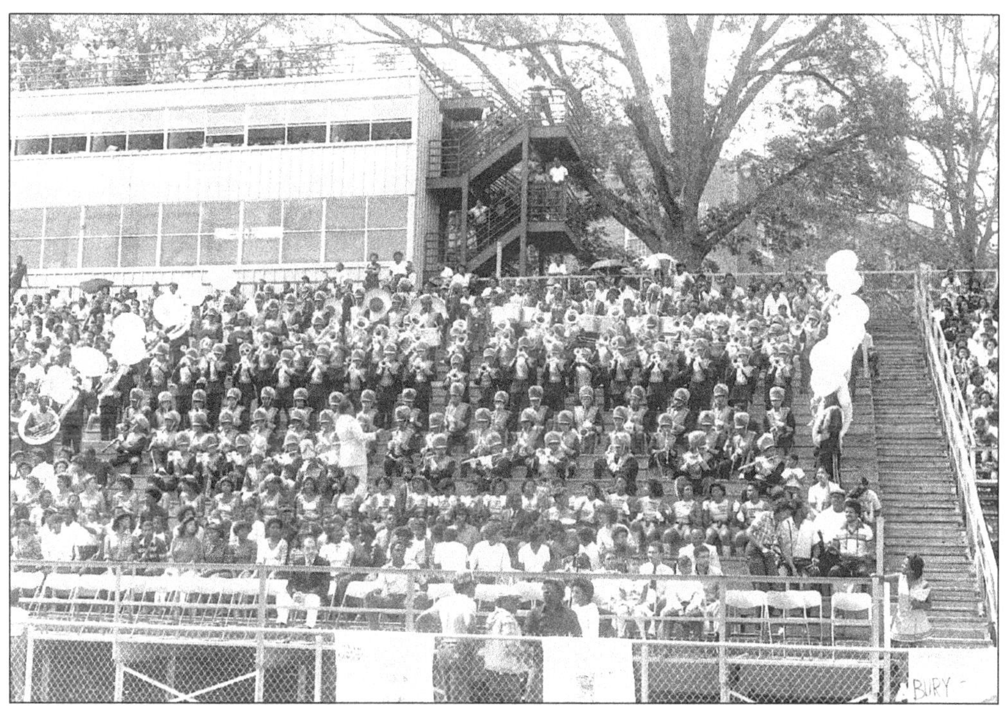

The band relaxes while waiting for their next routine and another touchdown for the Alcorn Braves. Though the year of this photograph is unknown, Alcorn's opponents in this game are likely either Mississippi Valley State University or Jackson State University.

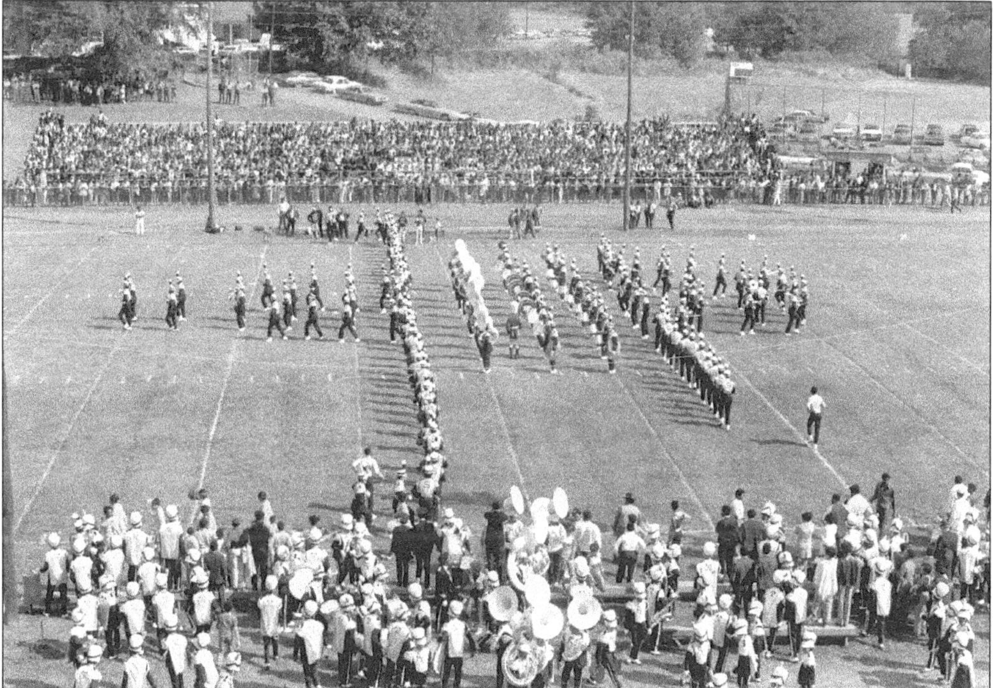

Alcorn's band has always played an important role in boosting the spirit of the team. Here, they perform a halftime during an Alcorn home game.

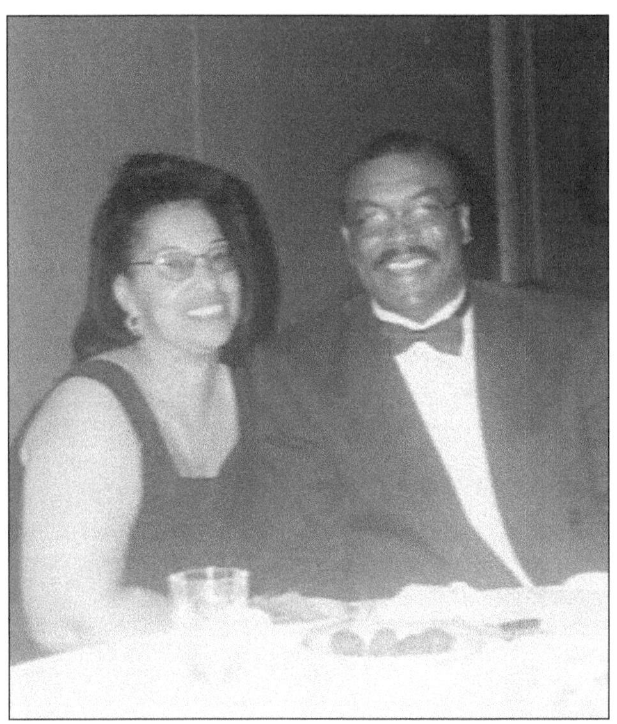

Head women's basketball coach Shirley Walker is Coach of the Year for the Southwest Athletic Conference (SWAC) and has been Coach of the Year several times. She is accompanied by her husband Lonnie Walker, an Alcorn graduate and former men's basketball coach.

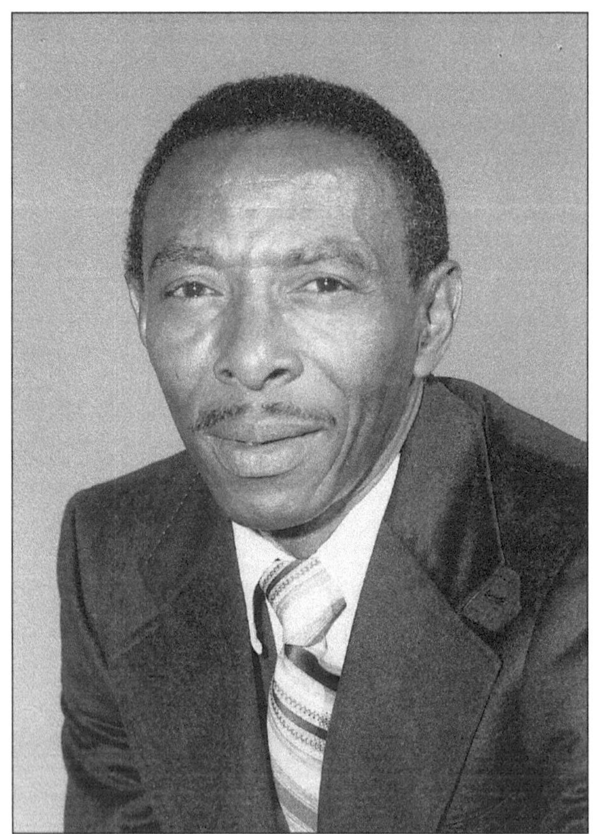

Head men's basketball coach David Whitney is Coach of the Year for the Southwest Athletic Conference (SWAC). He has been recognized as "Coach of the Year" several times.

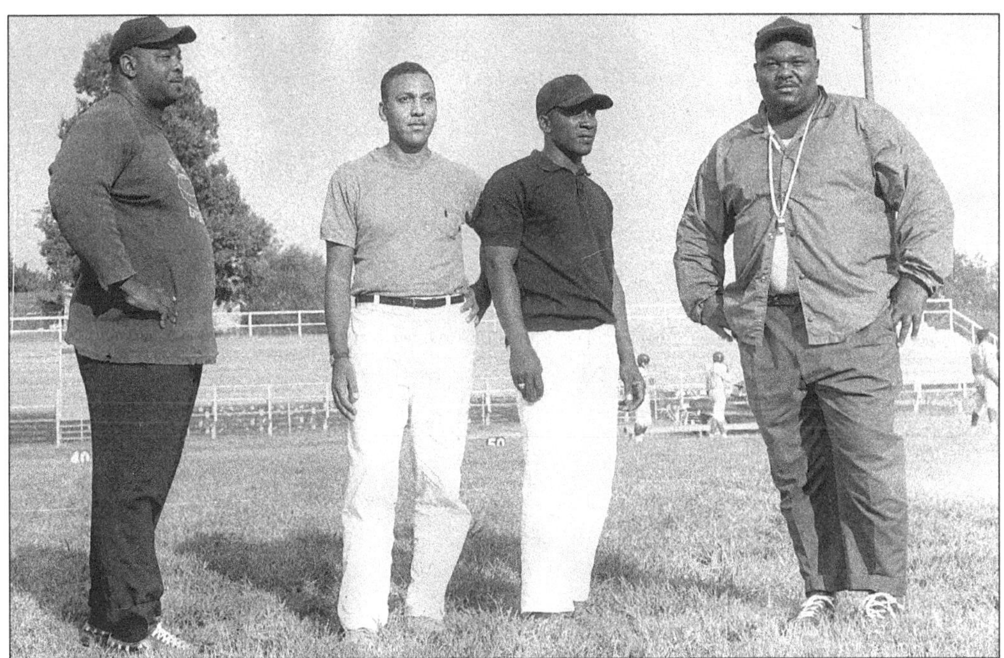

Seen here is the football coaching staff in 1961. From left to right are Coach Johnny Spinks, for whom the present stadium is named; Coach Grant Dungee, who also served as the track coach and the department chairman for Health and Physical Education; and two other dedicated Alcorn coaches.

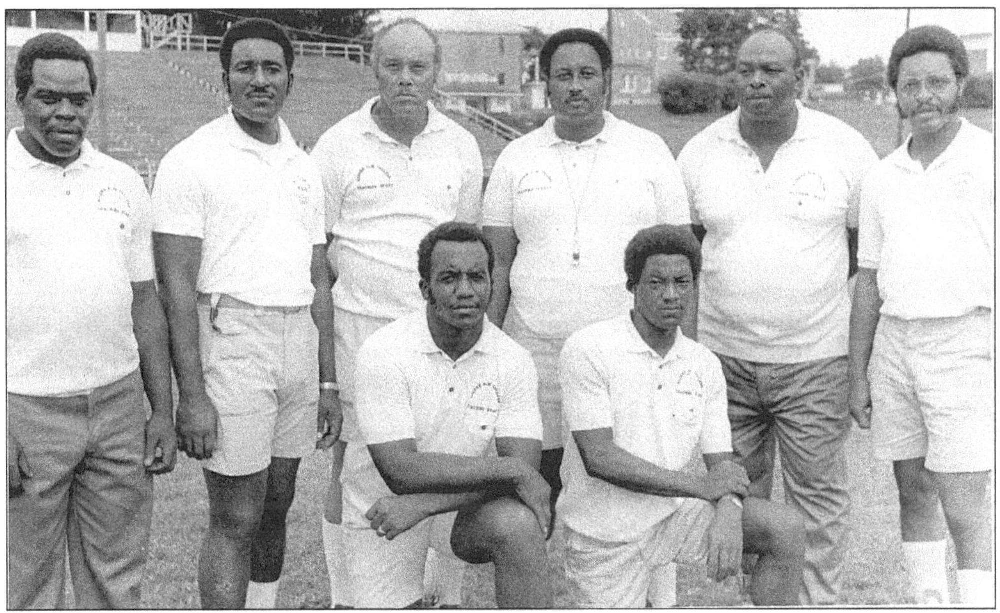

Featured in this photograph is the 1972 football coaching staff, under the leadership of Coach Marino Casem, "Godfather of the SWAC." Some of the coaches here include Willie McGowan, Archie Cooley, Theophilus Danzy, Jack "The Ripper" Spinks, and others.

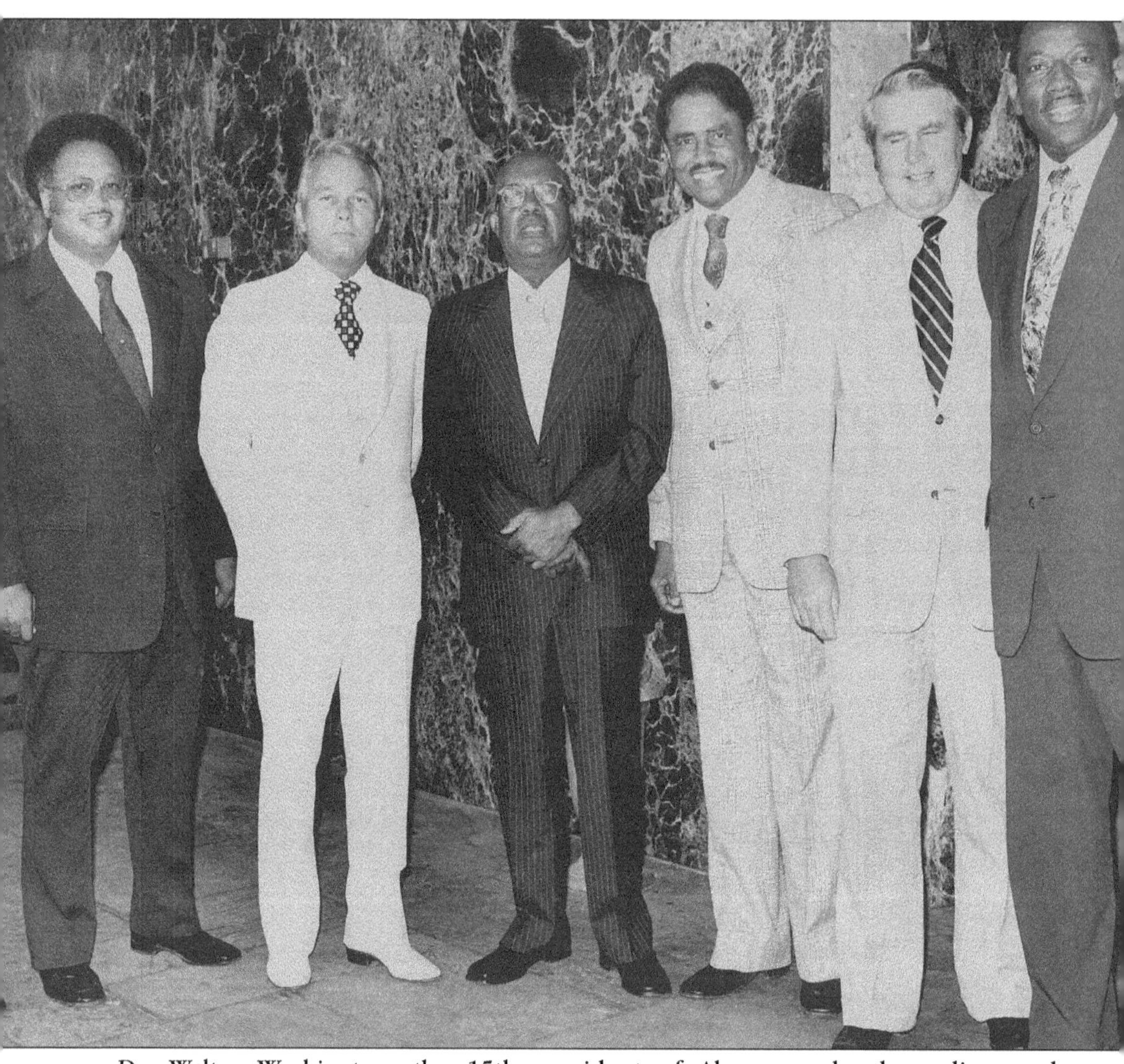

Dr. Walter Washington, the 15th president of Alcorn, and others discuss the Alcorn-Grambling football game that opened the Superdome in New Orleans, Louisiana. From left to right are Alcorn's coach Marino Casem; Louisiana governor Edwin Edwards; President R.W. Jones of Grambling; Grambling coach Eddie Robinson; Mississippi governor Bill Waller; and Dr. Walter Washington.

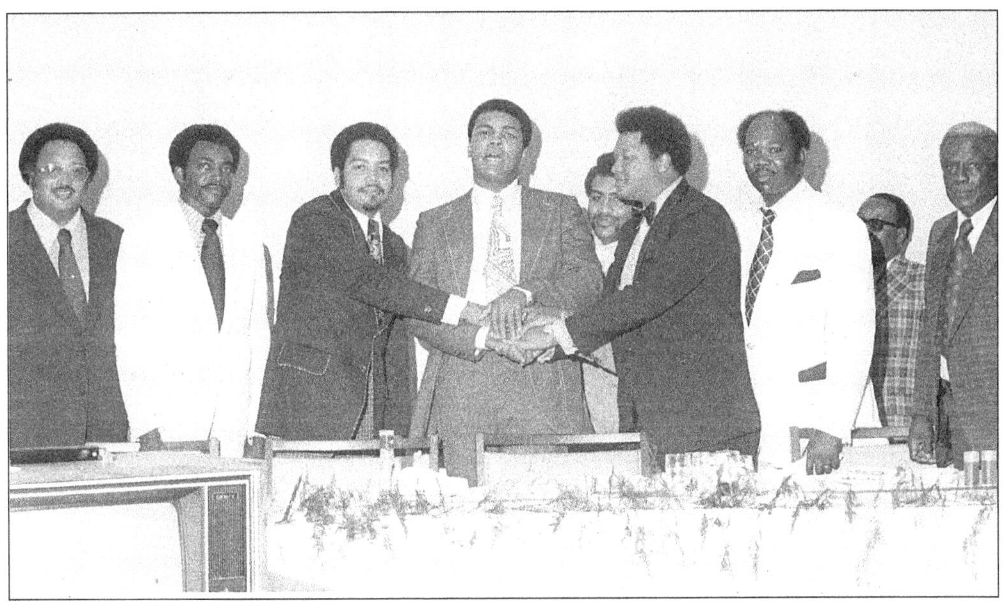

Mohammed Ali visits Alcorn and is welcomed by alumni and friends. Ali expressed a special interest in Alcorn and in its accomplishments, both athletic and academic.

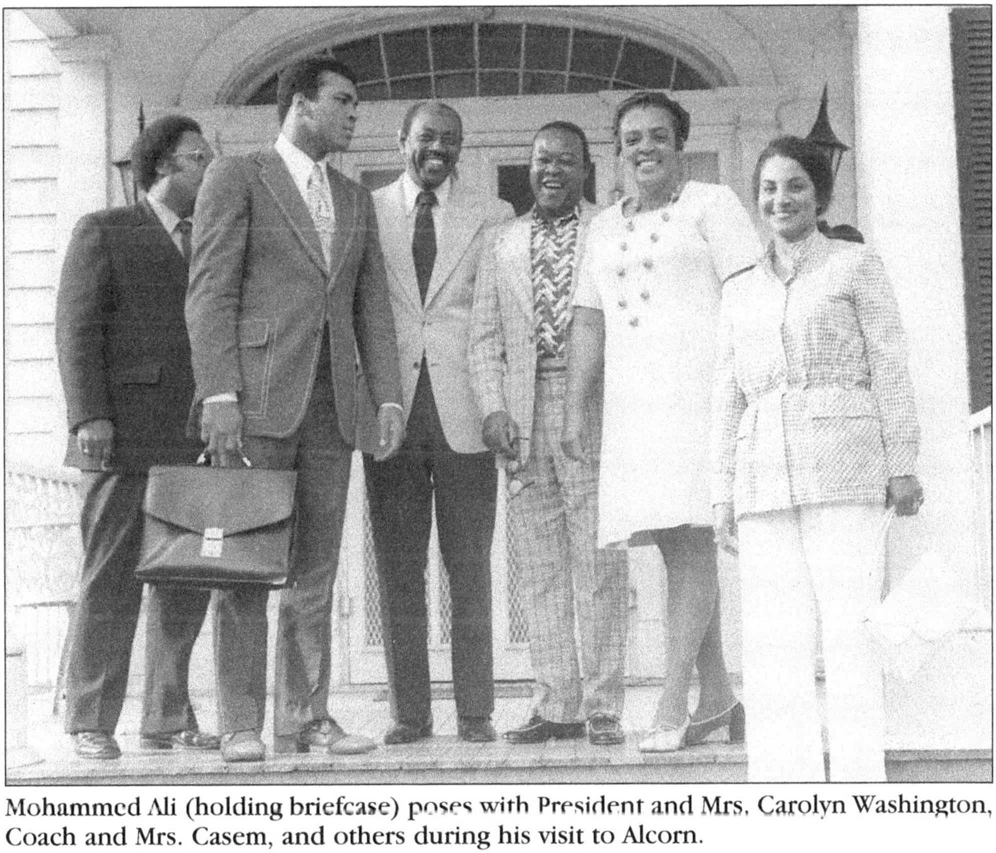

Mohammed Ali (holding briefcase) poses with President and Mrs. Carolyn Washington, Coach and Mrs. Casem, and others during his visit to Alcorn.

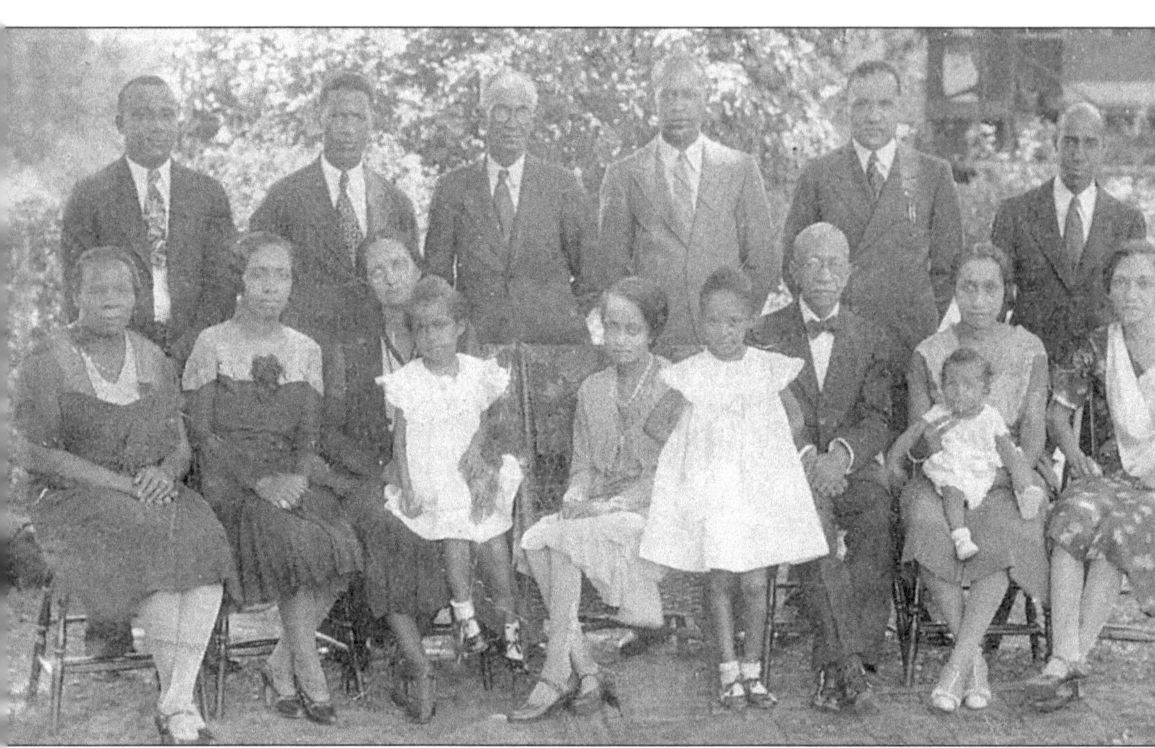

The family of President Levi J. Rowan is seen in this photograph taken in 1931. Rowan was the seventh president of Alcorn and was first elected to that position in 1905. The Rowan Model House is named in honor of his many accomplishments as Alcorn's president.

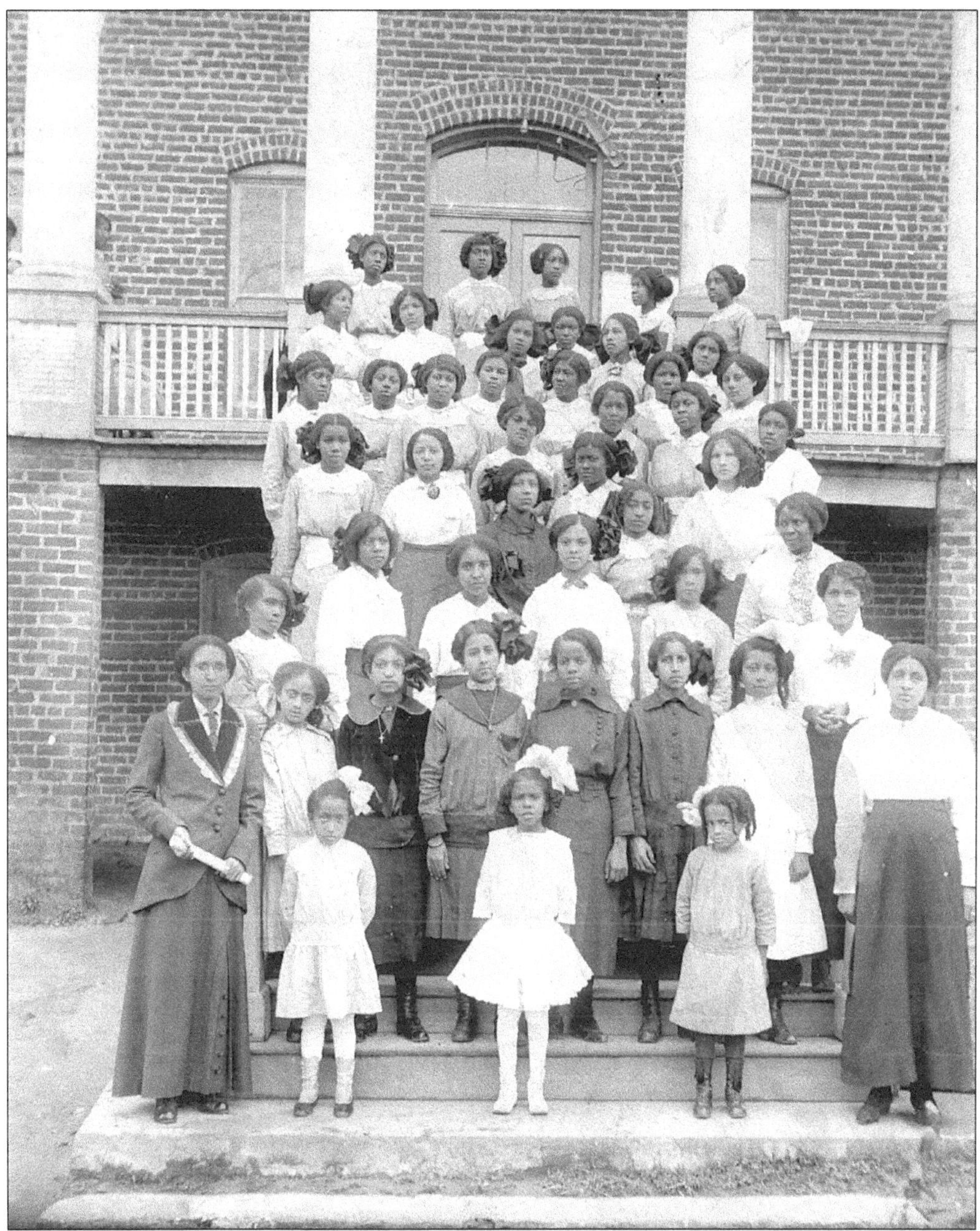

Alcorn was once a practice school in addition to a college. The students pictured here were enrolled in the practice school, an elementary school program that was housed on the campus and composed mainly of the children of Alcorn faculty and staff members. Alcorn students studying to become teachers utilized this facility as a hands-on training site.

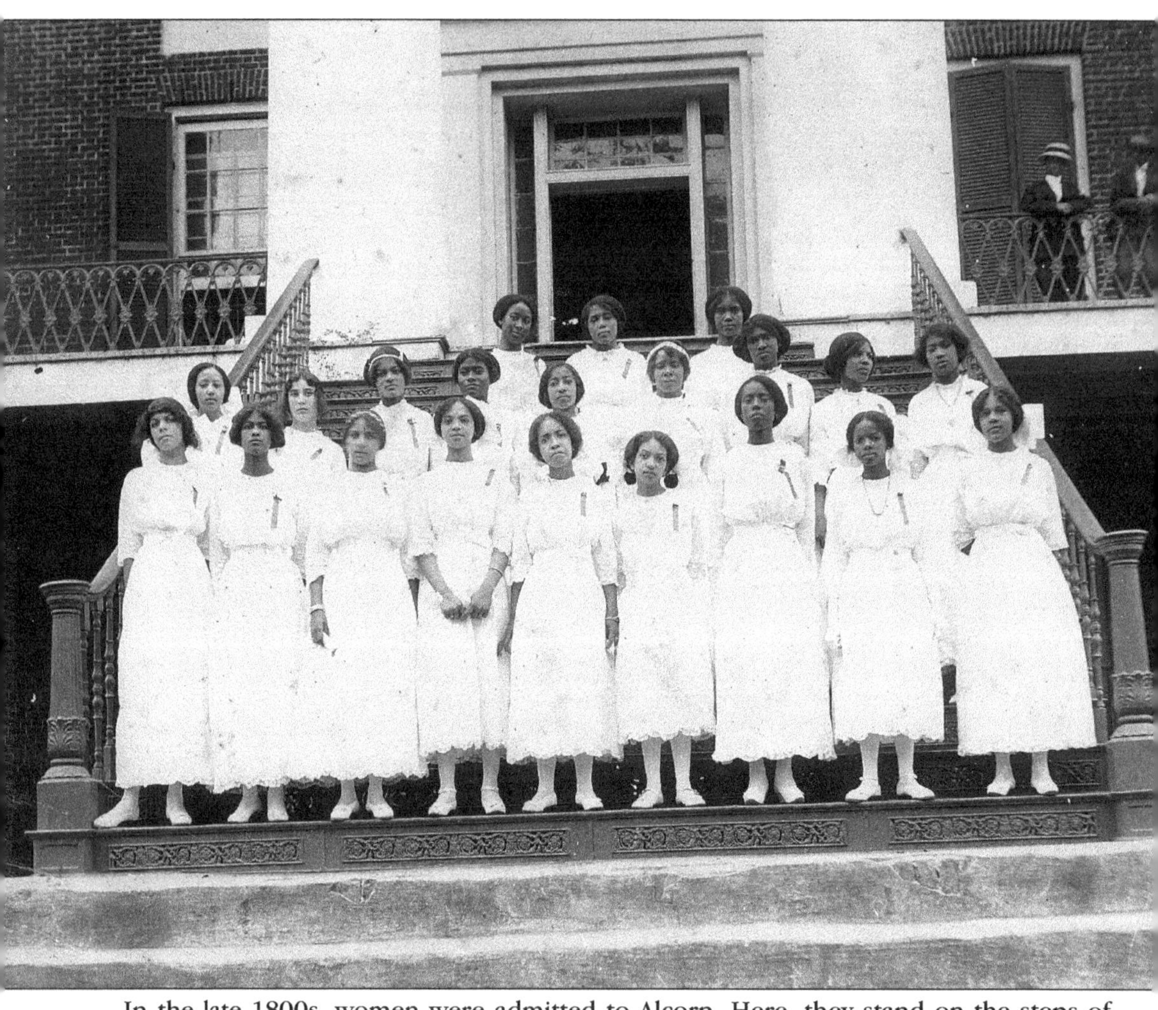

In the late 1800s, women were admitted to Alcorn. Here, they stand on the steps of the chapel, and two men in the right-hand corner appear very proud to have them as fellow classmates.

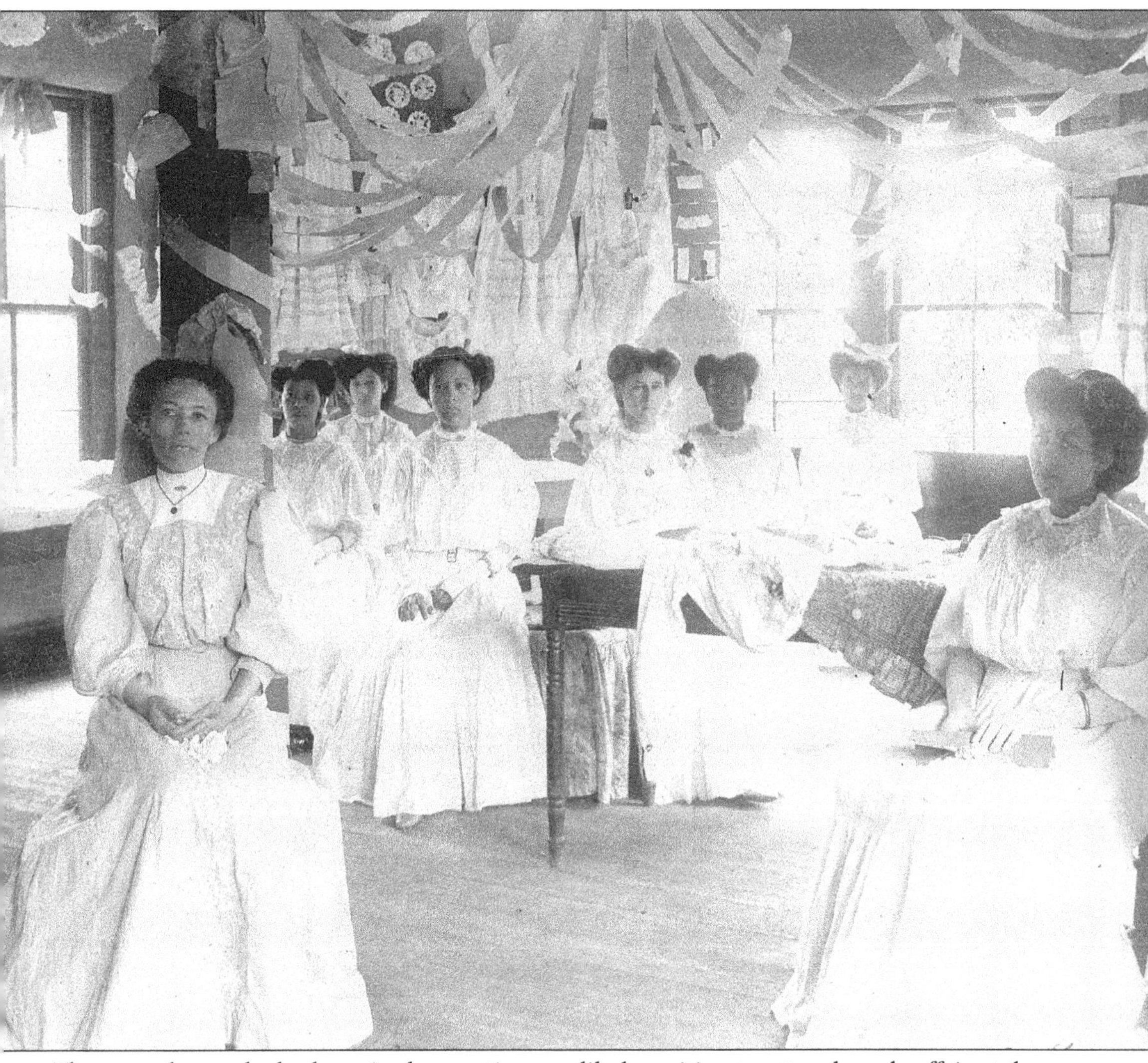

These students, decked out in dress attire, are likely waiting to attend a gala affair at the college. Alcorn students committed themselves to studying but also availed themselves of the opportunities to be involved in social activities.

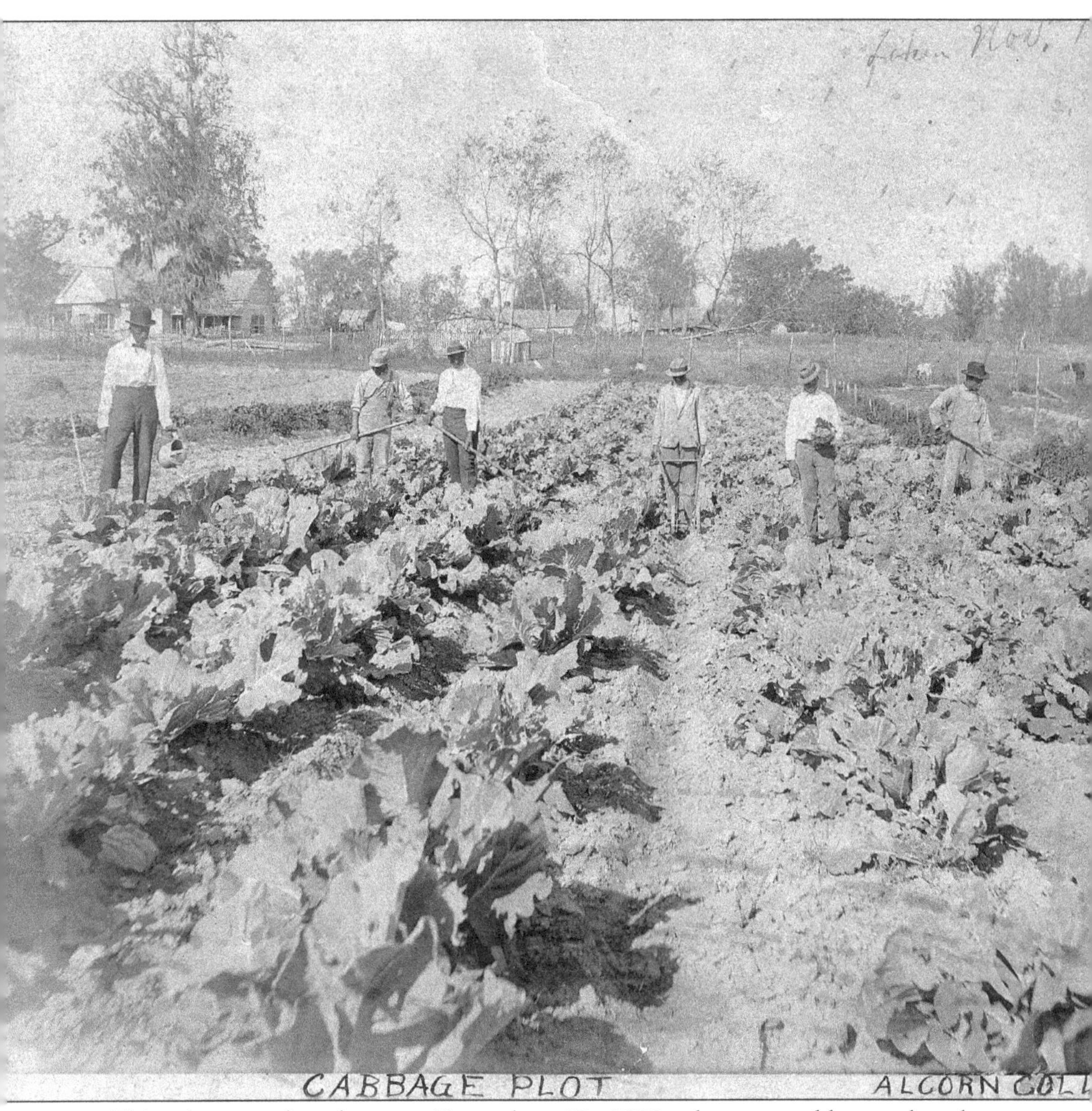

This photograph, taken on November 12, 1890, shows a cabbage plot that was planted and tended by college students, who learned to grow their own food and other survival skills.

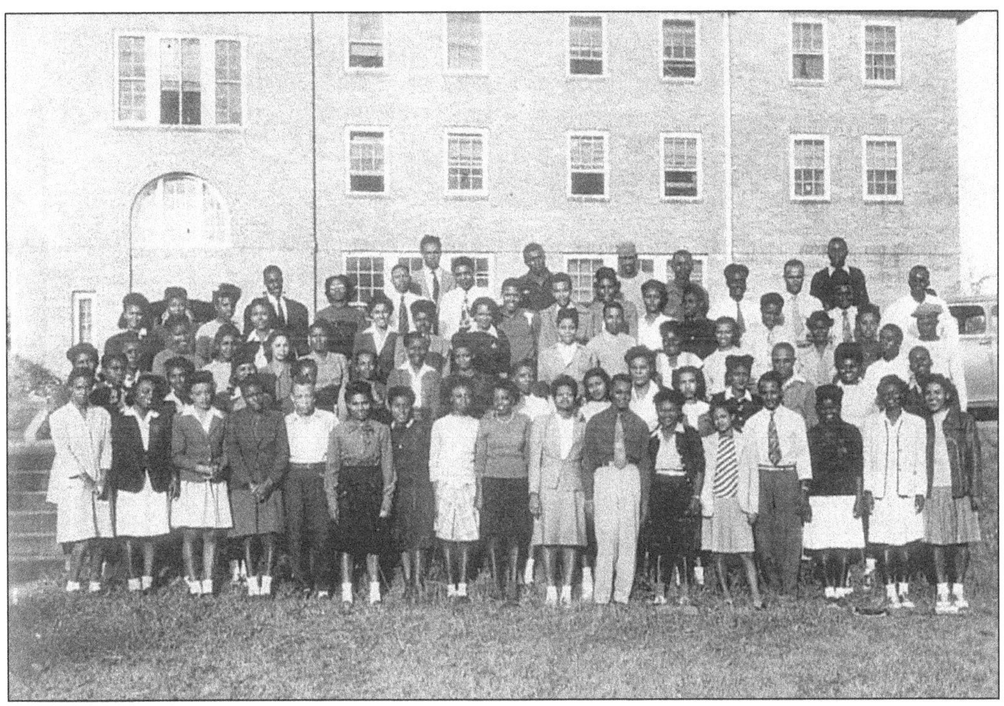

Members of Alcorn's freshman class of 1946 gathered for this picture and helped to preserve memories for years to come.

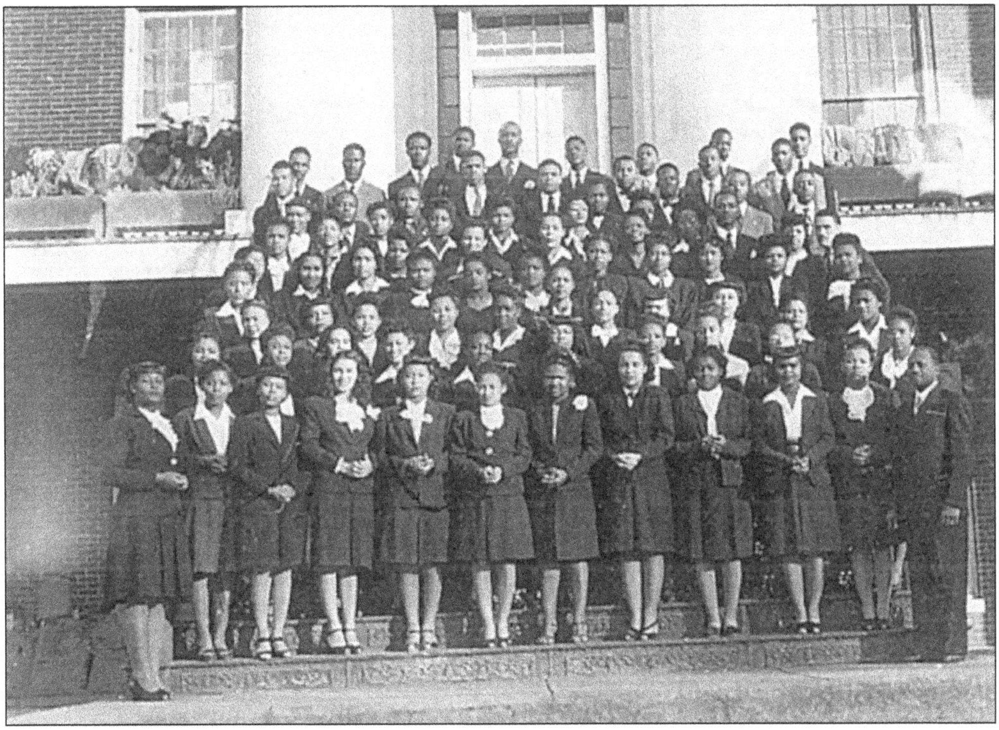

In 1947, members of the Alcorn Choir posed for this picture on the steps of the chapel. C.C. Bishop was the director and Herticene Jones was the pianist.

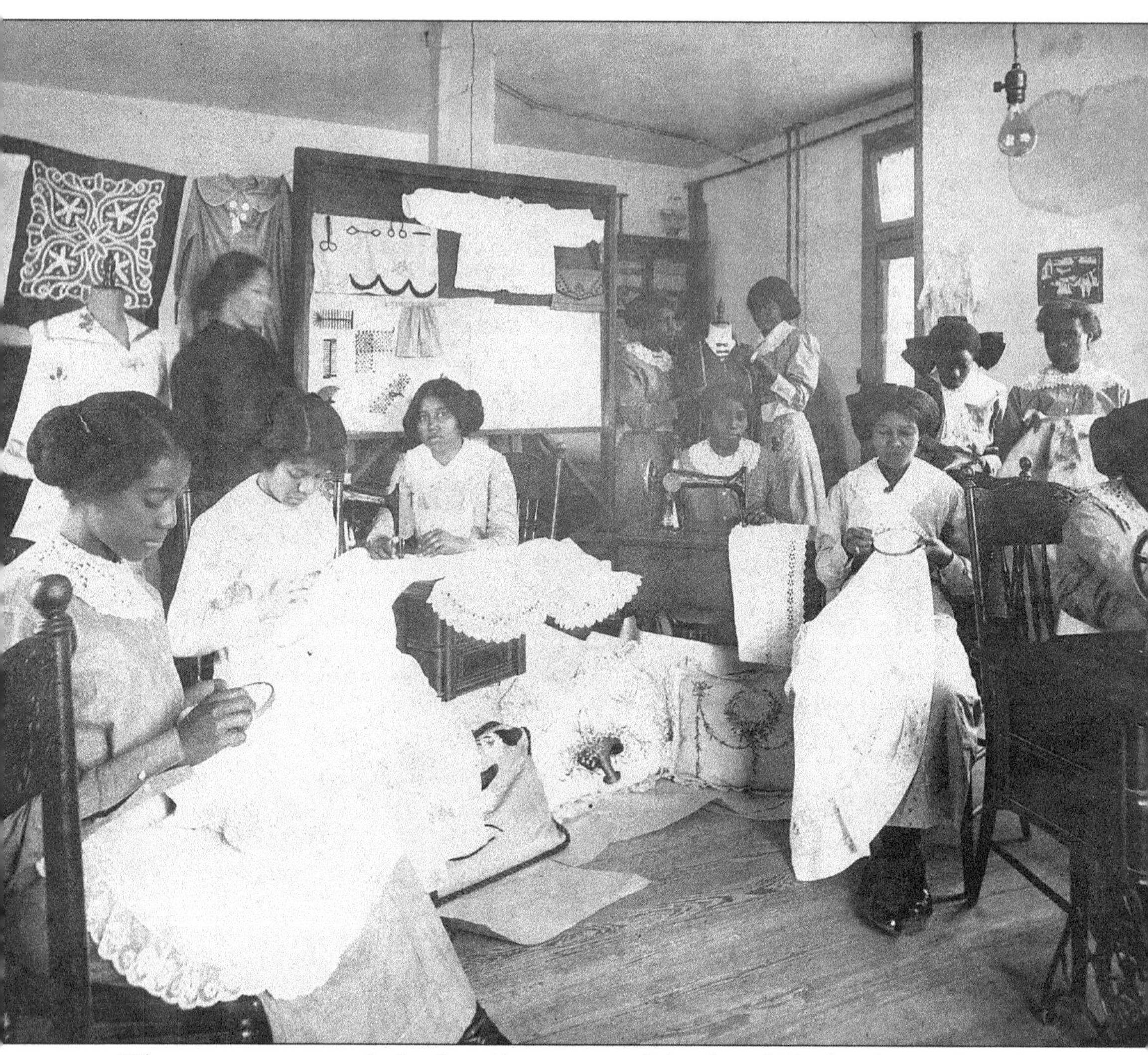

When women were admitted to Alcorn, one of the first skills they learned was how to sew and make their own clothes. This was a skill that enabled them to help their own families, as well as their community. These women perfected their skills and demonstrated great pride in their work.

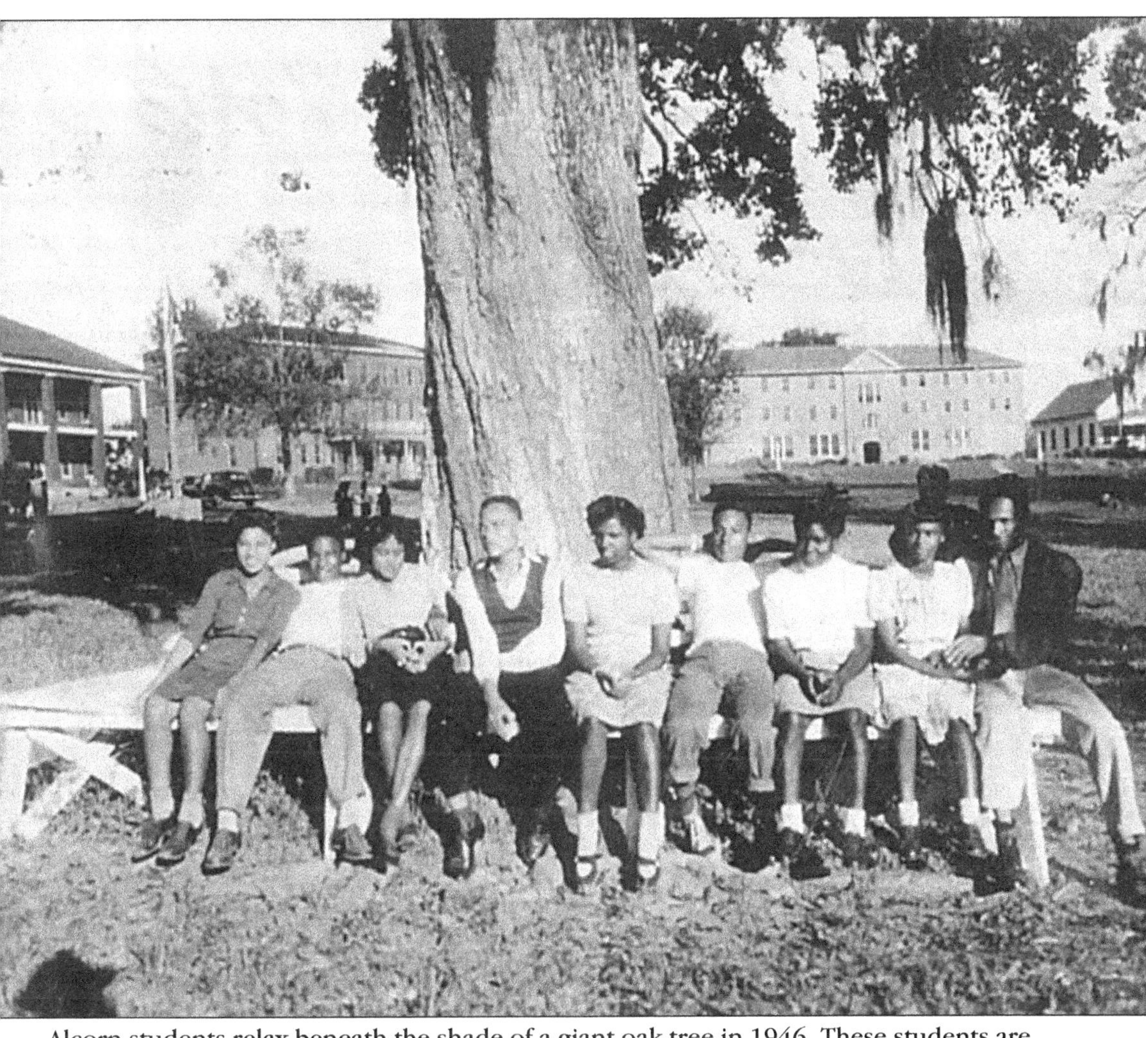

Alcorn students relax beneath the shade of a giant oak tree in 1946. These students are, from left to right, Lois Batts, Roy Rocker, Josephine Ward, Bo Wright, Helen Johnson Pointer, James Ford, Virginia Foster Henderson, Carolyn Brown, and Frank Gambrel.

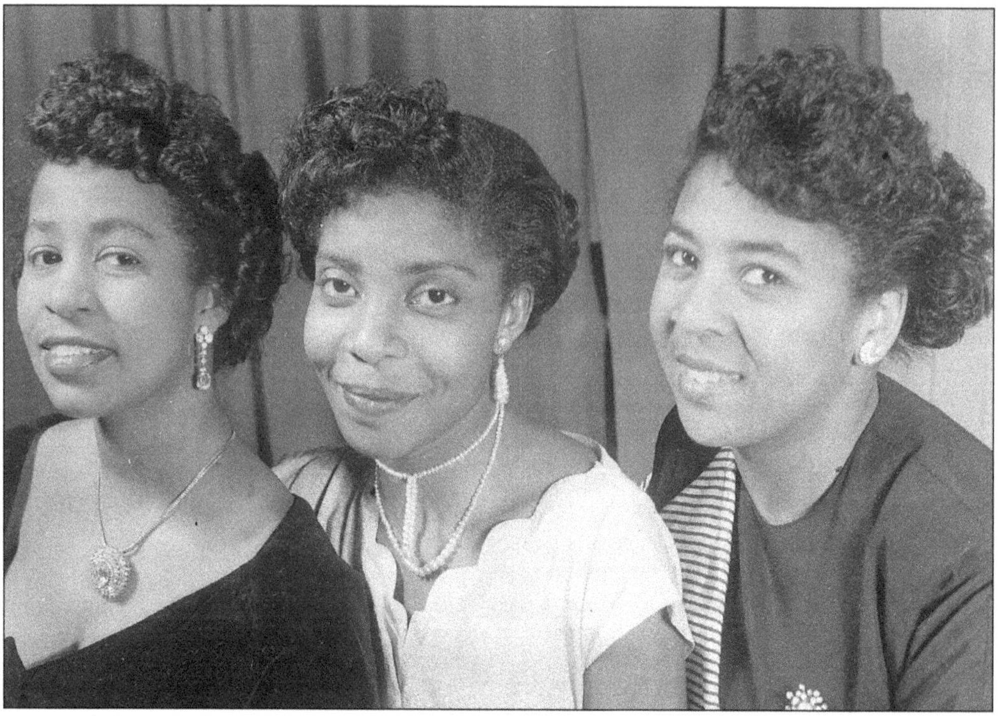

Pictured, from left to right, are Mary Goins Jackson, Billie Whitfield Barnes, and Marva Smith Russell as they flash that "Alcorn smile."

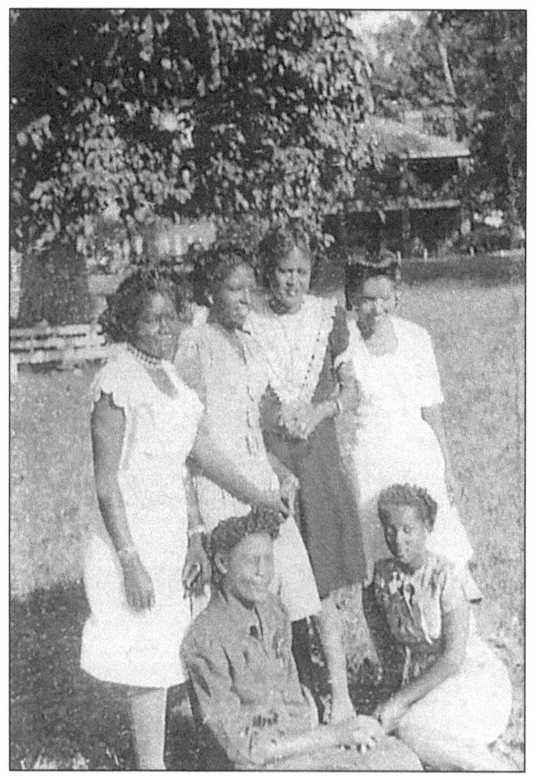

Alcorn students are pictured here in front of the dining hall on a Sunday afternoon in 1946. From left to right are (seated) Alfreda Greene and Roberta Anderson Brock; (standing) Virginia Foster Henderson, Helen J. Pointer, Josephine Ward, and Ruby Pearl Gray.

These Alcornites pose near Oakland Chapel. They are, from left to right, Willie Harper Wilson, unidentified, George Wilson, and Marva Smith Russell. The chapel, constructed in 1830, is one of the oldest buildings on the Alcorn campus.

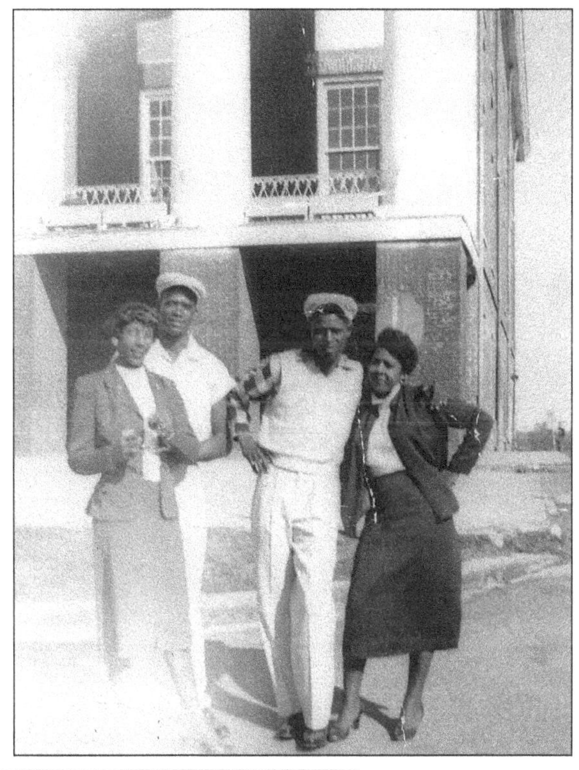

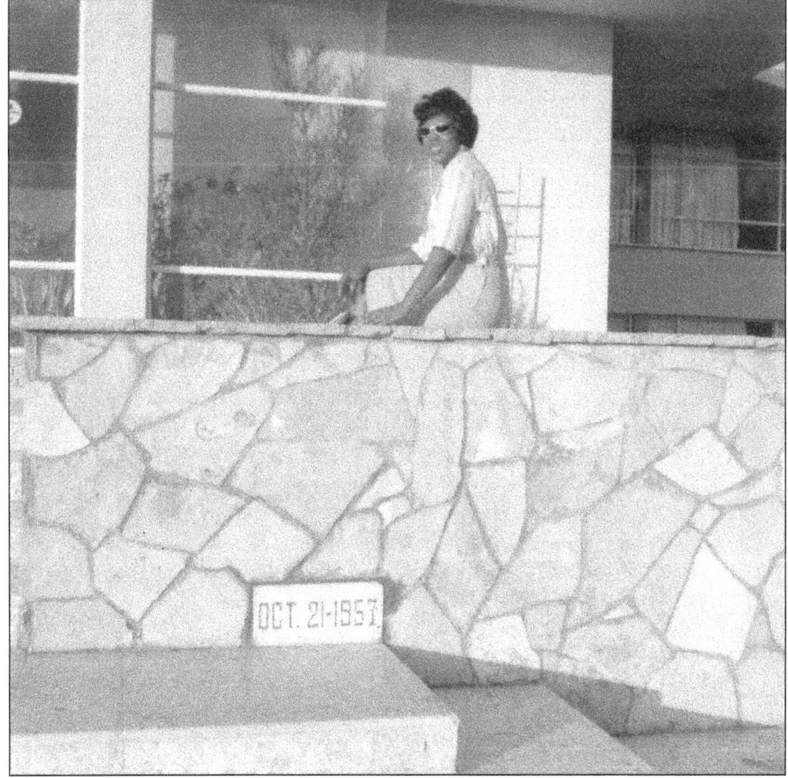

Mary Lizzie Smith is pictured in front of Alice Tanner, now a dormitory for men. The building, constructed in 1957 at a cost of $225,000, was named in honor of an Alcornite.

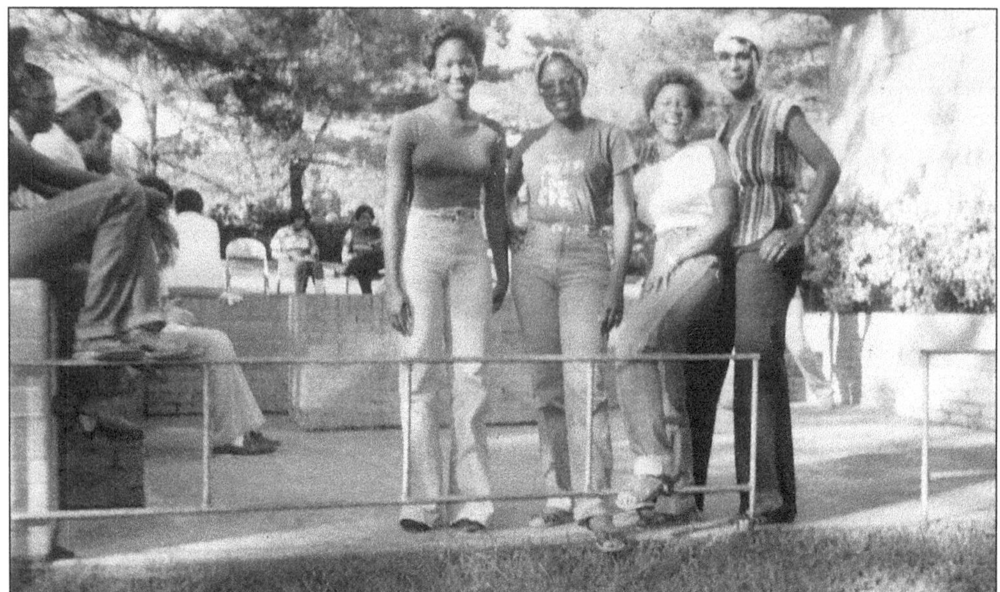

Transfer and freshman students learn early how to exude the Alcorn style. From left to right are Pamela Washington, Kimberly Jackson, Petera G. Washington, and Patricia Smith.

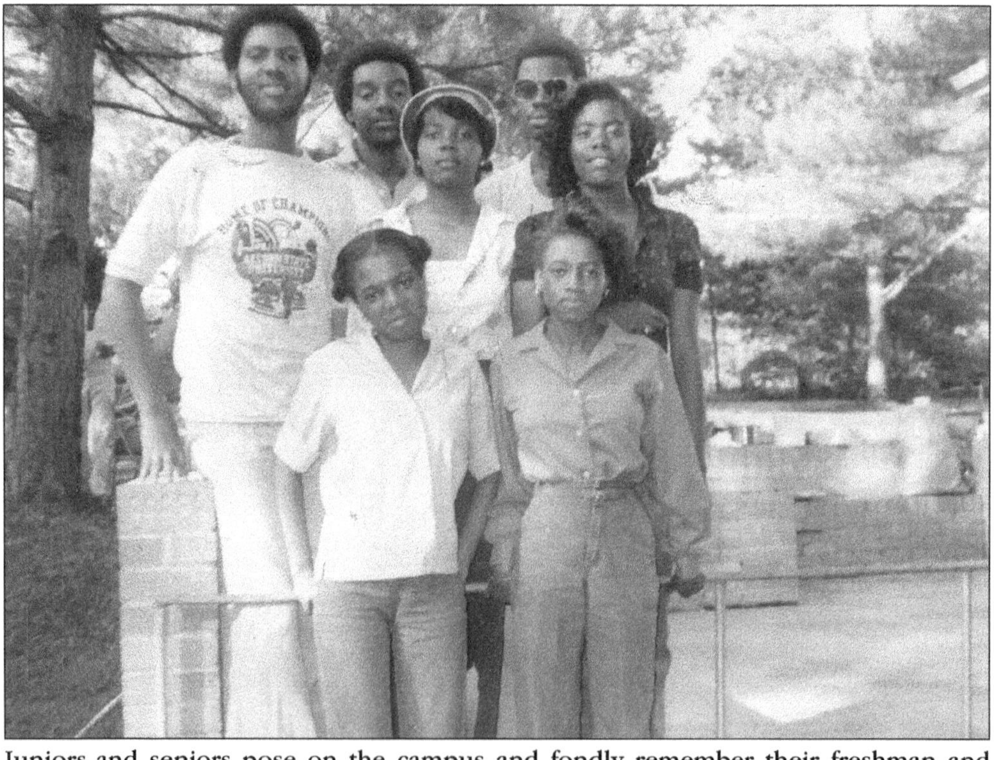

Juniors and seniors pose on the campus and fondly remember their freshman and sophomore years. From left to right are (front row) Valerie Spiller and Mable Burton; (second row) Dexter Holloway, Janice Johnson, and Alberta Jones; (back row) Stephen Earl and Secdonia Webb Jr.

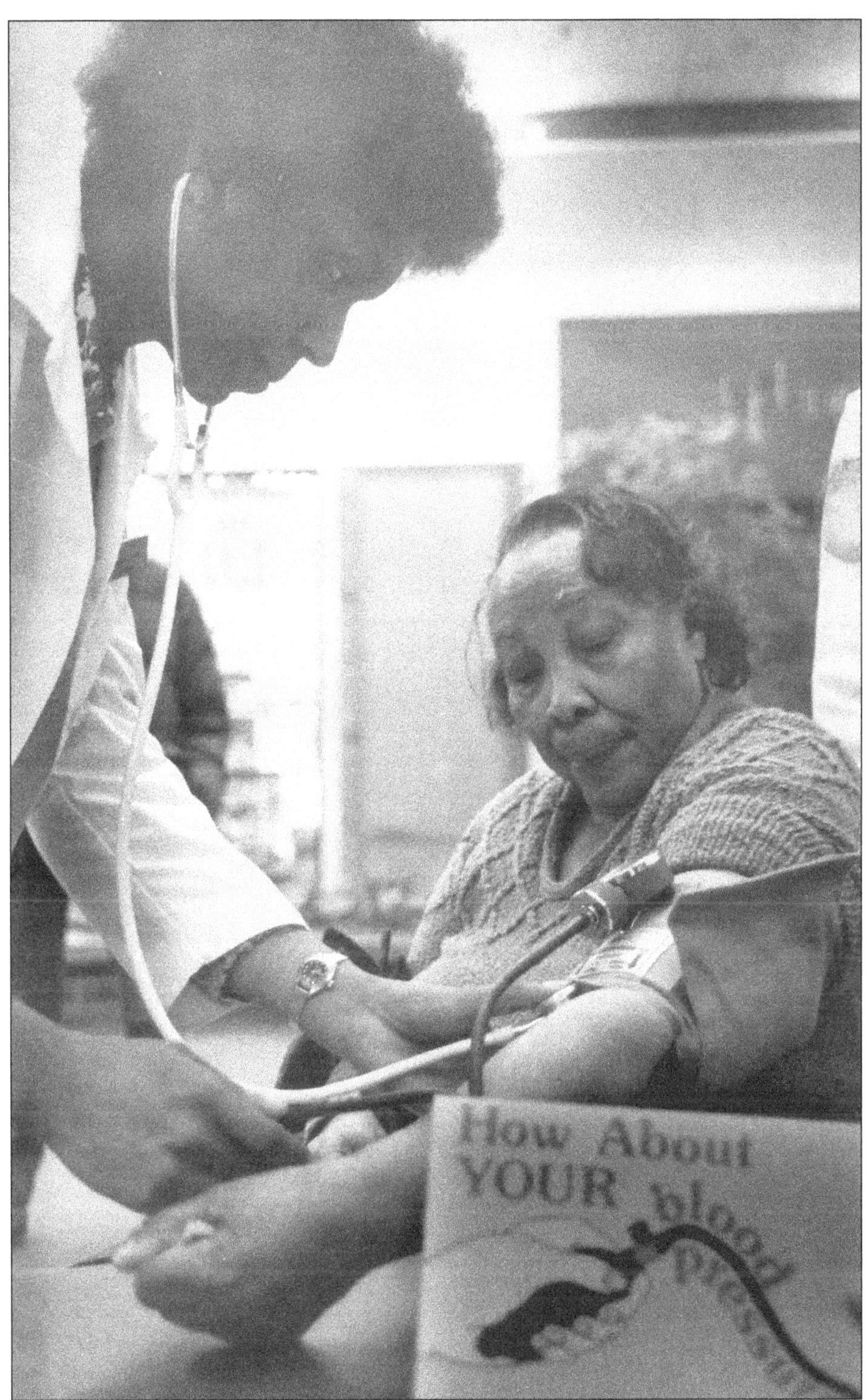

Alcorn nursing student Jacqueline Thompson learns to check blood pressure. The sign reads "How About Your Blood Pressure?" and a resident of Waterproof, Louisiana is finding out.

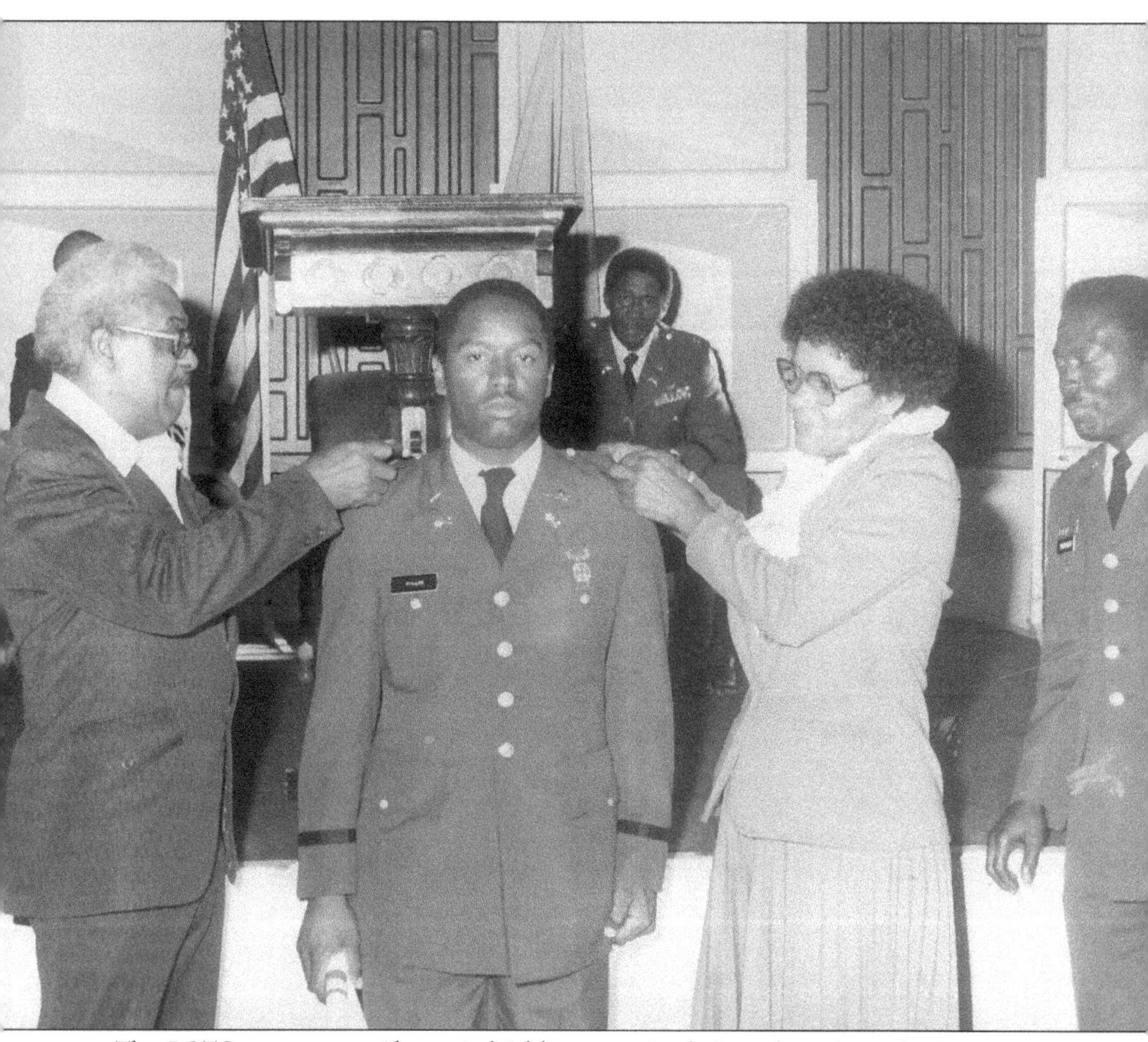

The ROTC program at Alcorn is highly recognized. Seen here is a pinning ceremony, which takes place each year upon completion of the program.

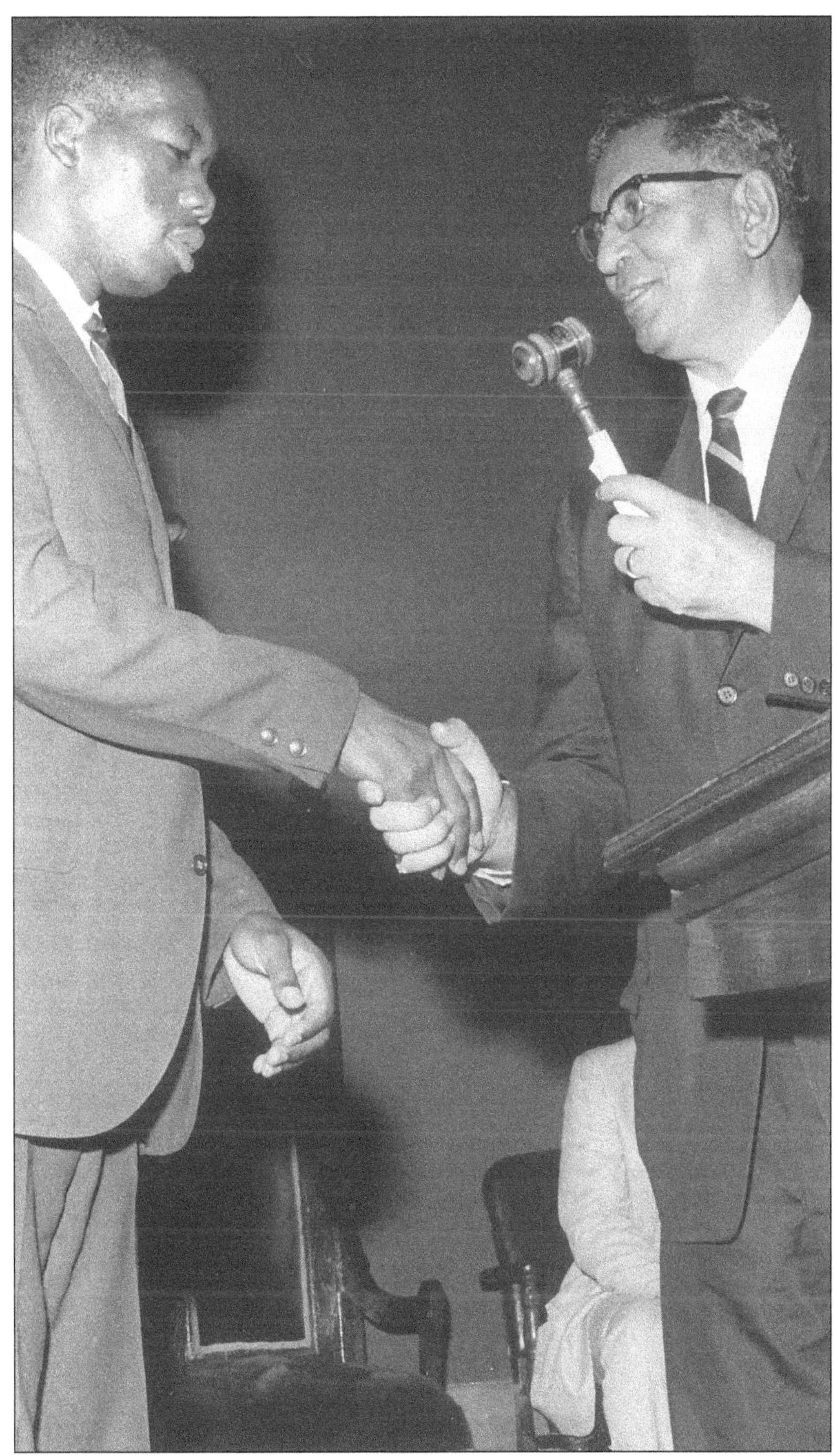

President Boyd, president of Alcorn from 1957 until 1969, gives the great Alcorn greeting and handshake at a college function.

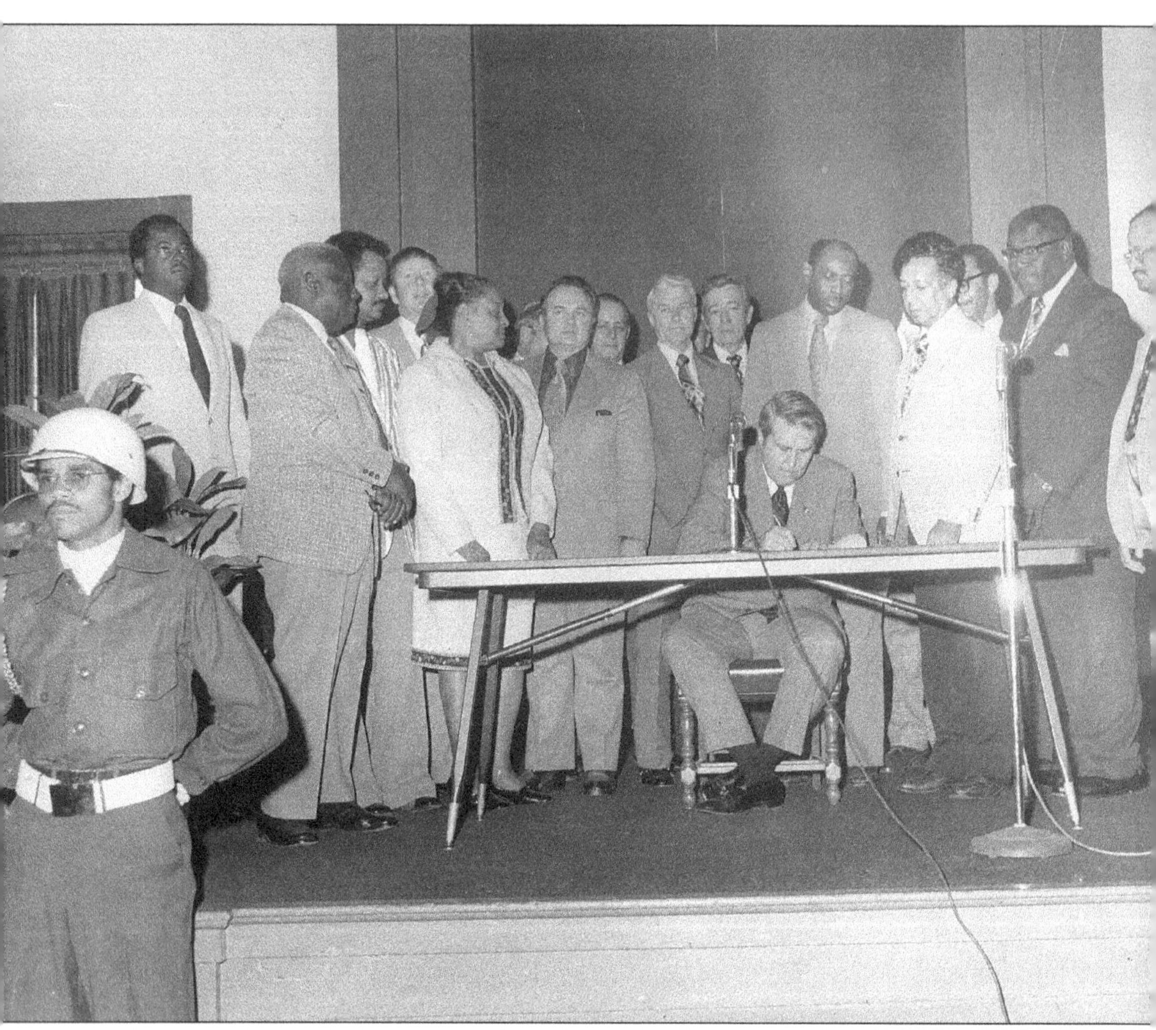

The name Alcorn Agricultural and Mechanical College was officially changed to Alcorn State University in 1974. The governor of Mississippi Bill Waller is pictured here signing the change into law.

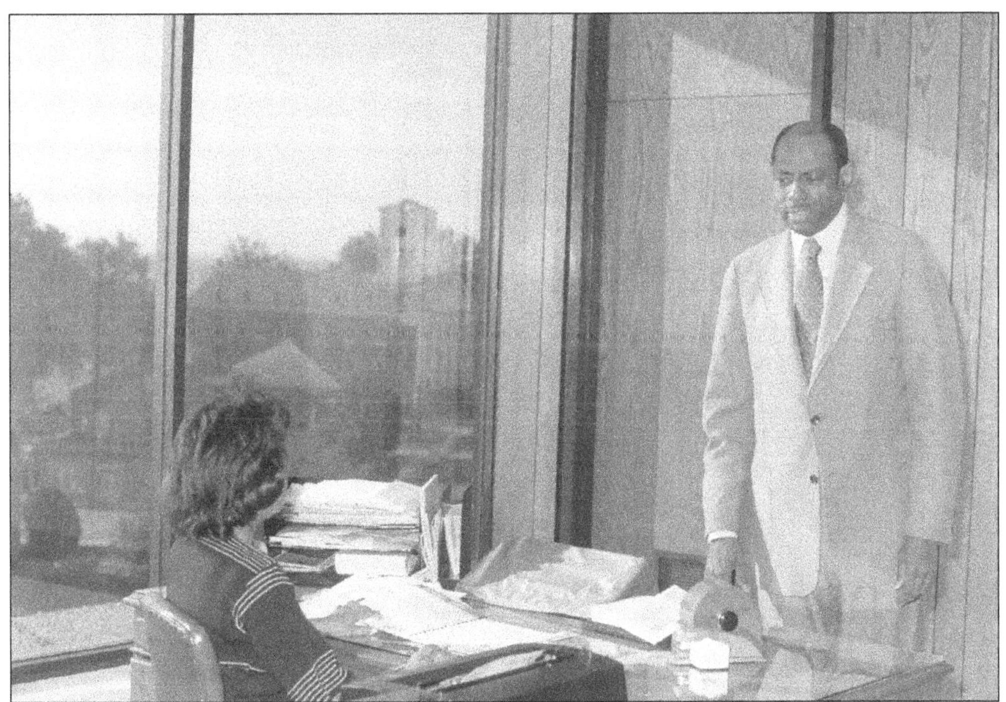

President Walter Washington and his executive secretary Erma Hawkins discuss the business of the university. Dr. Washington served as president of Alcorn for 25 years.

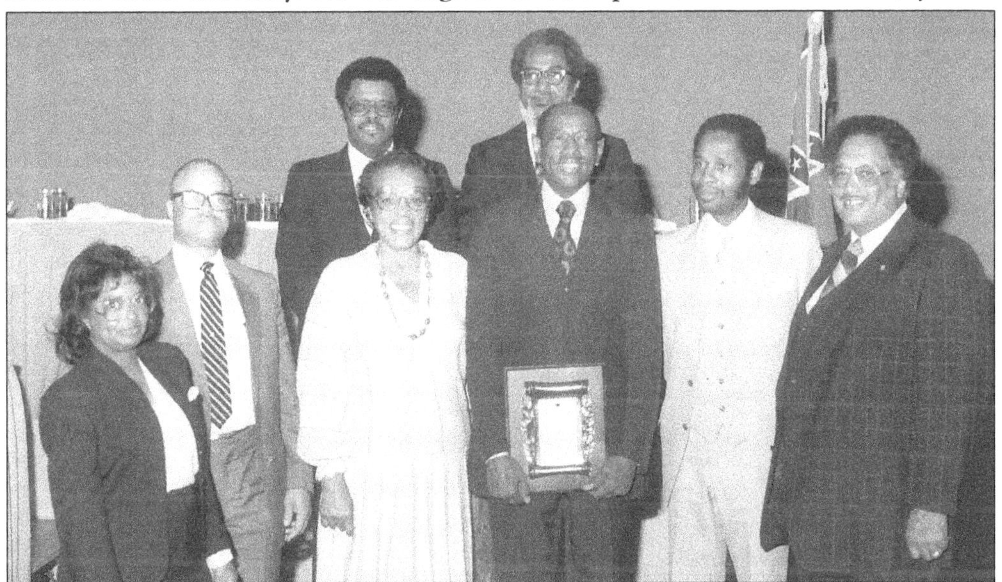

Dr. Walter Washington is pictured here after having received one of the many honors bestowed upon him during his tenure as president of Alcorn. Surrounding him, from left to right, are (front row) Erma Hawkins; Executive Vice President Rudolph Waters; Dr. Carolyn Washington, first lady; Dr. Franklin Jackson, the vice president of Institutional Advancement and Planning; and Coach Marino Casem; (back row) Dr. Malvin Williams, vice president of Academic Affairs; and Dr. Norris Edney, dean of the Graduate School and of Arts and Sciences.

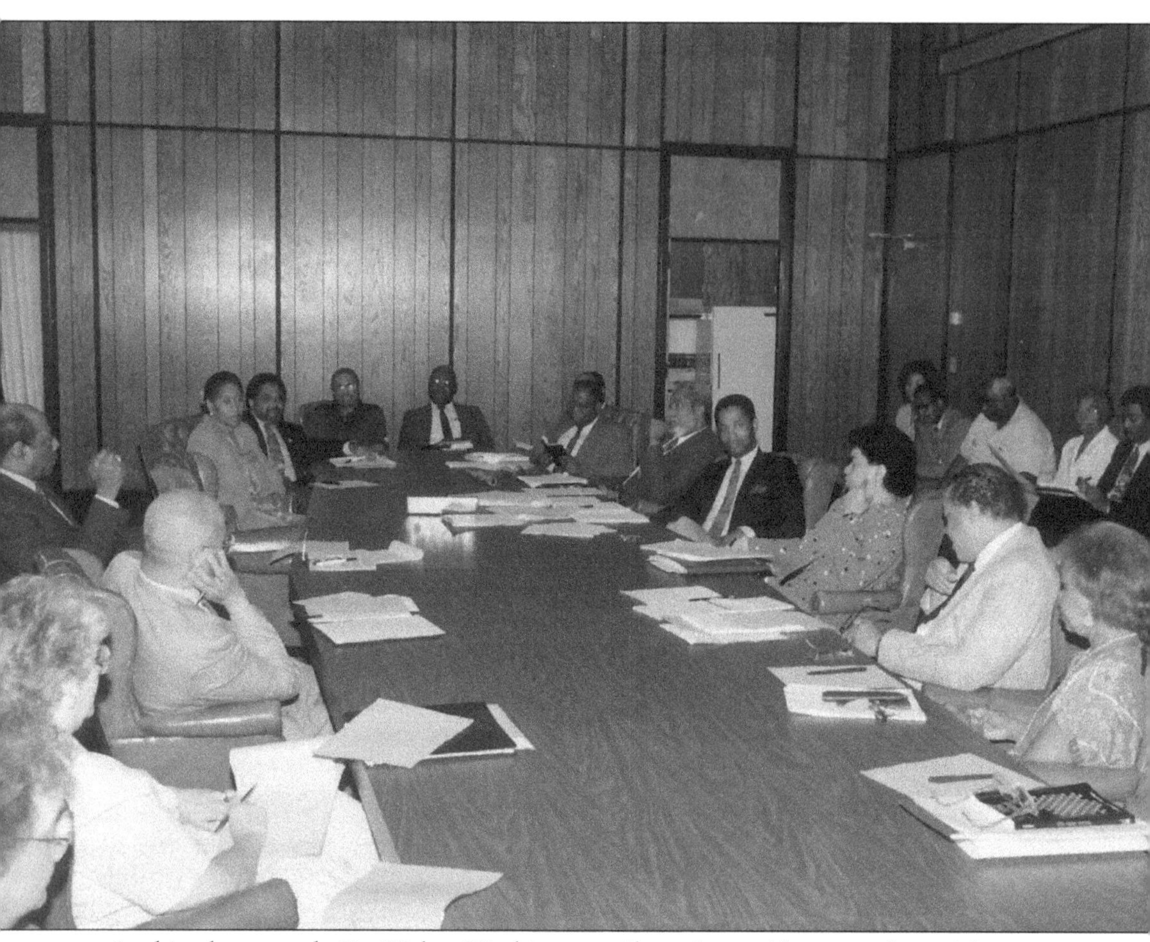

In this photograph, Dr. Walter Washington, Alcorn's president, confers with university administrators on accreditation and other issues of concern related to the overall growth and enhancement of the university.

Three

Miss Alcorn in the Early Years

Miss Alcorn has been selected by the student body on an annual basis as a representative who portrays Alcorn's commitment to excellence. The first Miss Alcorn was Henerine Simpkins Knaives (1926–1927), and the second Miss Alcorn was Emma W. Howard (1927–1928). Some of the women chosen as Miss Alcorn over the years are featured in this chapter; however, several portraits were not available for publication. Congratulations go to all of these women, those pictured and not pictured, for representing the Alcorn family in a most excellent and graceful manner.

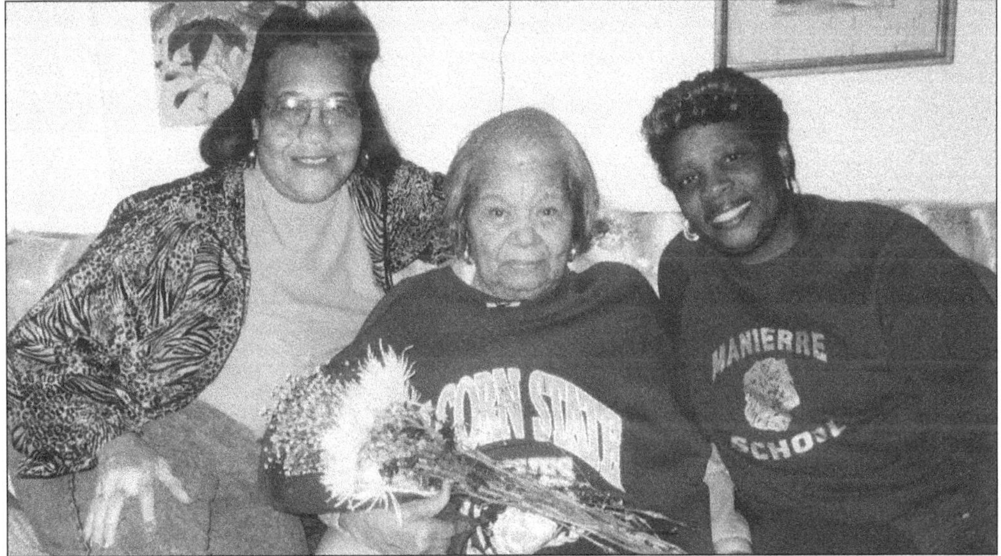

Emma W. Howard, Miss Alcorn 1928, is seated in the middle of Angie Roberson and Carolyn Ball. Howard lives in Chicago, Illinois, and continues to contribute to the Miss Alcorn Forever Club.

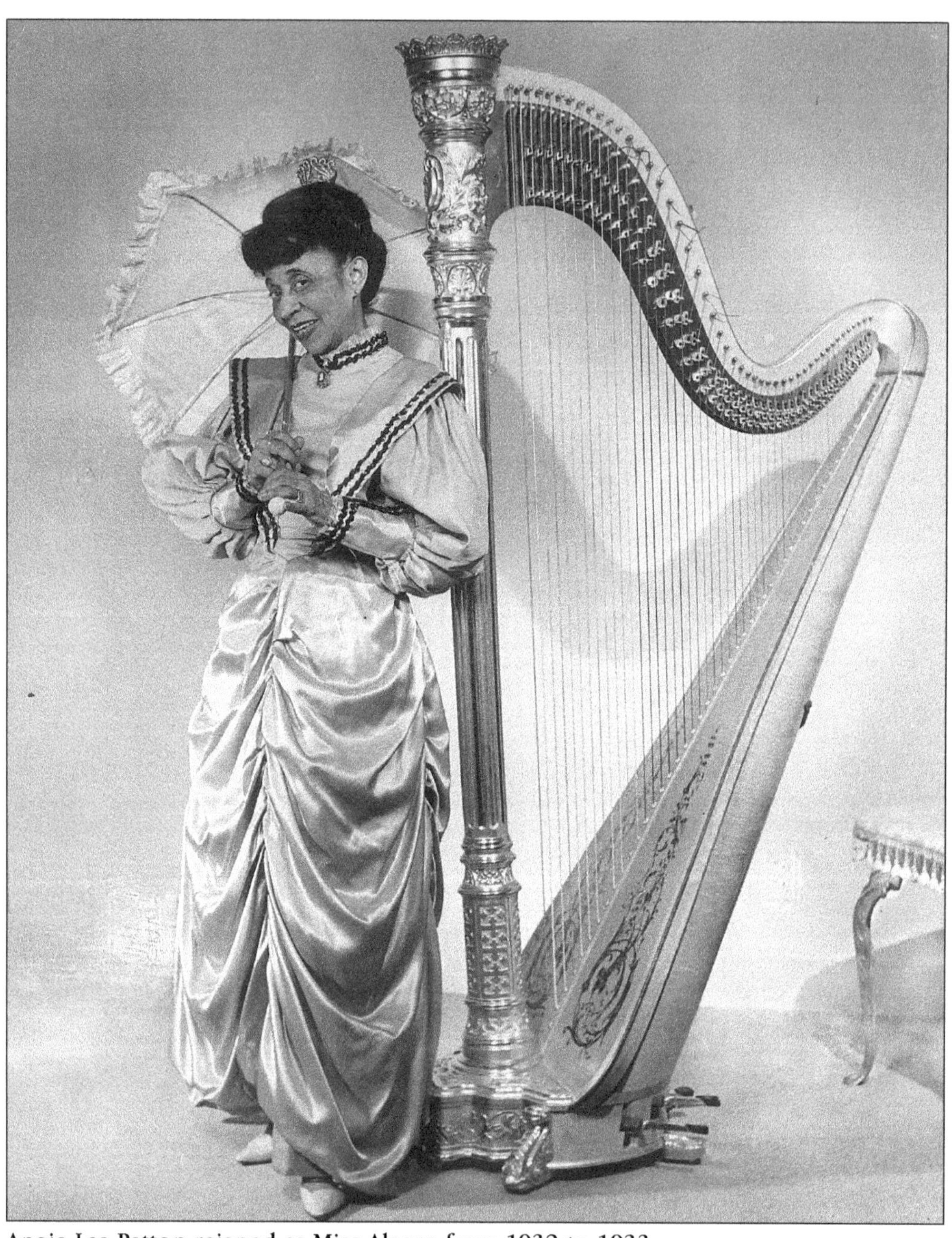

Angie Lee Patton reigned as Miss Alcorn from 1932 to 1933.

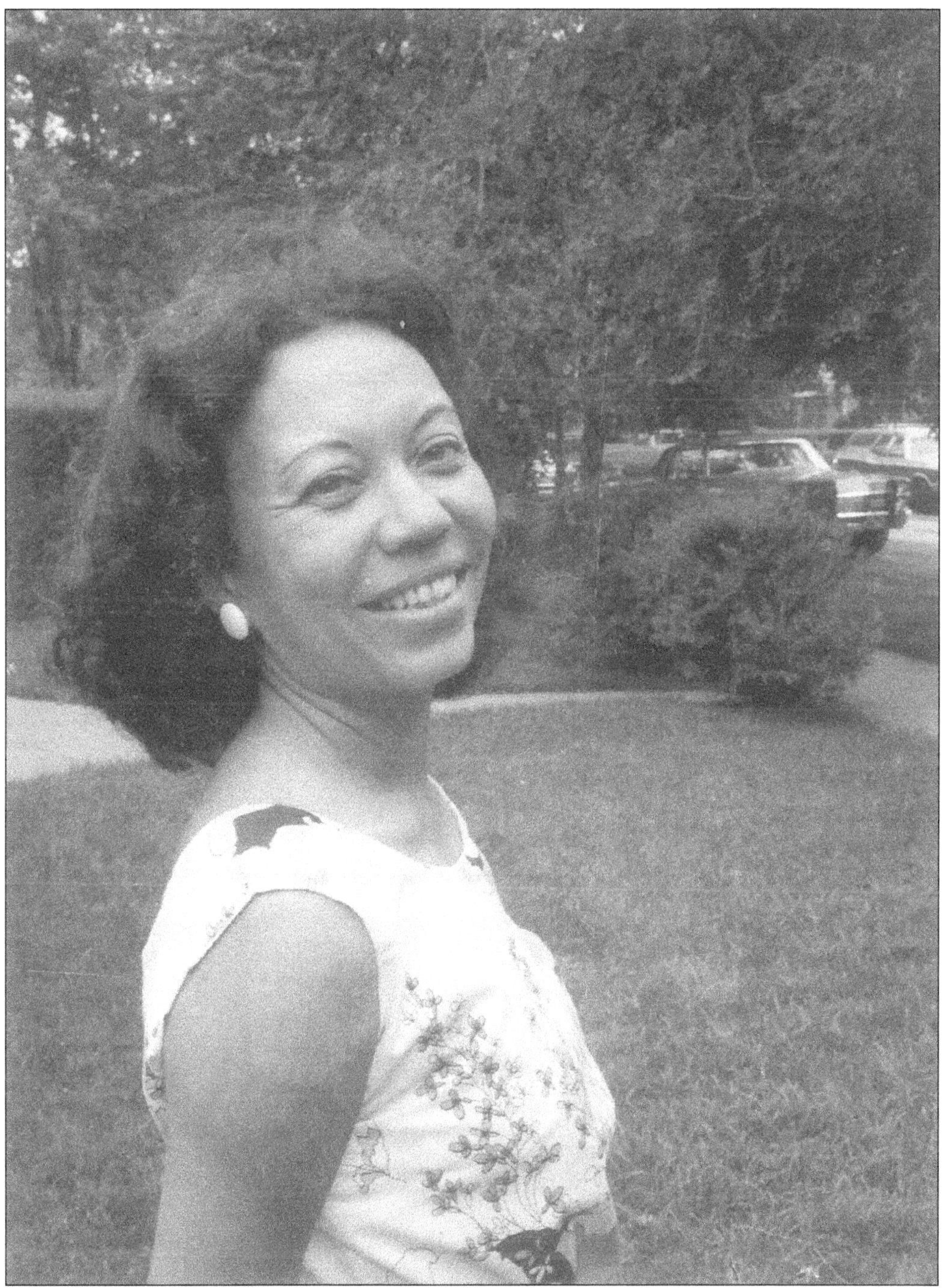

Janice Snodgrass Waters reigned as Miss Alcorn from 1945 to 1946.

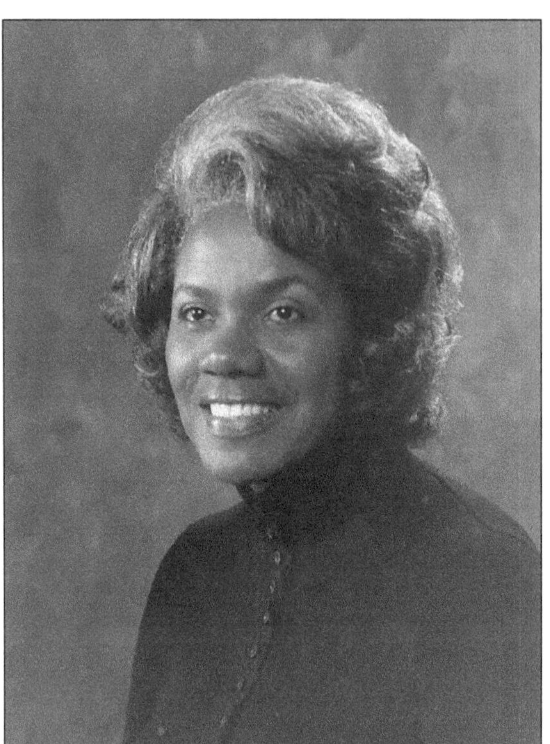

Kathryn Moore Jones reigned as Miss Alcorn from 1946 to 1947.

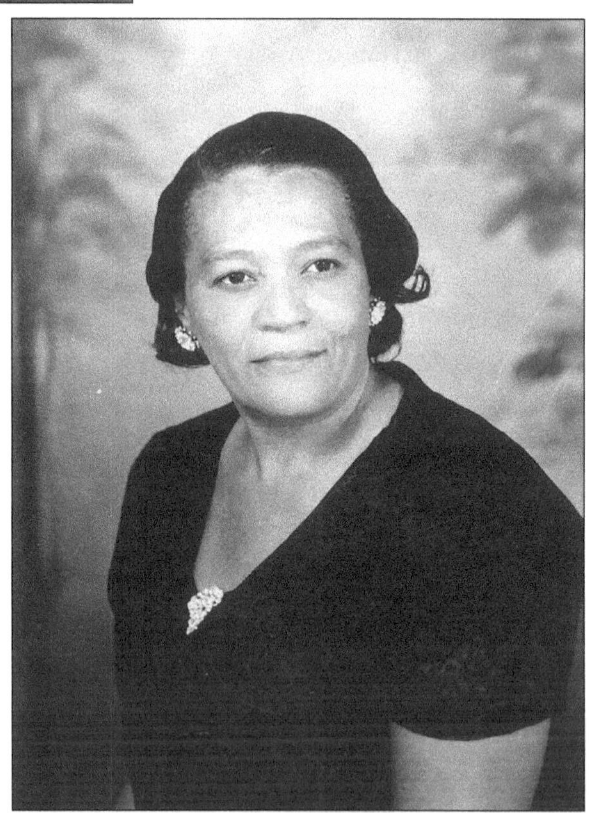

Henriene Simpkins Knaives was the first Miss Alcorn in the school's history and she reigned as Miss Alcorn from 1926 to 1927.

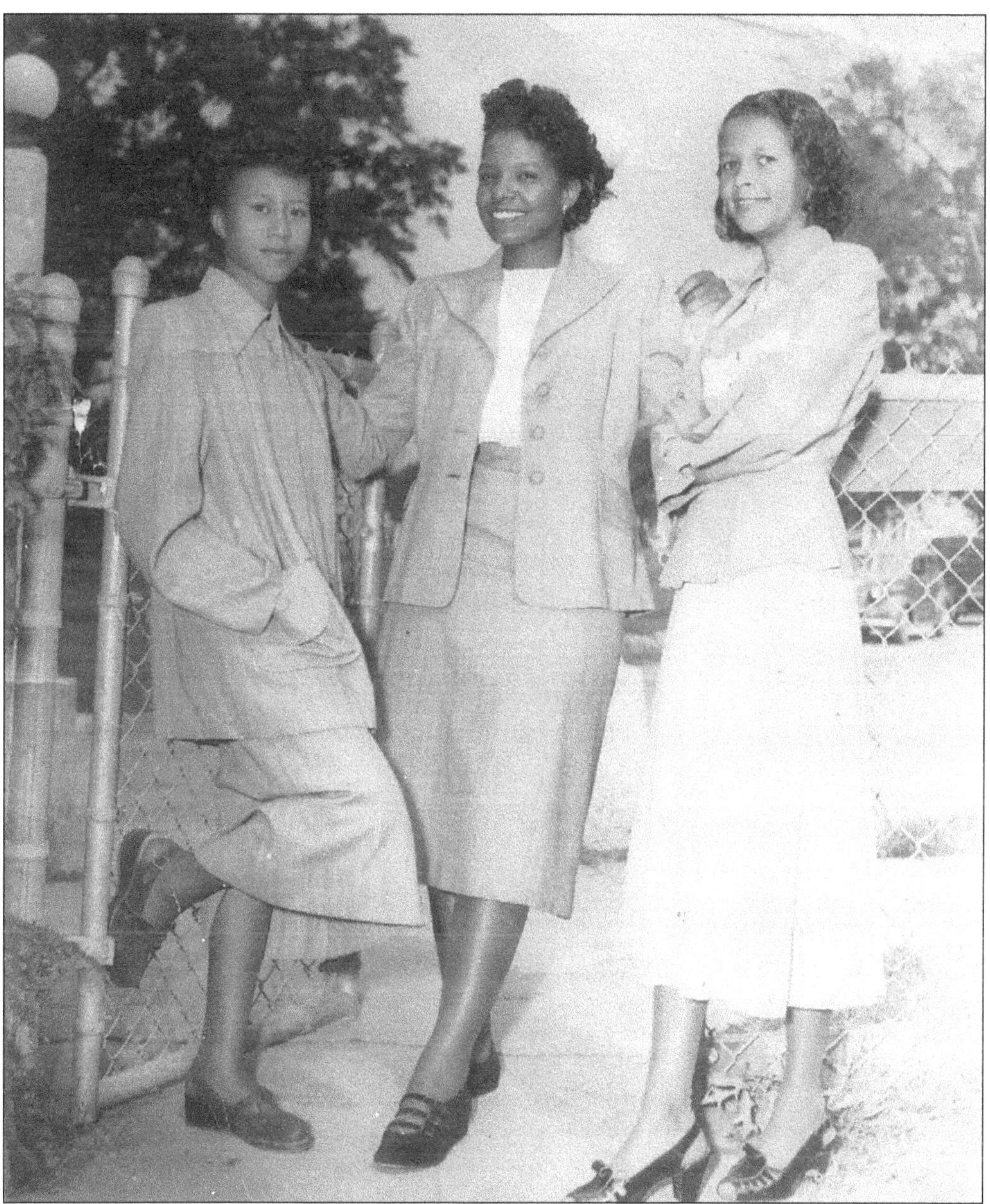

Helen J. Pointer (center) reigned as Miss Alcorn from 1949 to 1950. Her attendants were Ponjola Posey Andrews (left) and Alma Calcote (right). Pointer received a bachelor of science degree in Health Education in 1950 and worked as a special education teacher in Lansing, Michigan, for a number of years.

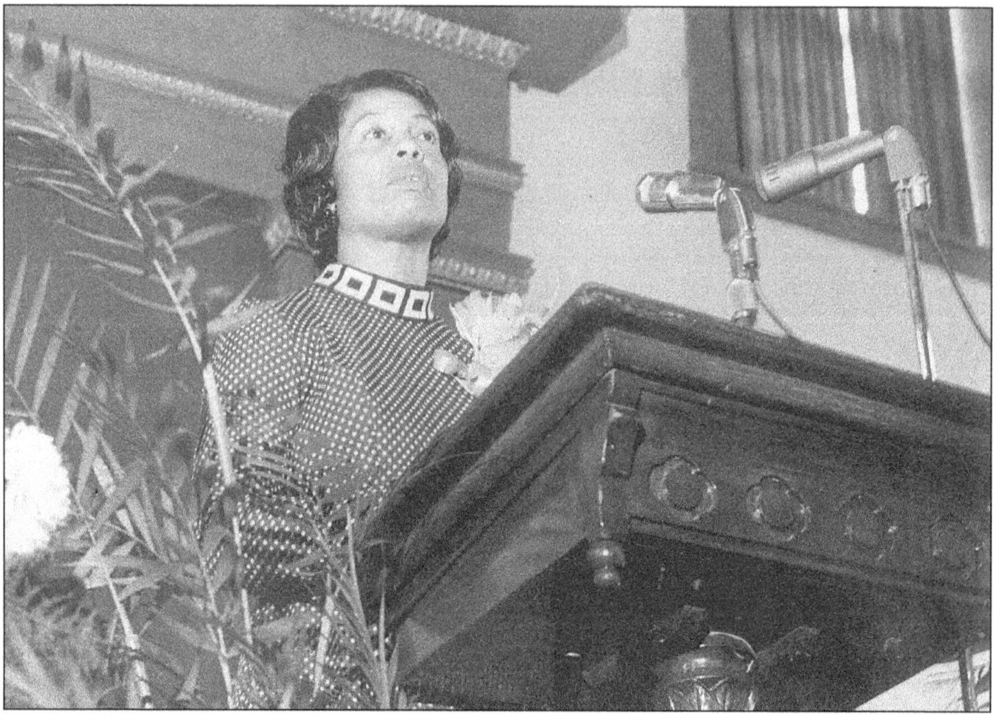

Annie Ruth Johnson Stepney reigned as Miss Alcorn from 1950 to 1951. At one time, she served as the president of the National Alumni Association and organized the Miss Alcorn Forever Club in 1992.

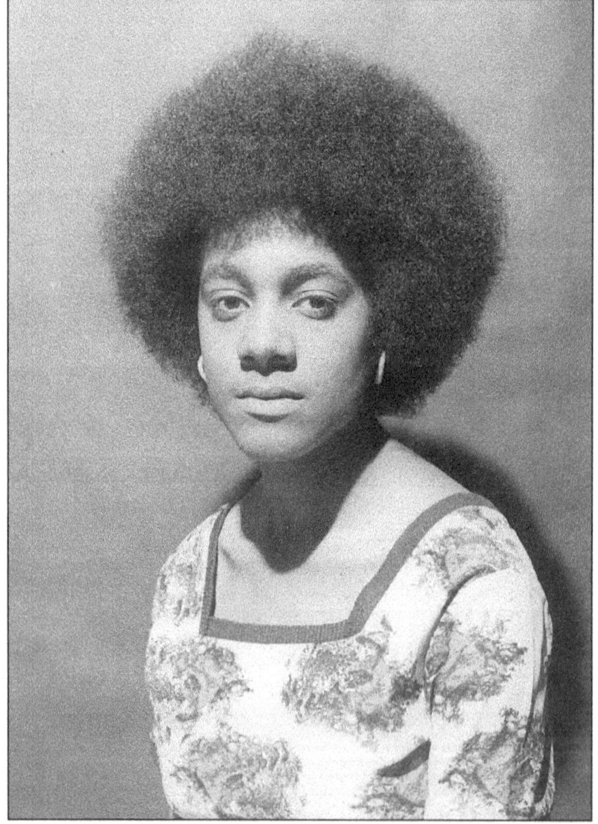

Carolyn Gamblin, a 1975 graduate, reigned as Miss Alcorn from 1973 to 1974. She was also the first black woman to graduate from the University of Mississippi School of Dentistry. Gamblin's mother, Bernice Gamblin, was Miss Alcorn 1951–1952.

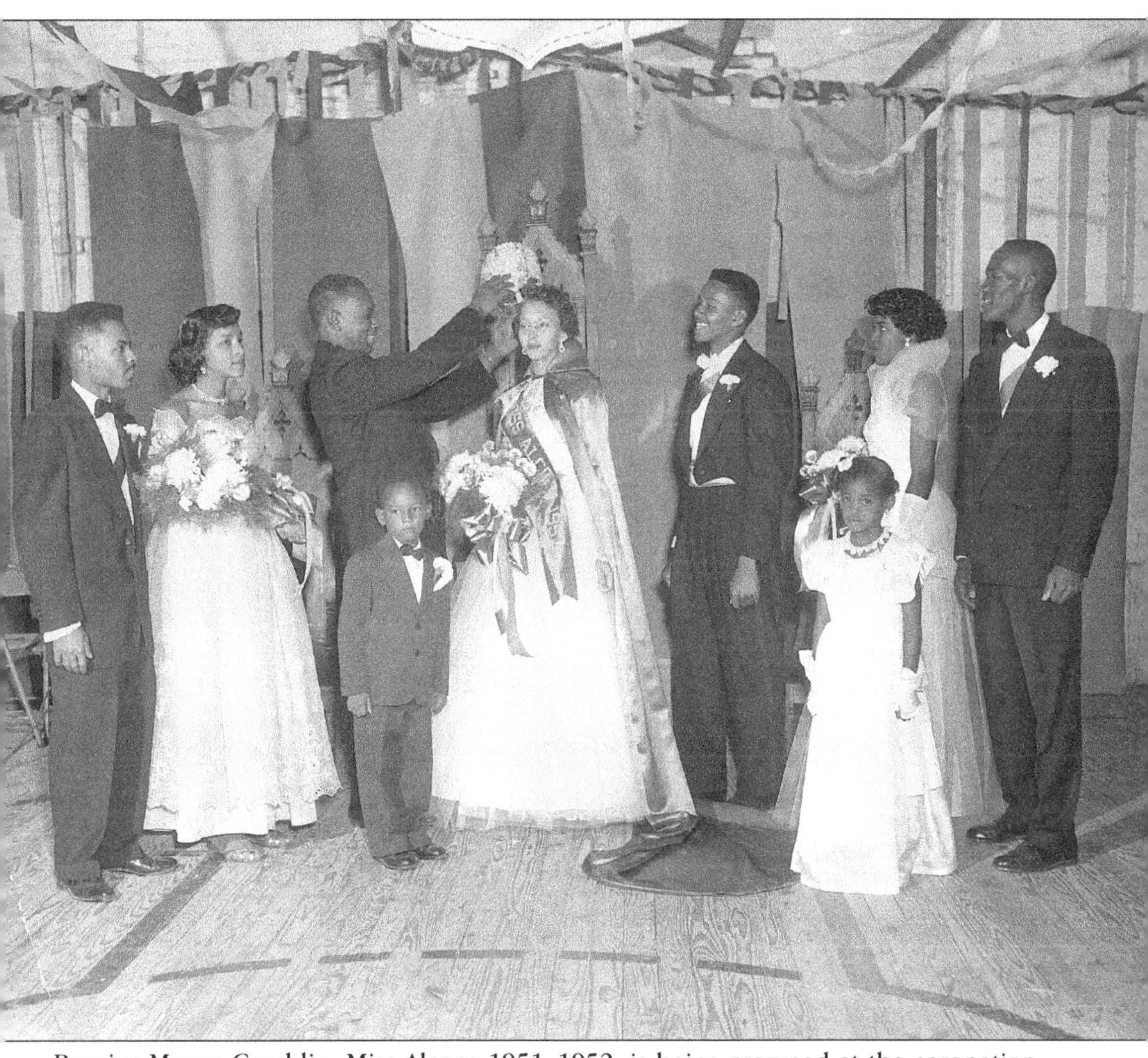

Bernice Moore Gamblin, Miss Alcorn 1951–1952, is being crowned at the coronation as her attendants look on. Her daughter, Carolyn Gamblin, would later win the same title in 1973–1974.

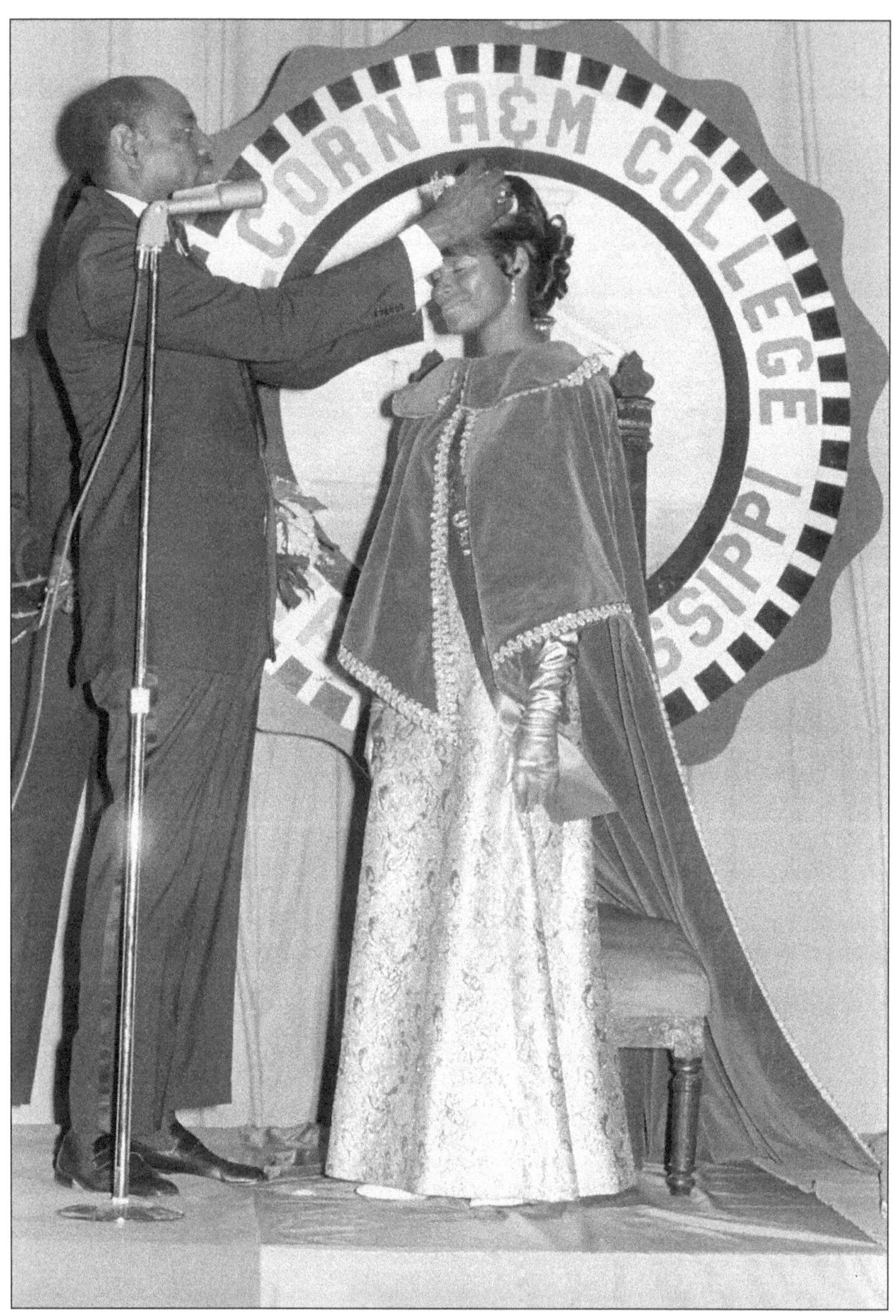

Shirley Barnes reigned as Miss Alcorn from 1971 to 1972.

Esther Jenkins Henderson reigned as Miss Alcorn from 1966 to 1967.

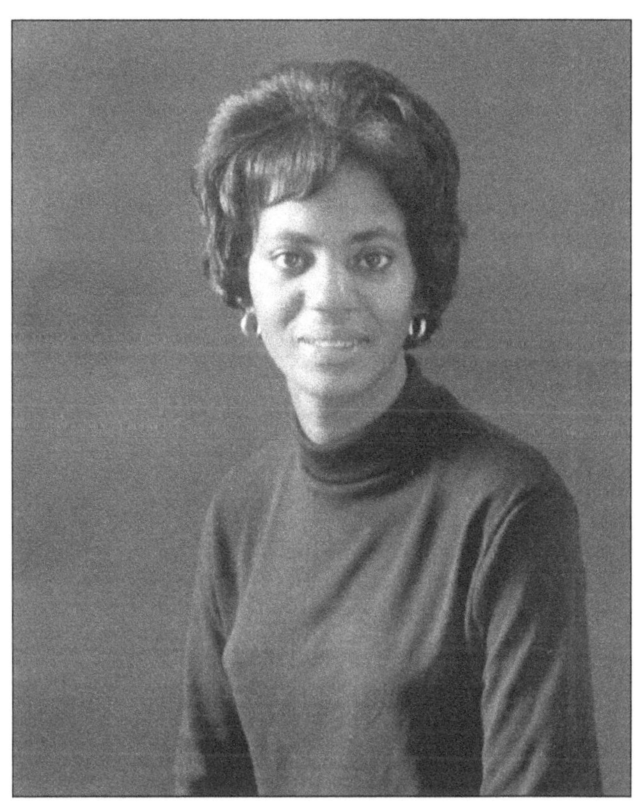

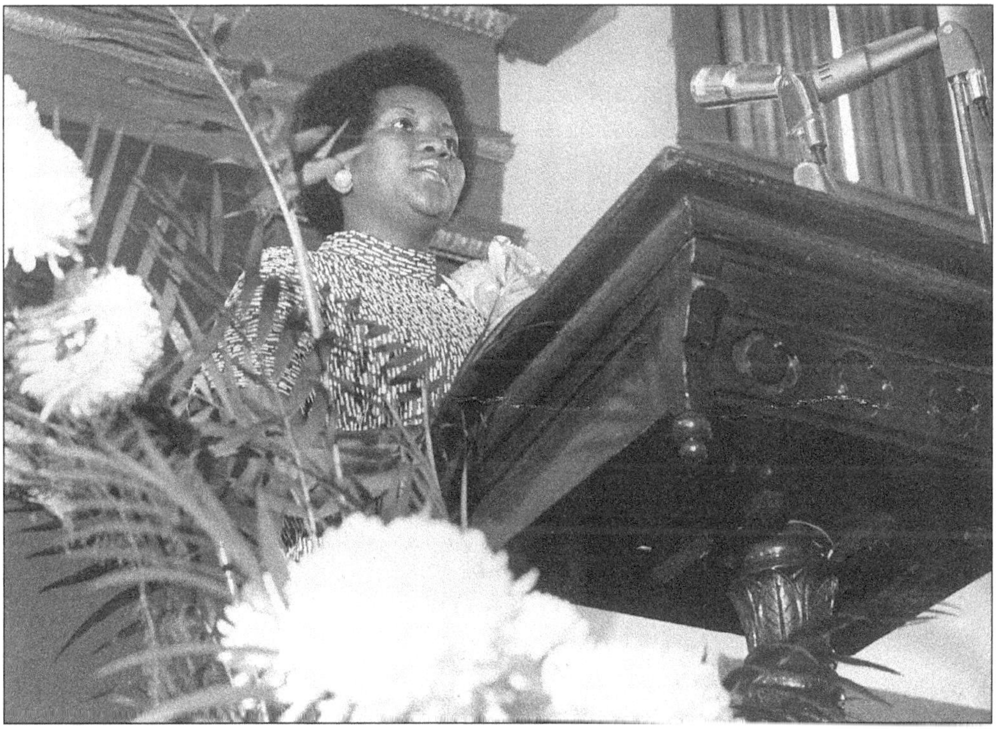

Lucille Smith Reese reigned as Miss Alcorn from 1967 to 1968.

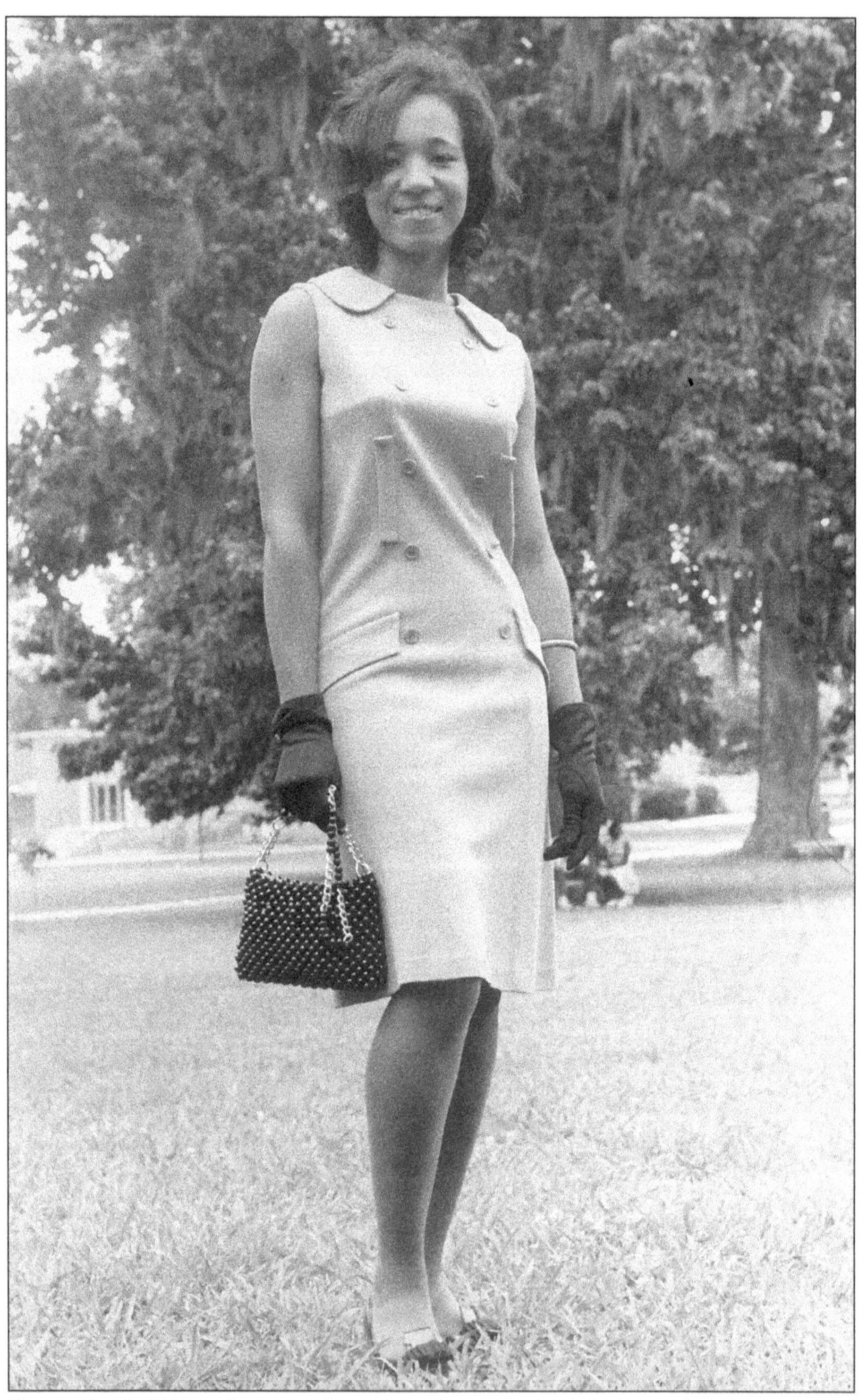

Ora Dean Marshall Powell reigned as Miss Alcorn from 1968 to 1969. She is a native of Liberty, Mississippi, and a 1969 Alcorn graduate who majored in elementary education. Ora Dean is a fifth-grade teacher in Hopewell Junction, New York.

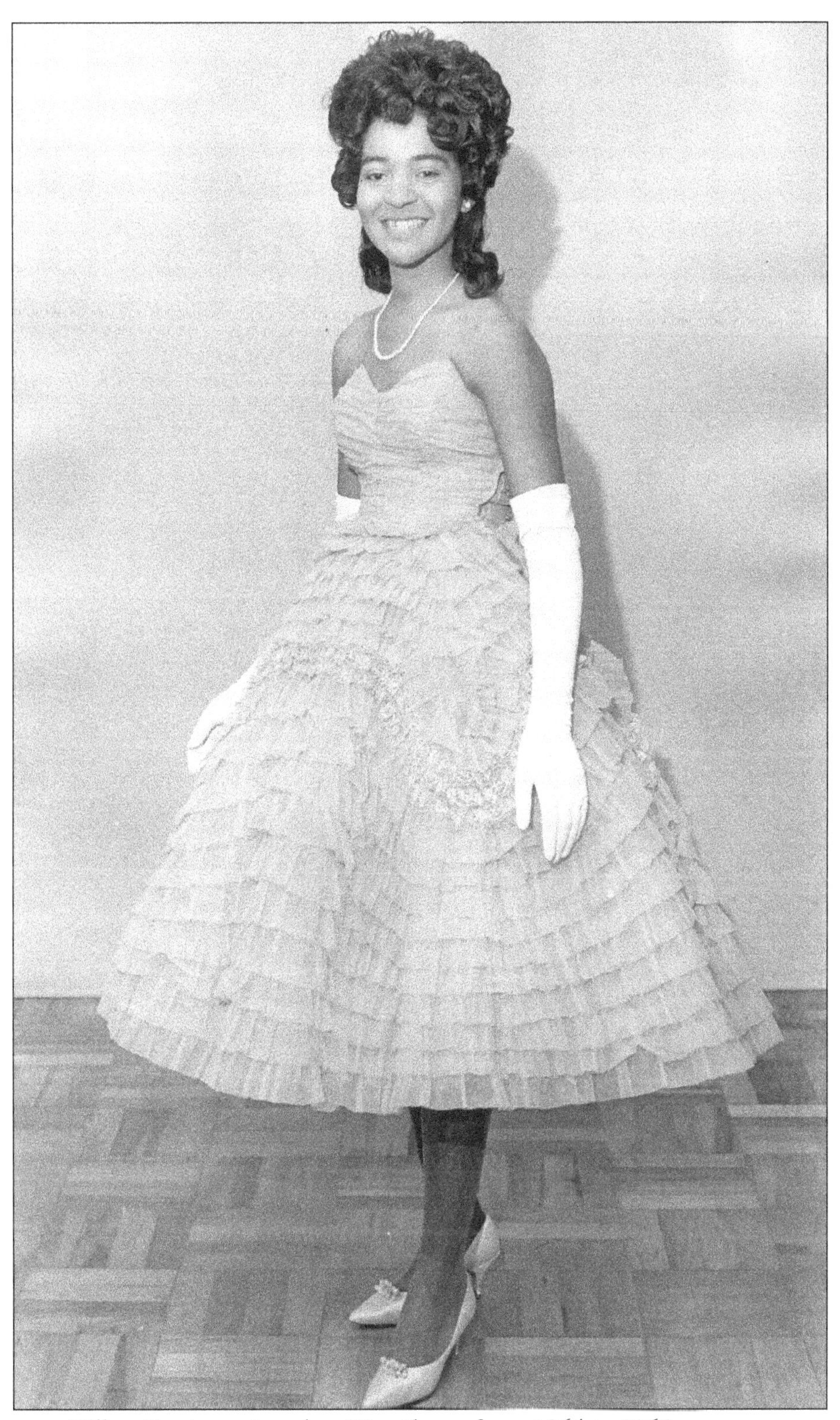

Berneyye Dillon Steptoe reigned as Miss Alcorn from 1964 to 1965.

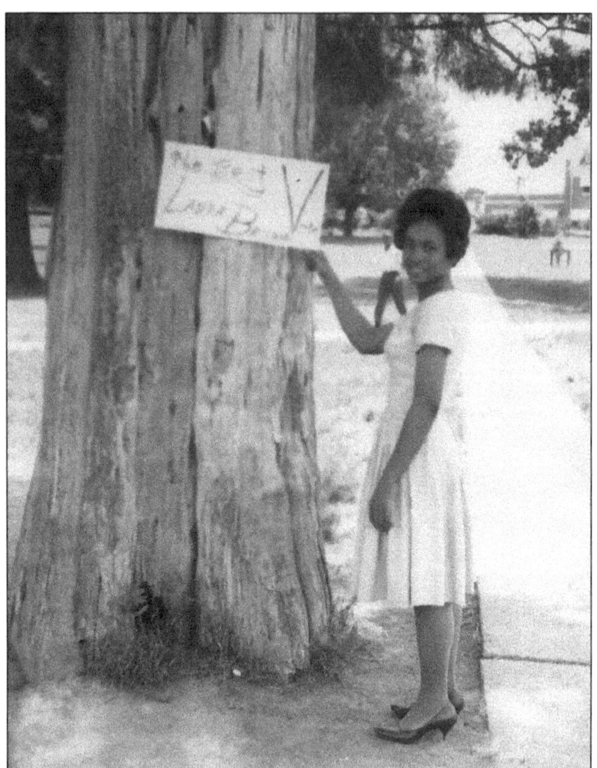

Laura Brown Nelson, a native of Vicksburg, Mississippi, reigned as Miss Alcorn from 1963 to 1964. While at Alcorn, Nelson was a member of Alpha Kappa Alpha Sorority and was an Alpha Phi Alpha sweetheart.

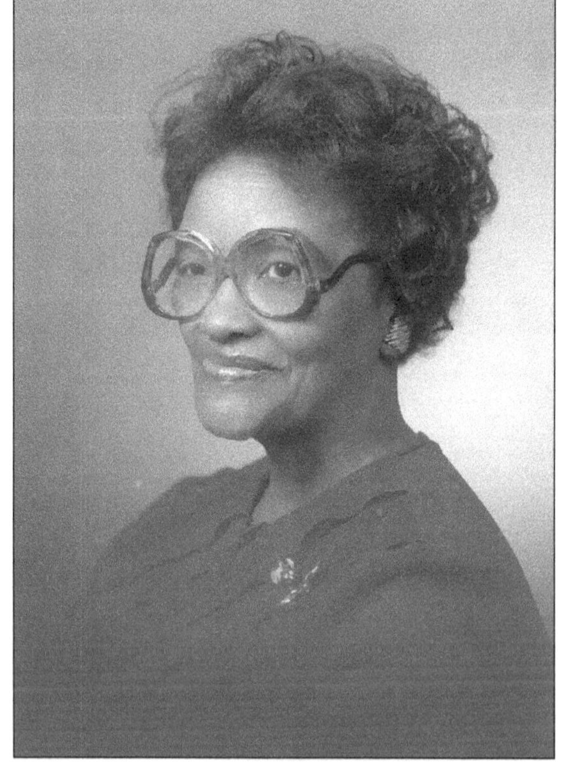

Vera Hendricks Bryant, a native of Magnolia, Mississippi, reigned as Miss Alcorn from 1956 to 1957. Bryant served as the supervisor of instruction in the South Pike County School District for many years. She also served as the assistant secretary of the Miss Alcorn Forever Club and was named Alcornite of the Year in 1983.

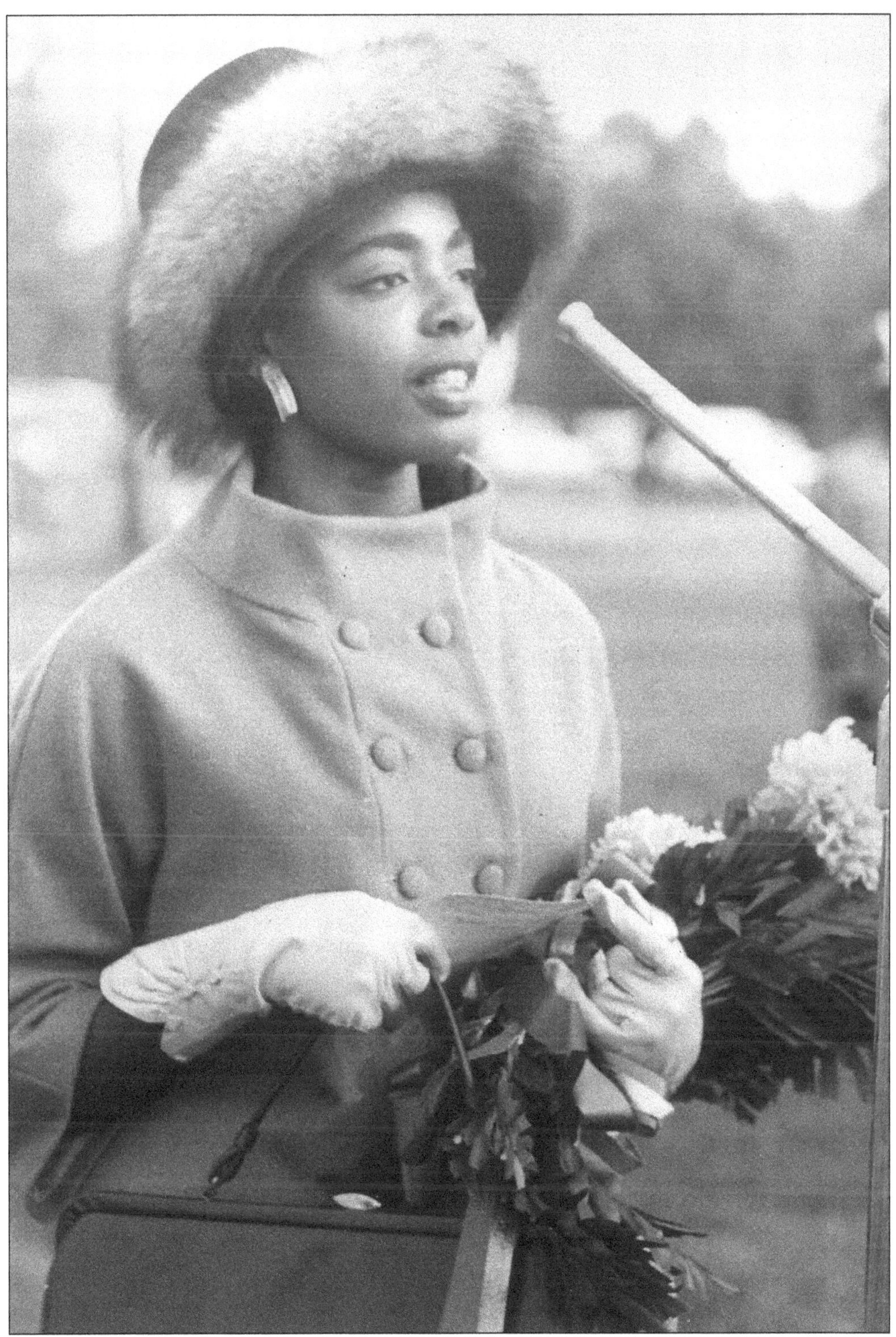

Veronica Levison Richardson reigned as Miss Alcorn from 1962 to1963. She is a native of Leland, Mississippi, and is currently an elementary principal in Washington County.

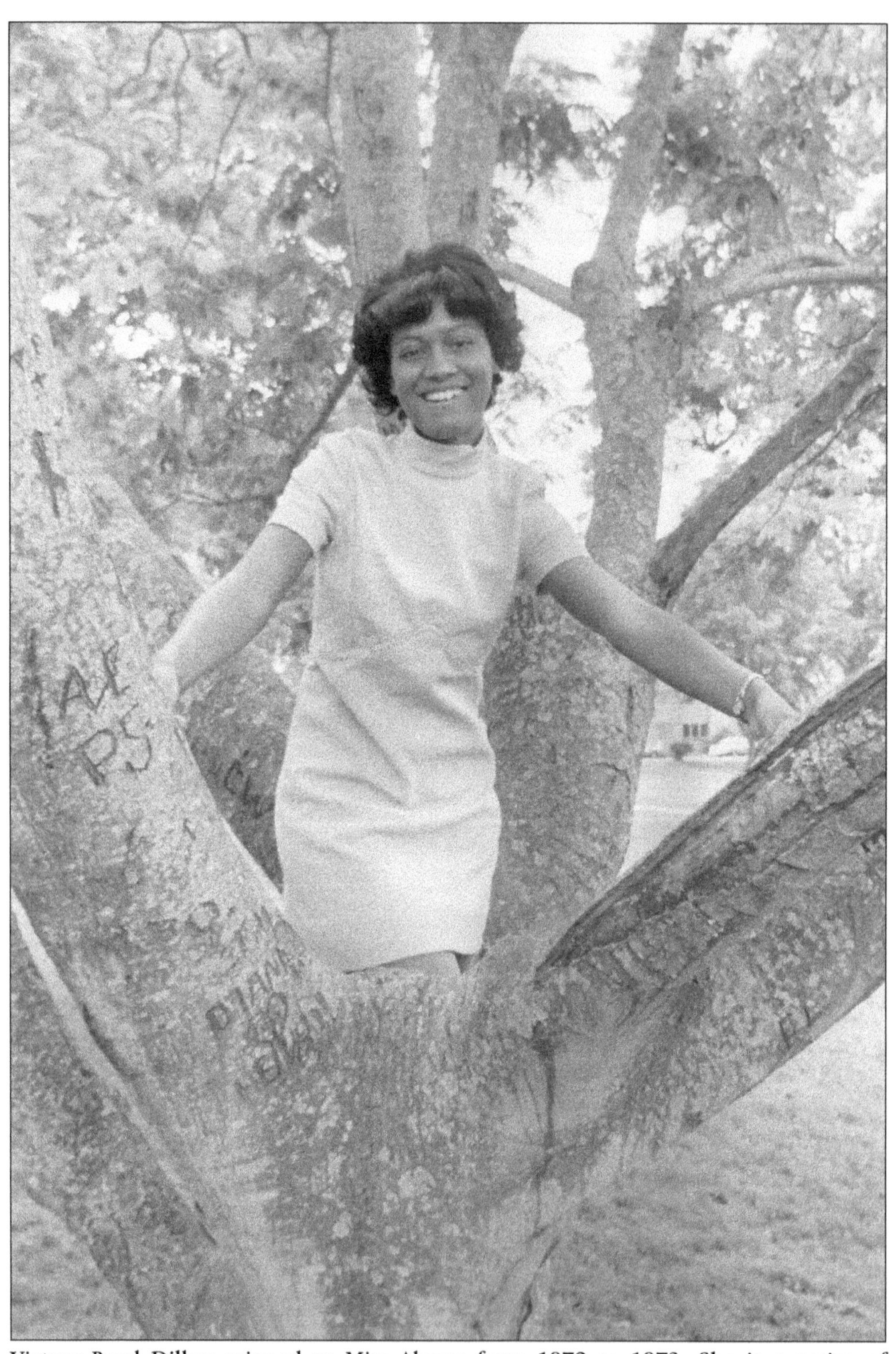

Victory Pearl Dillon reigned as Miss Alcorn from 1972 to 1973. She is a native of Magnolia, Mississippi, and was a business education major.

Dorothy Hayes Overstreet reigned as Miss Alcorn from 1941 to 1942 and received her degree in 1942 She is a retired teacher from the Detroit public school system.

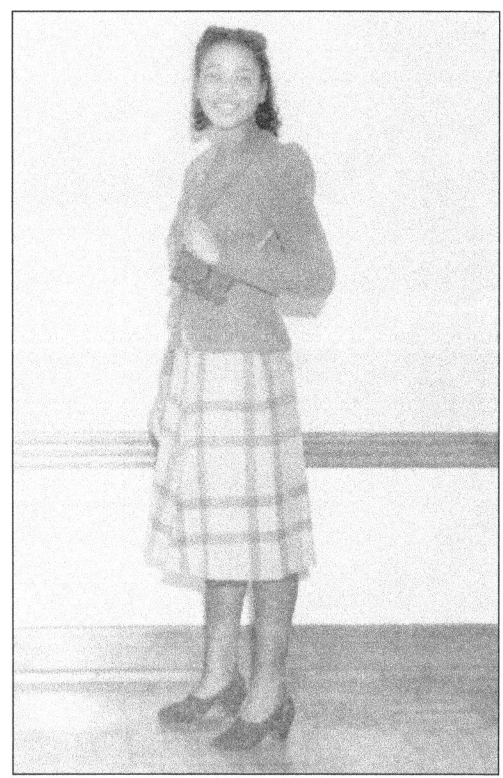

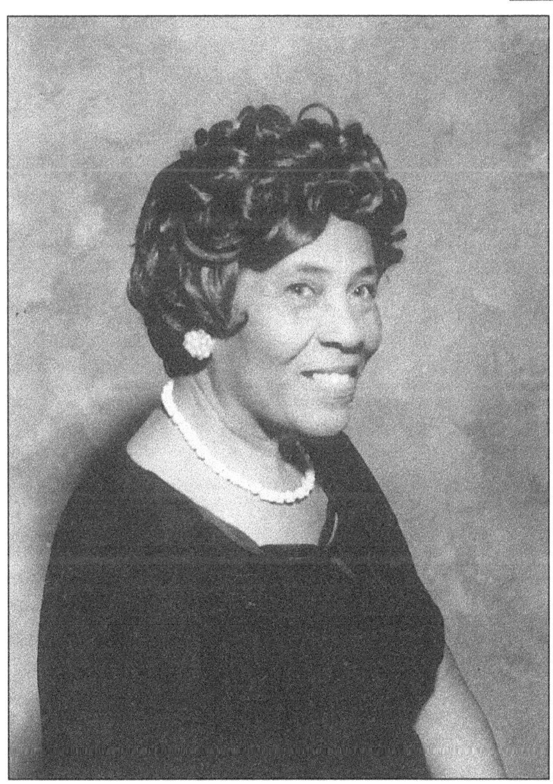

Lillian O. Palmer reigned as Miss Alcorn from 1931 to 1932.

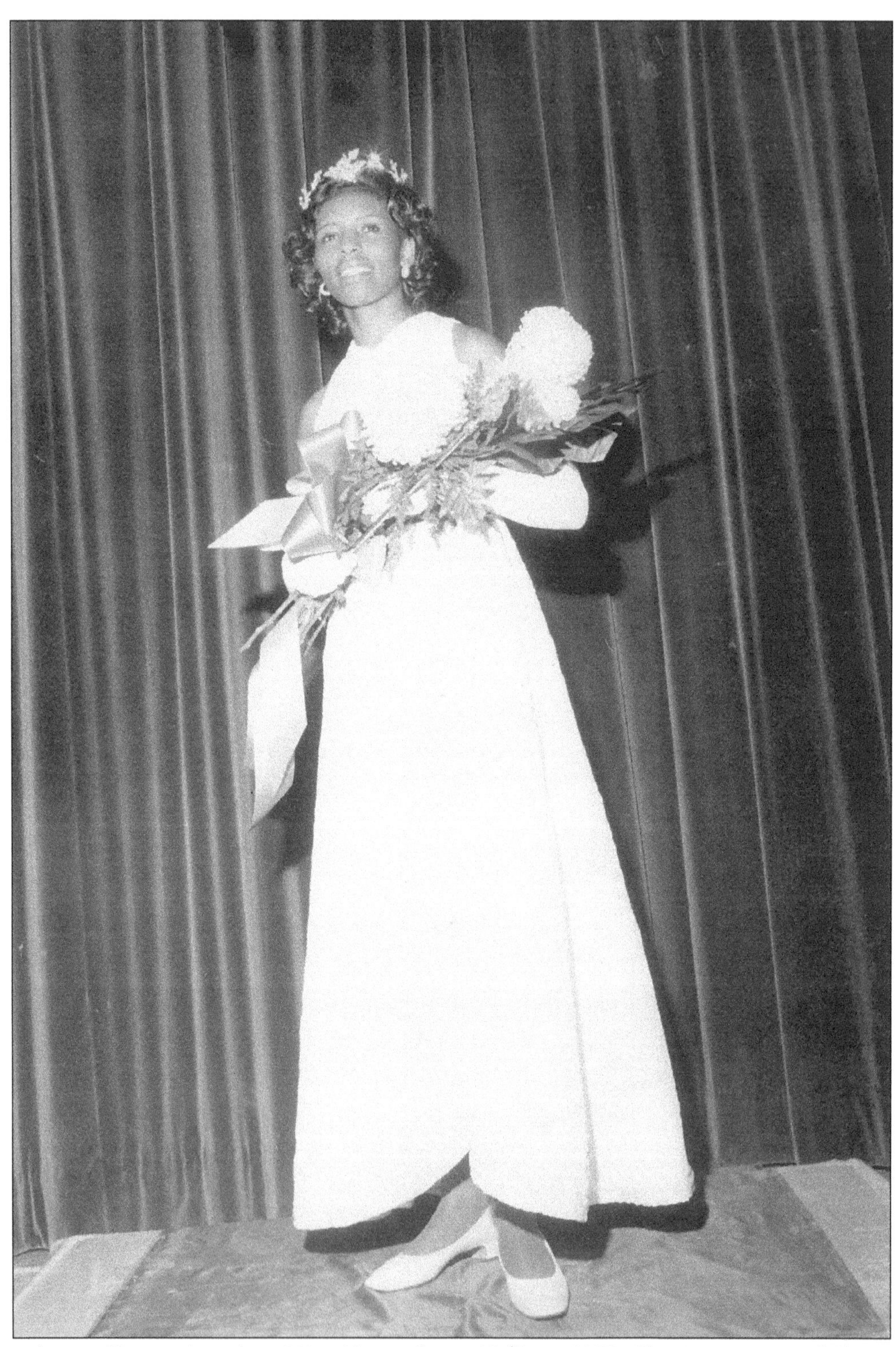

Rebecca Shaw reigned as Miss Alcorn from 1969 to 1970. She is a native of Shaw, Mississippi, and currently resides in Mount Boyou, Mississippi.

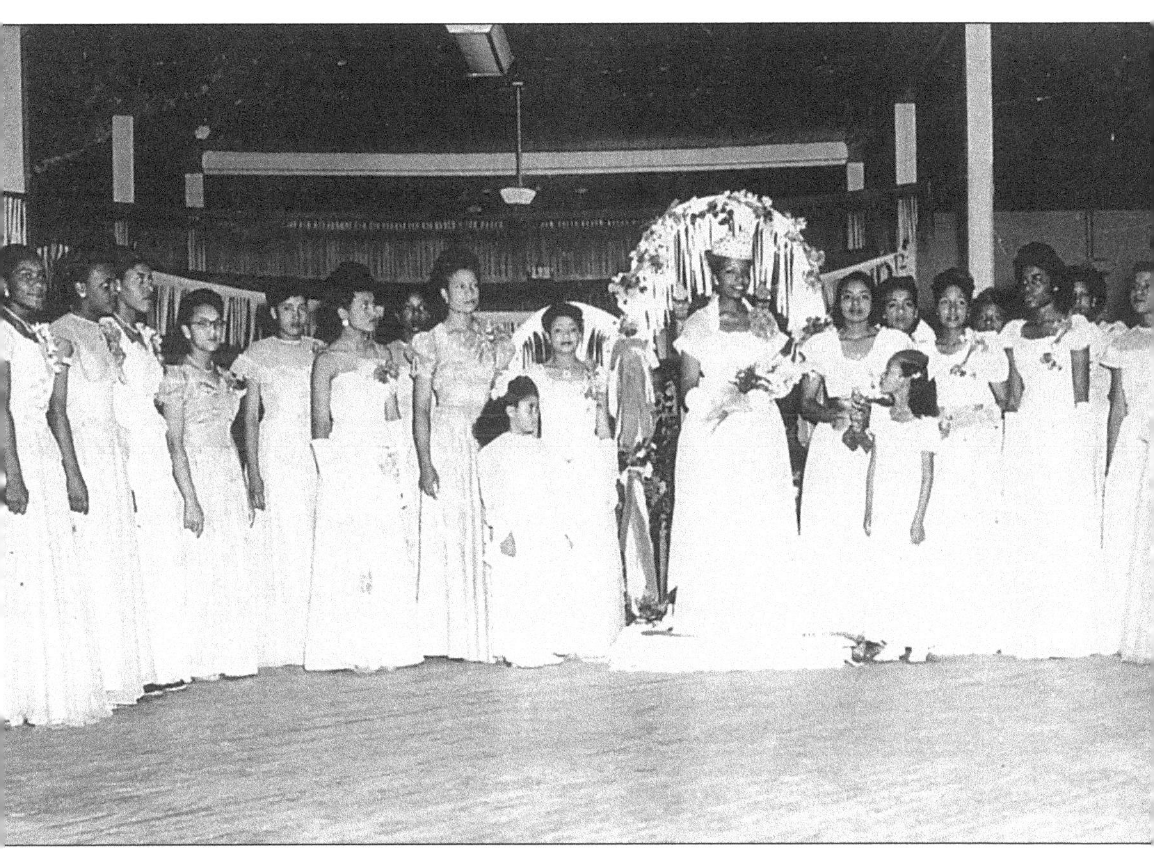

Alcorn's first Coronation Ball in honor of Miss Alcorn was held in 1949. In that year, Miss Alcorn was Helen Johnson Pointer, and she was crowned by Margie Price Funchess (on her right), the 1948–1949 Miss Alcorn.

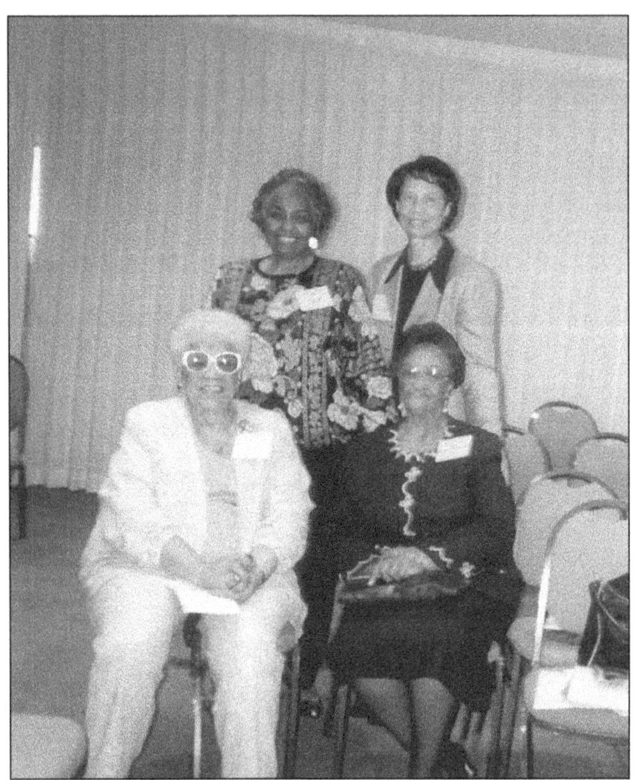

The Miss Alcorn Forever Club officers are, from left to right, (seated) Gladys Noel Bates, treasurer and Miss Alcorn 1936–1937; and Vera Hendricks, assistant secretary and Miss Alcorn 1956–1957; (standing) Helen Johnson Pointer, secretary and Miss Alcorn 1949–1950; and Ann Johnson Stepney, president and Miss Alcorn 1950–1951.

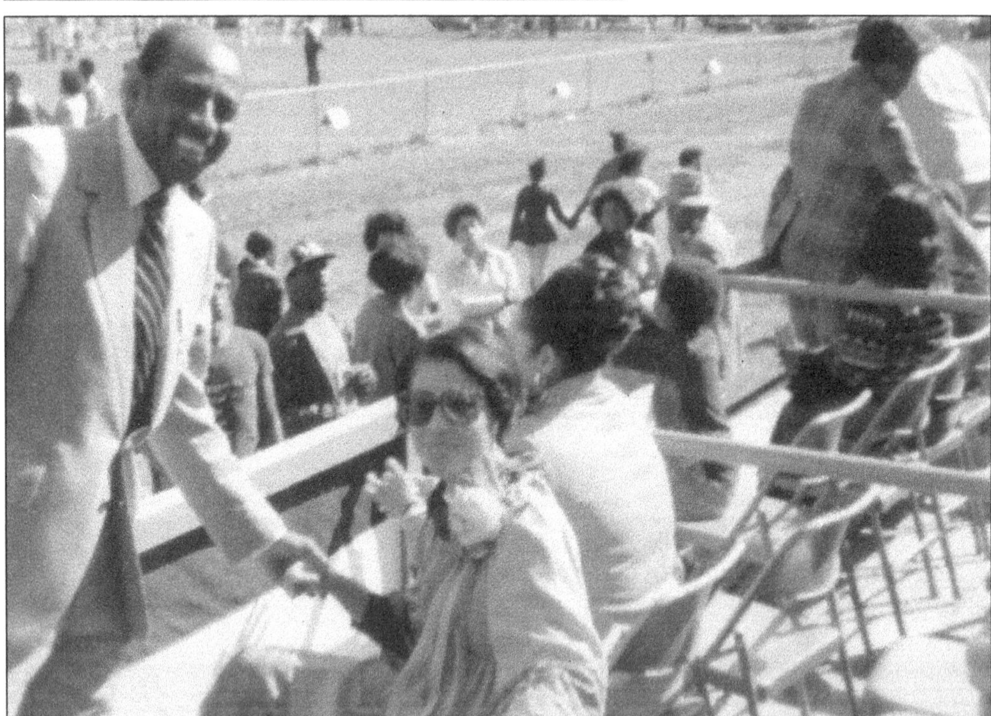

President Walter Washington always greeted the Miss Alcorns, and a special area was always reserved for them when they returned to campus for games and other functions.

Four

Alumni on the Move

Alumni of Alcorn are always on the move. Alcornites are involved in many endeavors, and demonstrate true leadership in all of their ventures. Alcornites gather together for special functions and always enjoy reuniting with fellow alumni.

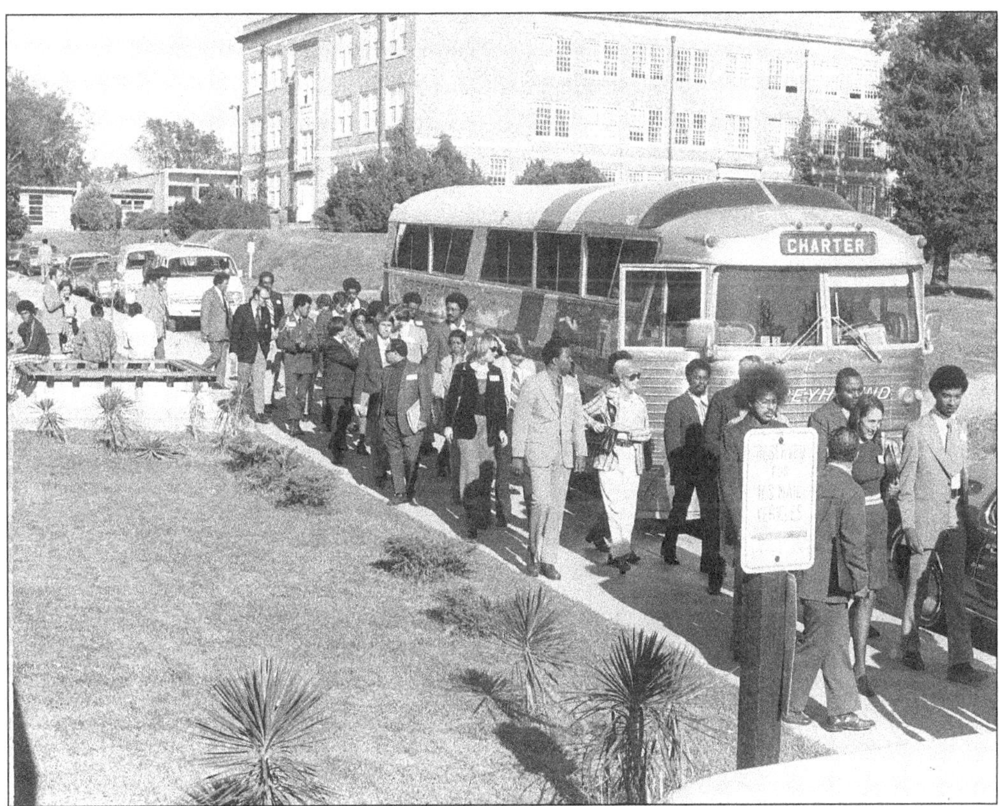

Alumni who have returned to campus prepare for a series of meetings and campus activities. Alcornites always look forward to homecoming, mid-winter conferences, and alumni weekends.

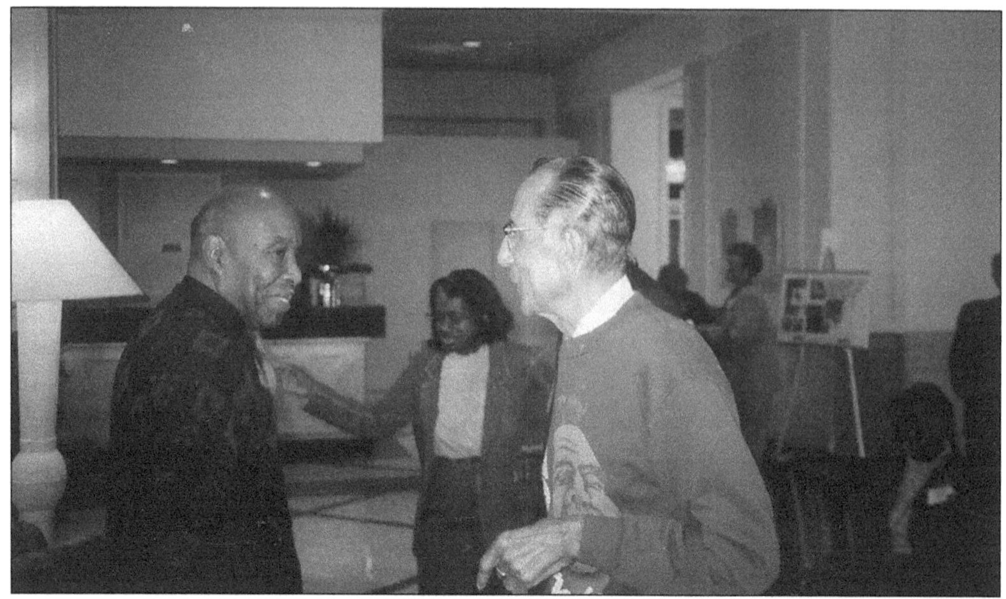

D.W. Wilburn and Mac Payton, Class of 1950, are always on the move for Alcorn. Wilburn served as the registrar at Alcorn for many years and recently donated more than $100,000 to the university. Payton, an army veteran, and his wife, Gertrude, have established an endowment and scholarship fund through the University Foundation for Alcorn.

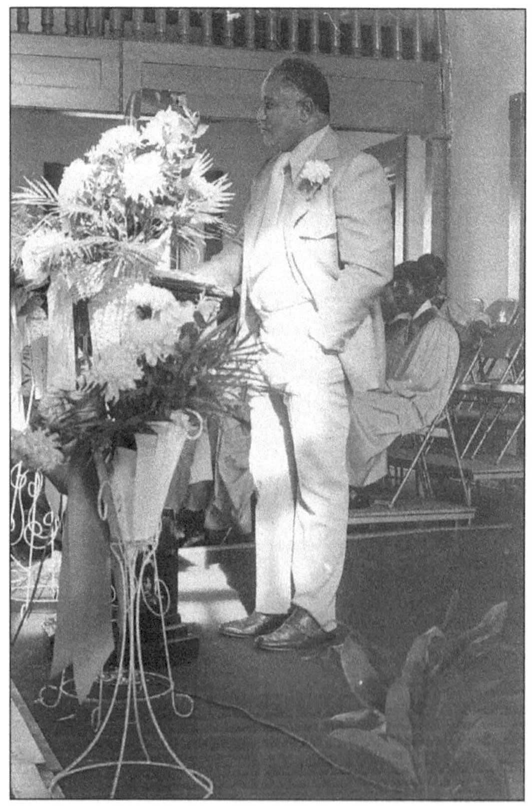

Dr. Felix Dunn, M.D., speaks to Alcorn students in Oakland Memorial Chapel. He encourages youths to always climb to the top and strive to be successful in whatever they do.

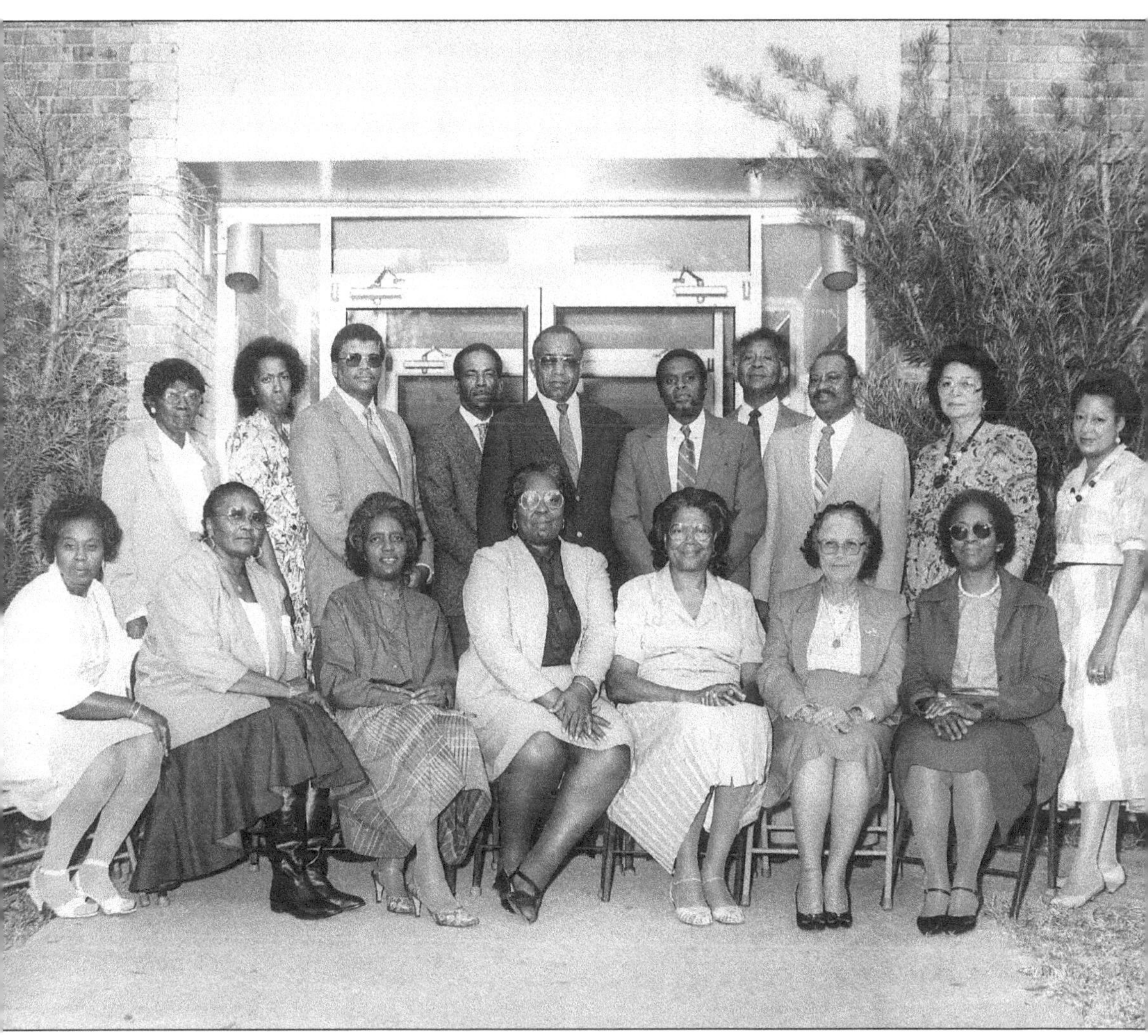

The Laurel-Jones County chapter of Alcorn alumni posed for this picture after a meeting in 1988. Pictured, from left to right, are (seated) Andrea Mae Martin, Aleace Cunningham (president at the time), Ermina Peyton, Lizer Marshall, Leatha Beard, Mary Jane Collins, and Wilma Fortenberry; (standing) Carolyn Sue Owens, Mattie Thomas (current president), Dr. I.L. Thomas, Roman L. Prater, Randolph Barnes, Frankie D. Peyton, Charles Barnes, James Minor, Winnie Hollingsworth, and Berdine Crosby.

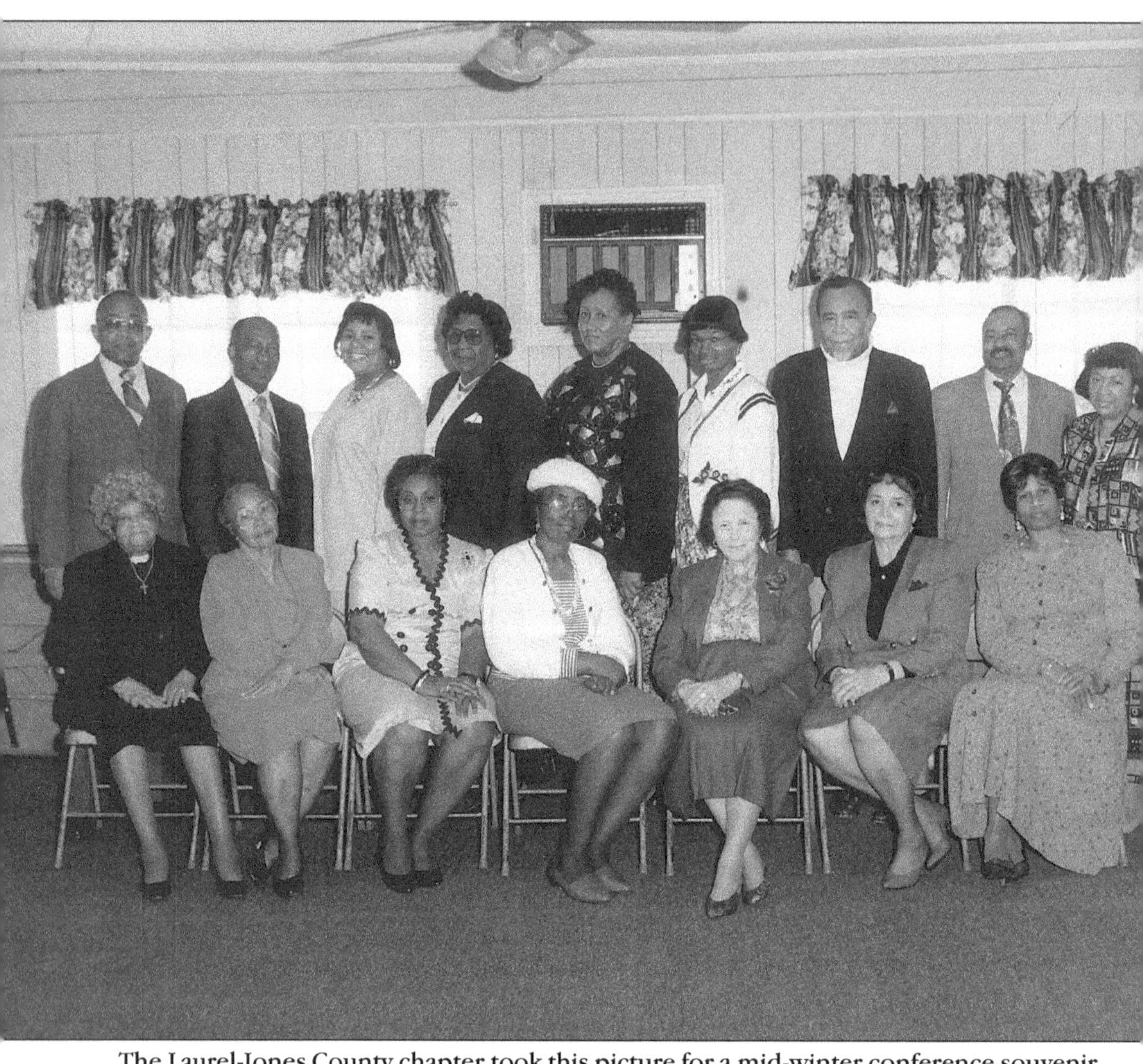

The Laurel-Jones County chapter took this picture for a mid-winter conference souvenir booklet. They always support the efforts necessary to ensure a successful conference and other university activities regardless of the sponsoring chapters.

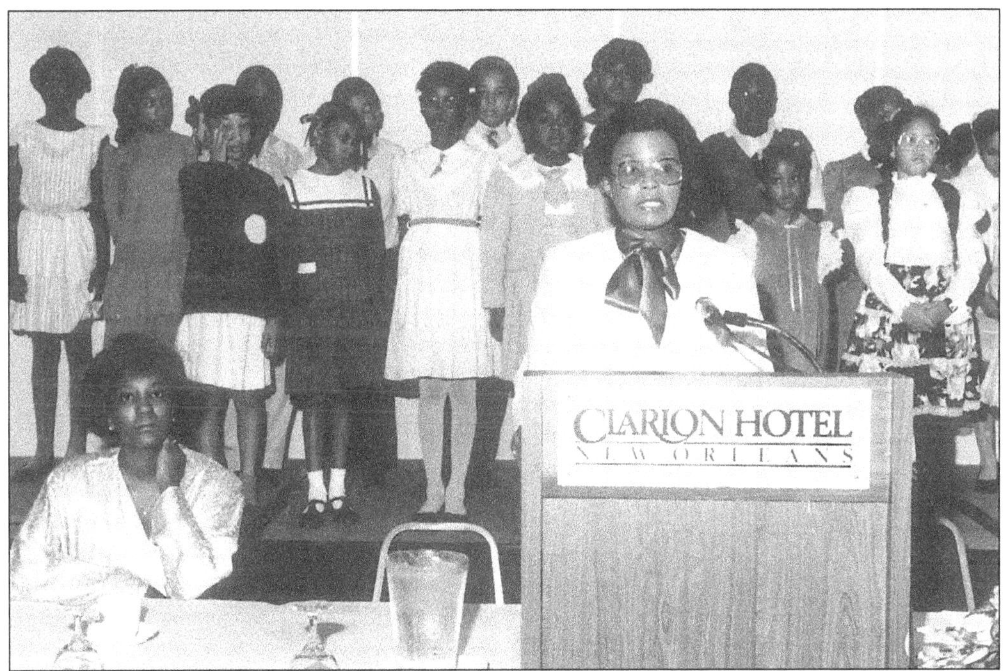

This mid-winter conference was hosted in New Orleans, Louisiana. The New Orleans chapter president at the time, Audrey Washington, welcomed everyone to the conference. Eula Beckwith, seated on the left, chaired the conference, and the young people on stage provided entertainment.

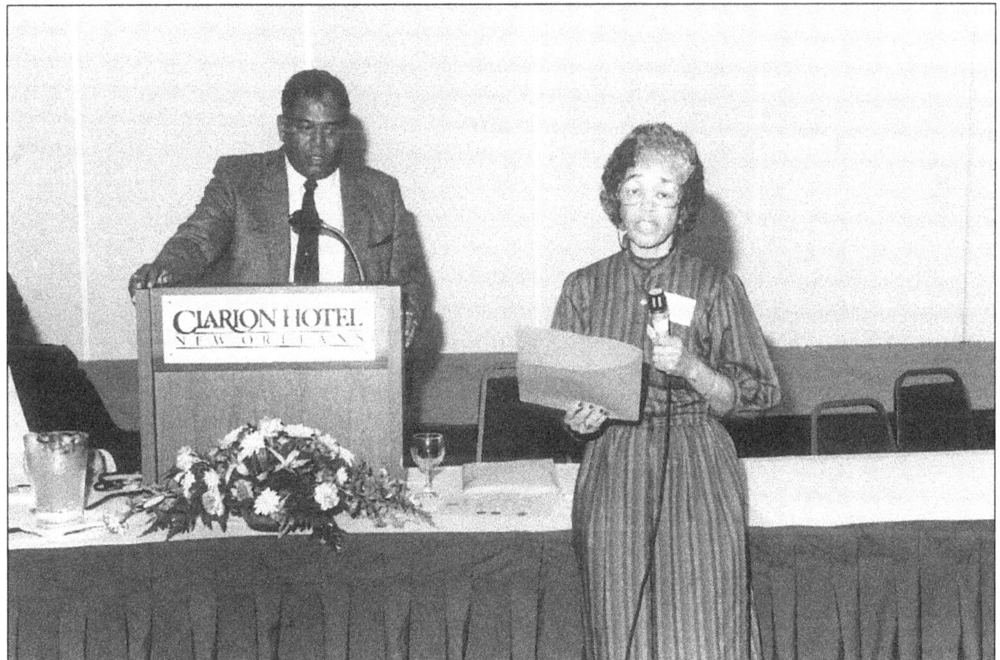

Mary Prater Demby reads a letter from the mayor of Los Angeles at the conference in New Orleans. In the letter, the mayor invites the alumni association to Los Angeles for the 1987 conference. National Alumni president Luther Alexander listens attentively.

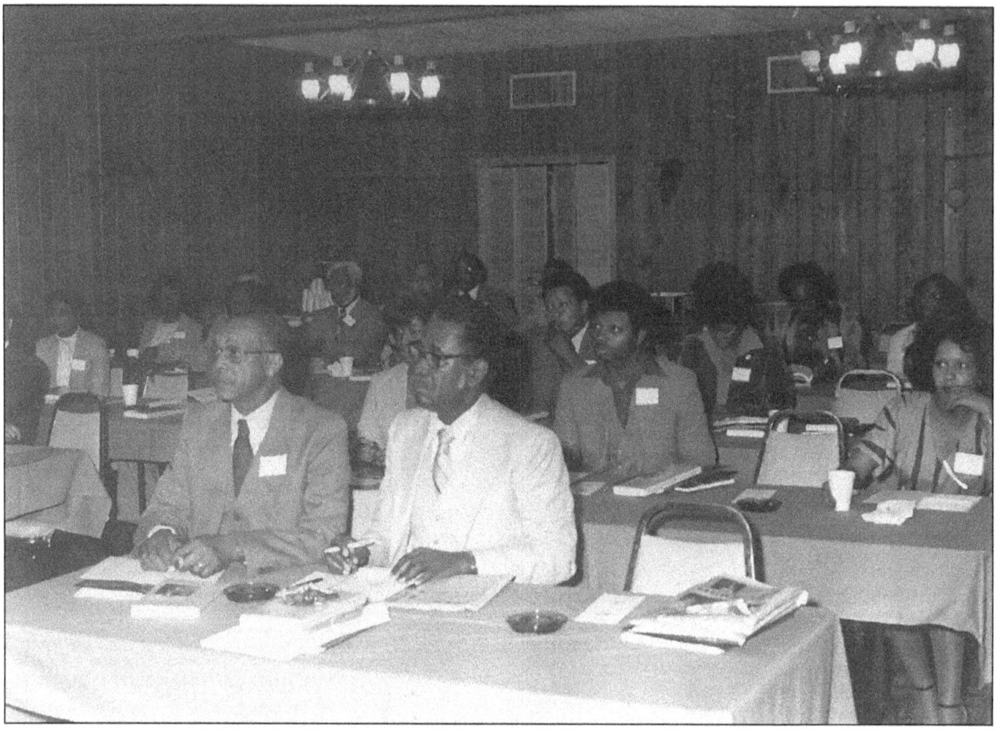

Alumni members participate in a workshop held at a mid-winter conference. Workshops feature many aspects of the university's overall functions.

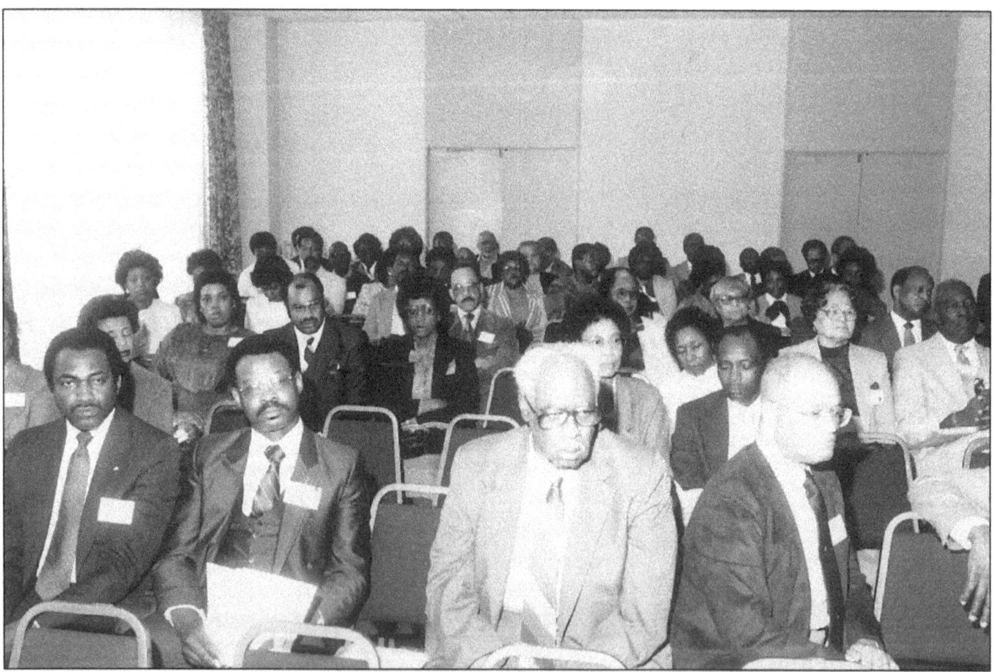

Alumni members participate in a business meeting at a mid-winter conference. They commit themselves to being aware of the happenings at their alma mater.

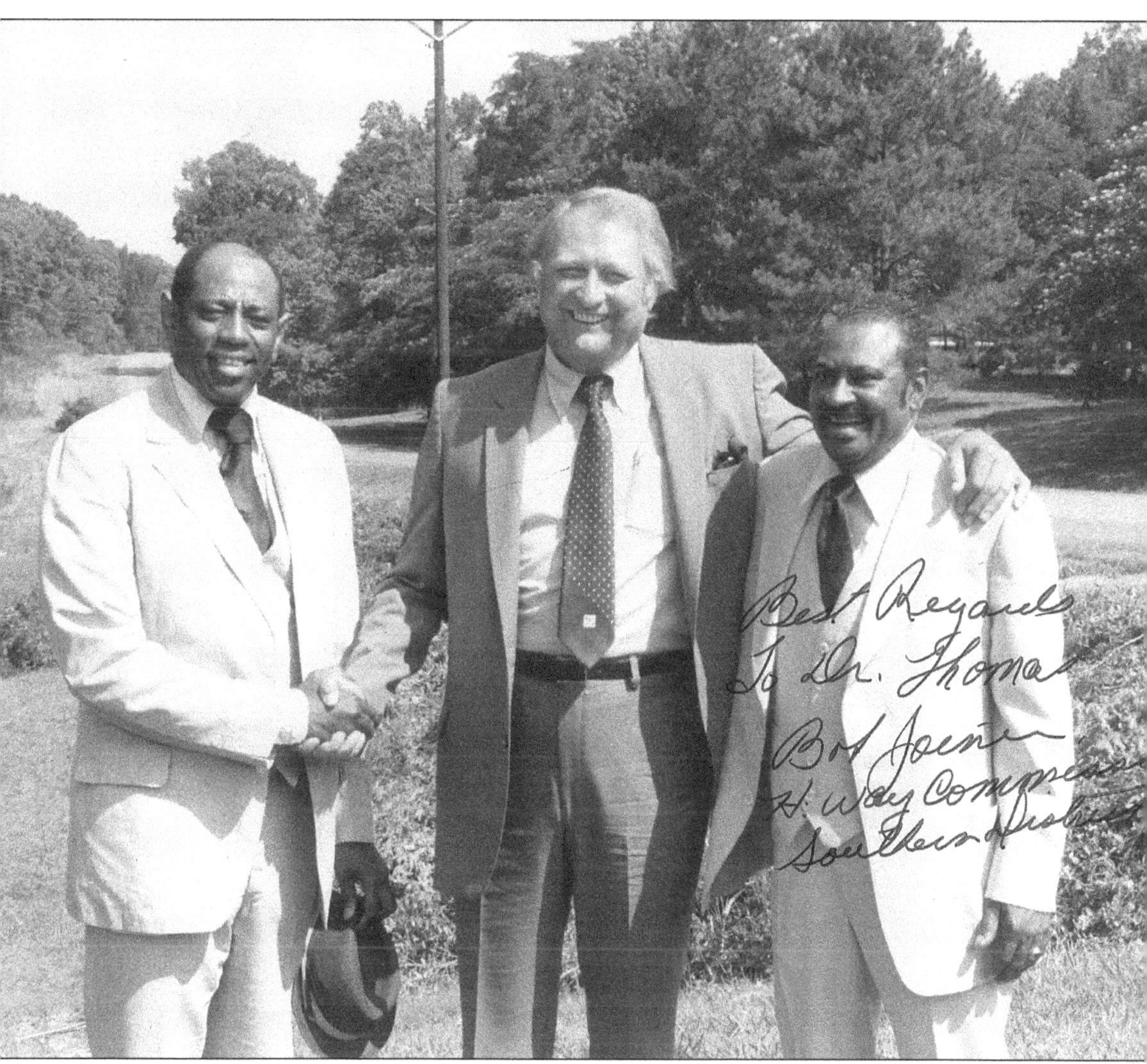

Dr. Walter Washington, Dr. I.L. Thomas, and Bob Joiner attend a ground-breaking ceremony for the new highway to the Alcorn State University campus. Dr. Thomas was one of the alumni instrumental in making this project a reality.

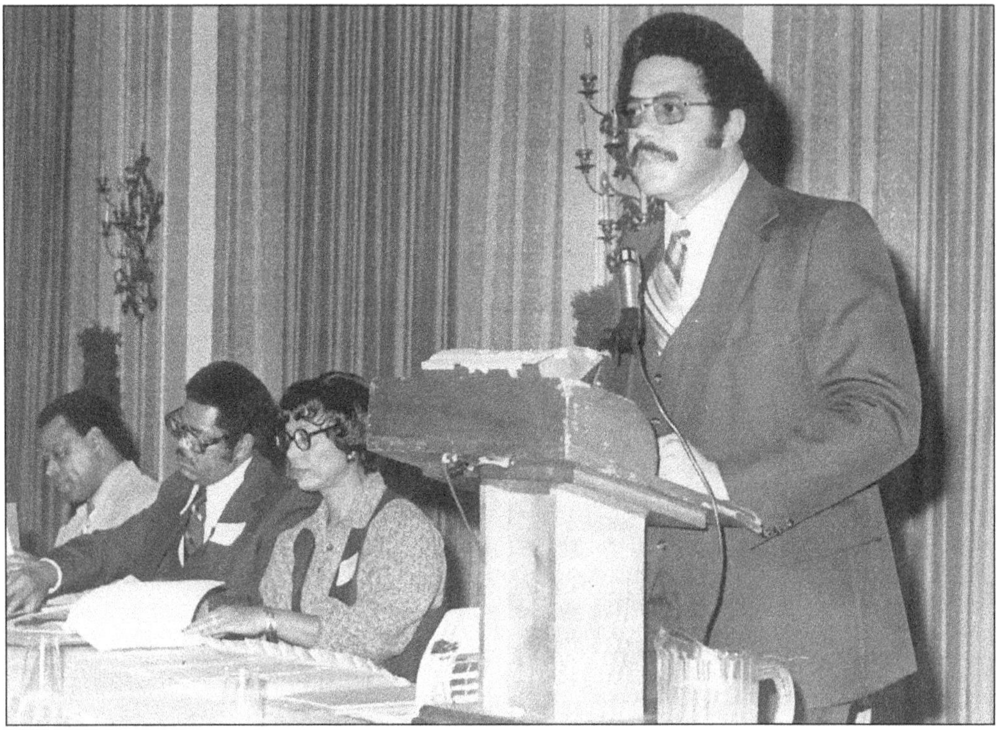

Charles Beckwith speaks to an alumni group at a mid-winter conference in New Orleans, Louisiana, where he served as chapter president. He is an Alcorn graduate and is currently employed with the Department of Labor in New Orleans.

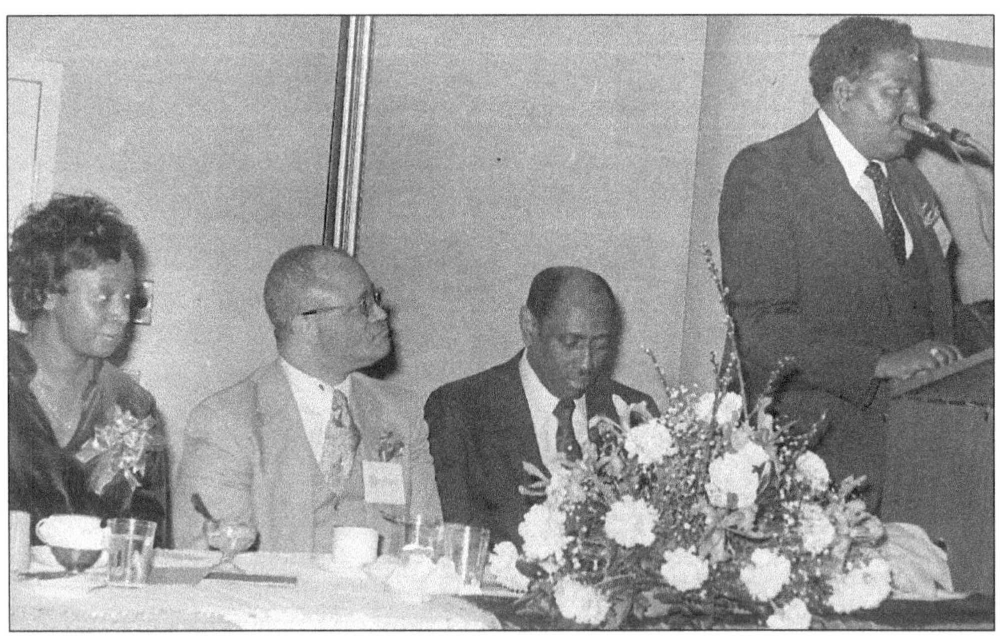

Luther Alexander, longtime National Alumni president, addresses the alumni group during an almuni weekend activity, the annual awards night banquet.

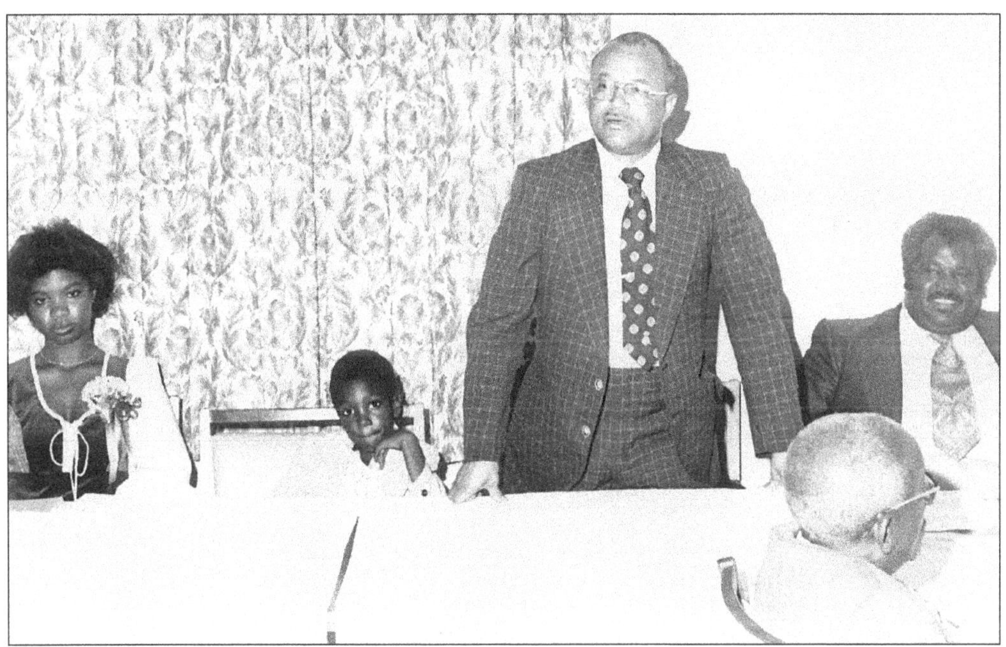

Rudolph E. Waters, executive vice president at Alcorn, is seen here addressing alumni during an alumni weekend meeting that is held annually on the Alcorn campus.

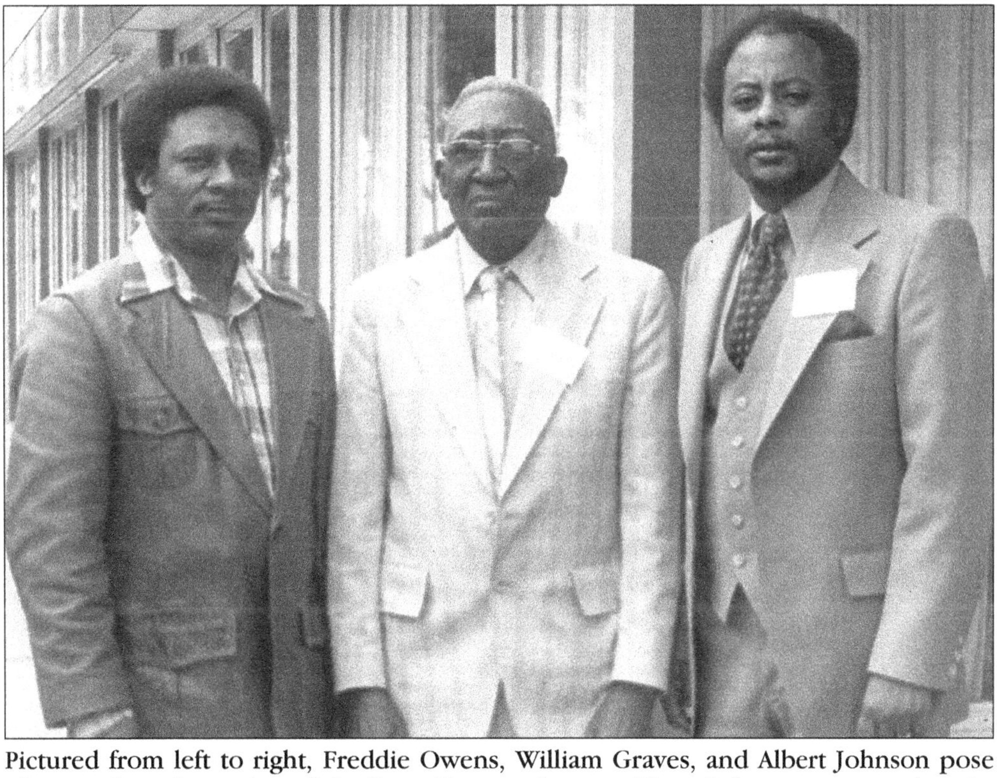

Pictured from left to right, Freddie Owens, William Graves, and Albert Johnson pose after an alumni meeting of the Scott County chapter. Albert Johnson was a university representative at the meeting.

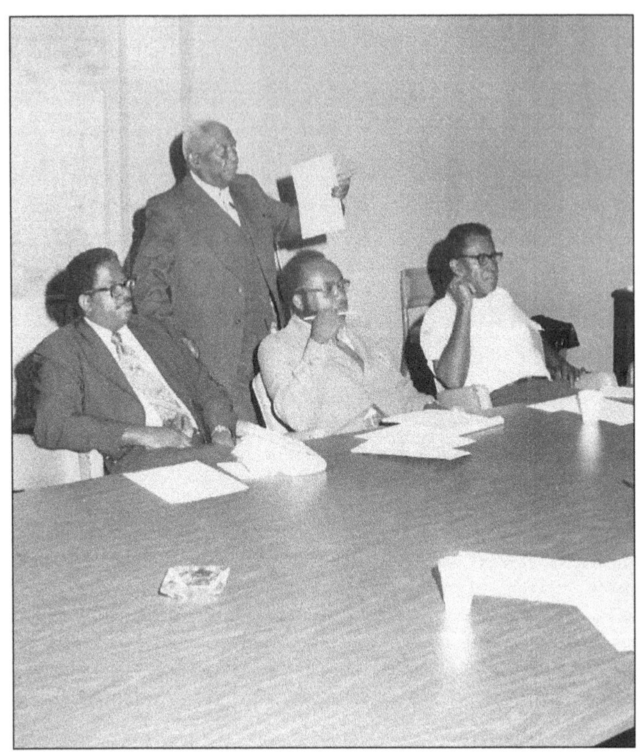

Alcornites continuously engage in the business of recruitment at Alcorn. Here, they discuss recruitment, financial aid, and other issues related to the admission of students. "Mr. Alcorn," William S. Darby shares his strategy, which often involved transporting students in his own vehicle to Alcorn. He encouraged others to do the same.

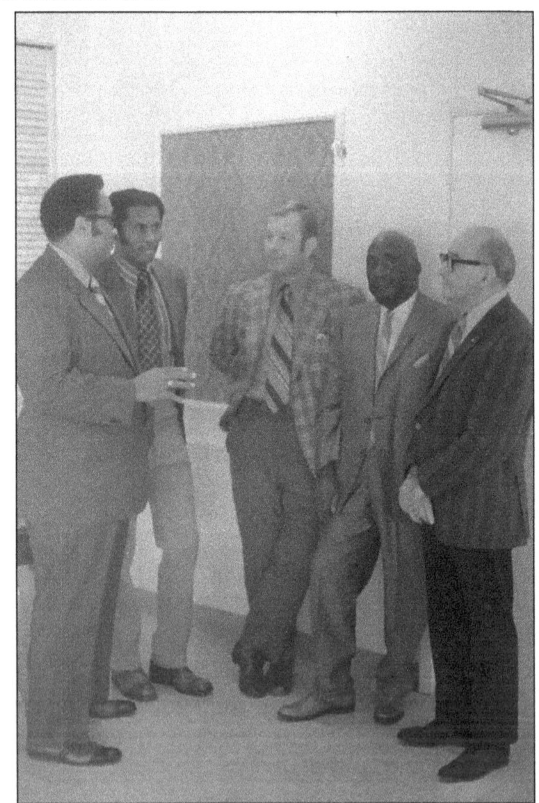

Alcornites always have the university's interests at heart. Speaking with this group of guests are W.S. Demby (second from the right) and Jim Stirgus (second from left). Both men are past National Alumni presidents.

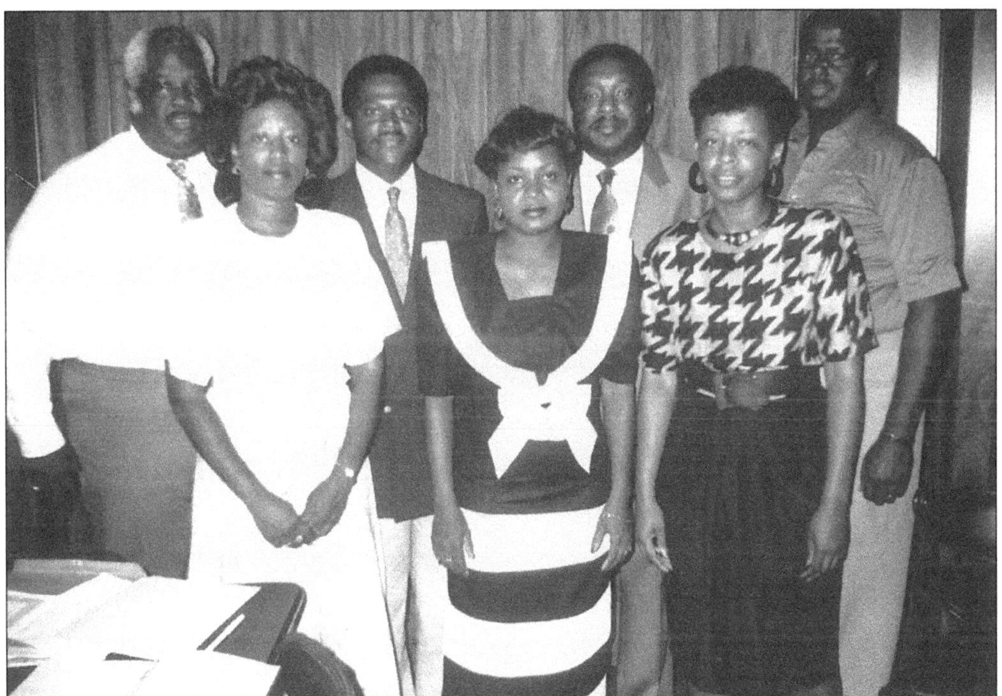

The Shreveport-Bossier chapter's chartering ceremony included, from left to right, the following: (front row) Lorine H. Pullen, Evelyn B. Dawson, and Earlene R. Thompson; (back row) Henry Houze Jr., Jerry Paige, Willie McPhearson, and John E. Walls. Houze and Walls were alumni representatives at the chartering ceremony.

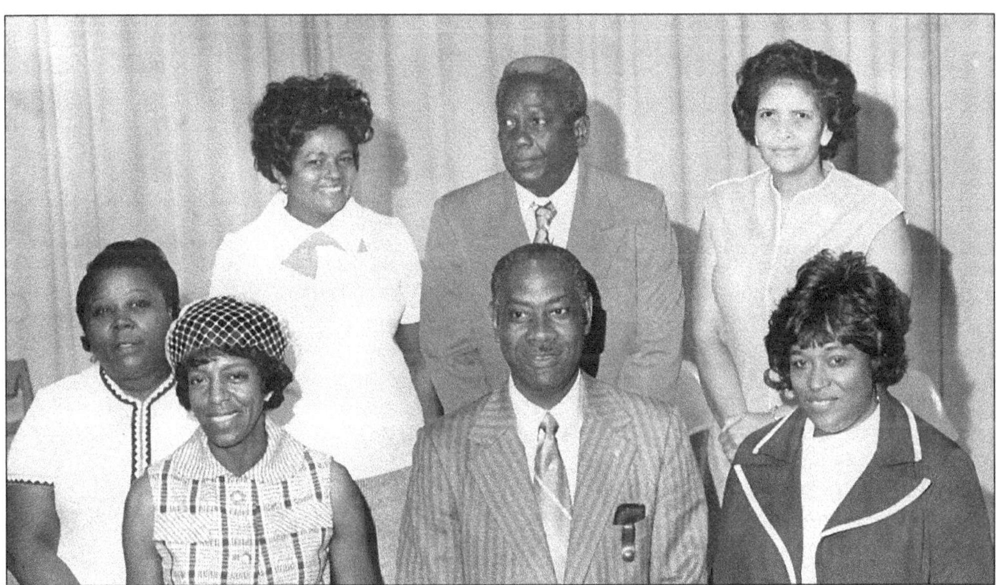

These members of the Class of 1947 pose for a picture on the campus while attending alumni weekend activities.

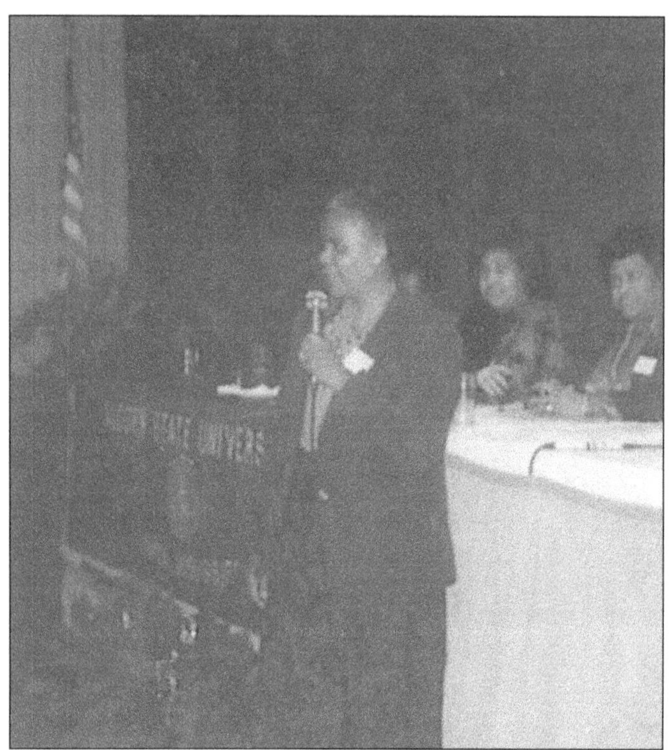

Dr. Alpha Lockhart Morris gives the Hall of Honors Report at a mid-winter conference. The Hall of Honors Report is an announcement of alumni selected, according to established criteria, for recognition of their achievements in the areas of alumni, athletics, and service. Dr. Norris is a 1952 graduate of Alcorn and was recognized in 1993 by the Mississippi legislature as outstanding faculty. She was Alcornite of the Year in 1988 and was born in Taylor, Mississippi.

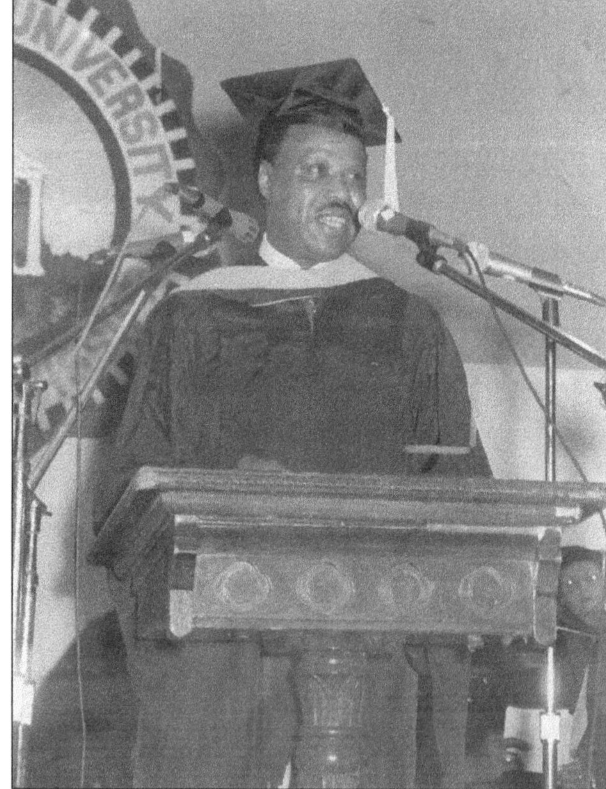

Jewell Lockhart serves as the keynote commencement speaker at his alma mater. He was a 1956 graduate of Alcorn and a 1982 Alcornite of the Year. He was born in Taylor, Mississippi, and has served as treasurer for the National Alumni Association since 1963.

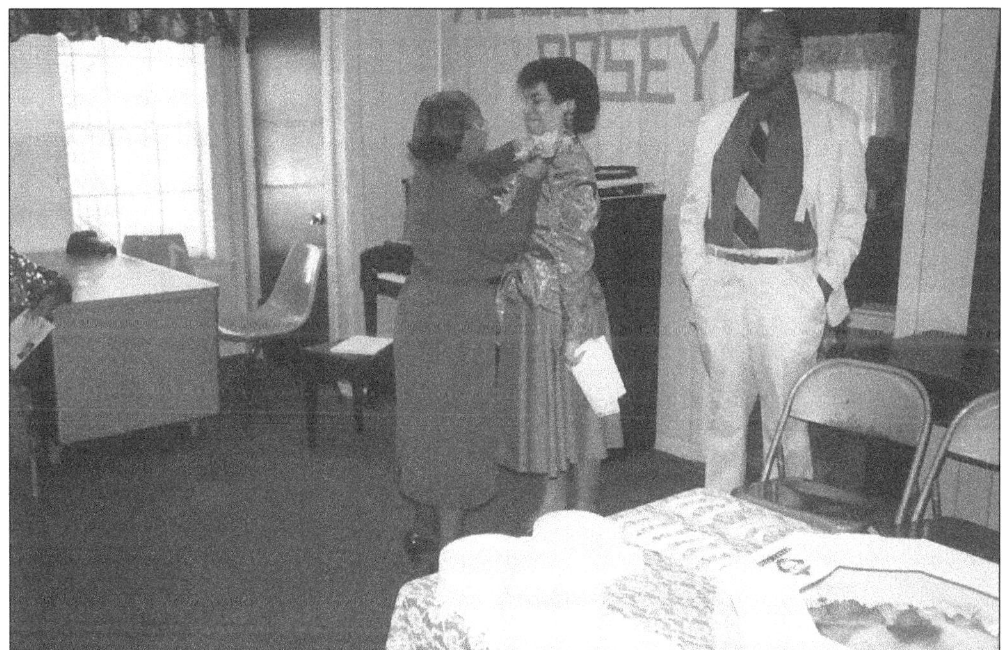

The Laurel-Jones County chapter sponsors an autograph party for Dr. Josephine M. Posey, author of *Against Great Odds: The History of Alcorn State University*. A corsage is pinned on her by Omega Davis as Frankie Peyton looks on.

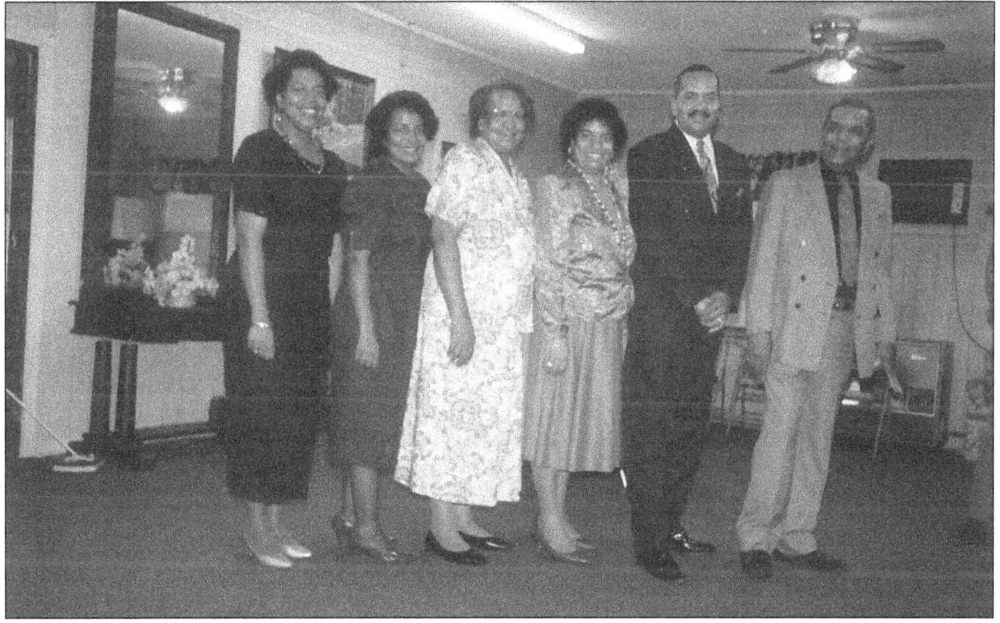

Dr. Posey's family attends a book-signing ceremony sponsored by the Laurel-Jones County chapter. Standing from left to the right are Connie McCann Fairley (sister), Helen McCann Milloy (sister), Aline McCann (mother), Dr. Posey, John Calvin McCann (brother), and the late Mr. Calvin McCann (father). Both of Dr. Posey's sisters and her brother are graduates of Alcorn. Her parents did not attend college, but all of their children consider them to be "Honorary Alcornites," for they too love Alcorn.

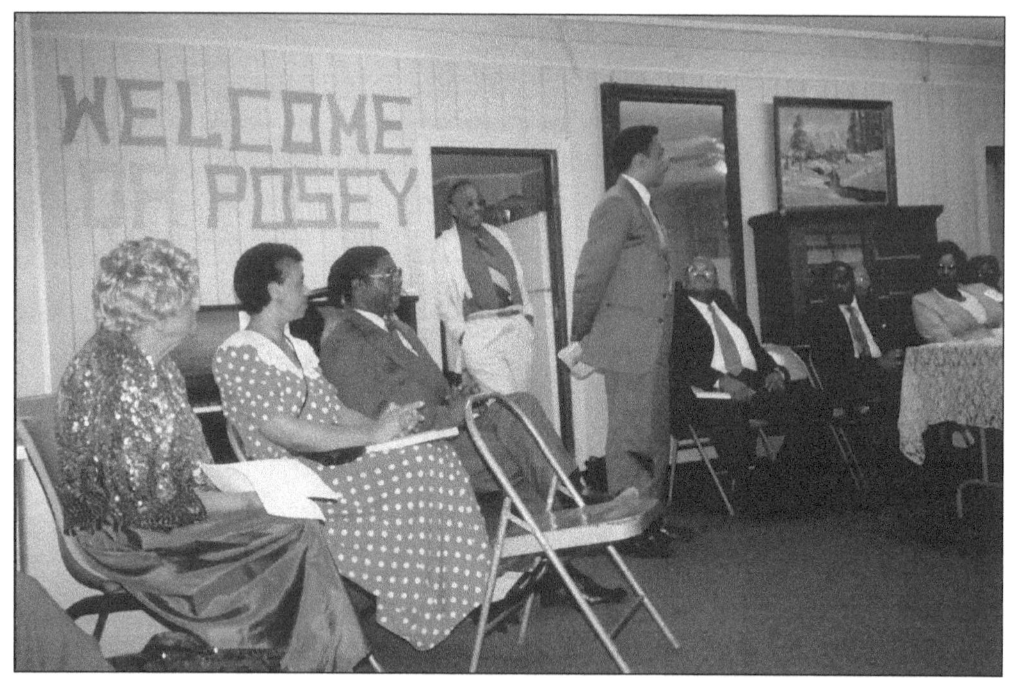

Charles Davis, director of Alumni Affairs, speaks at a book-signing ceremony for Dr. Josephine Posey sponsored by the Laurel-Jones County chapter. Her cousins Leola (Class of 1964) and Charles Beasley (Class of 1963), second and third from left, were in attendance. They are Alcornites who fell in love, graduated, and married.

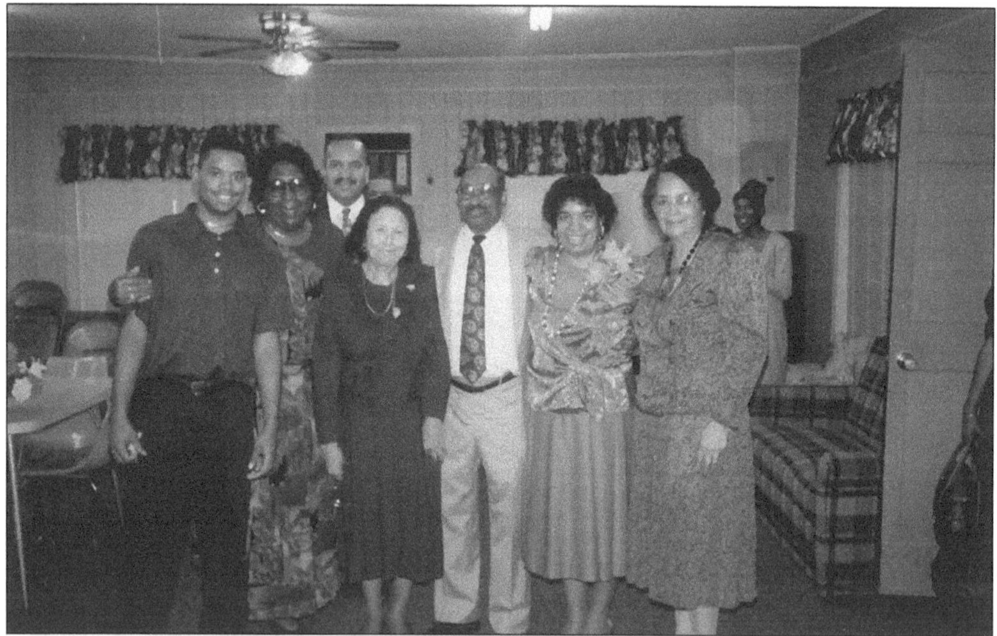

Dr. Posey had many relatives in attendance at the book-signing ceremony. From left to right are Carlos (son), Lillie Garner (cousin), John (brother), Mary Collins (cousin), Dr. I.L. Thomas (uncle), Dr. Posey, Mattie Thomas (aunt), and her niece Kristin, smiling in the background. Kristin will attend Alcorn beginning in the fall of 2000 as a freshman.

This group of Alcornites is pictured in front of Lanier Hall. They are on the campus for one of the annual homecoming celebrations.

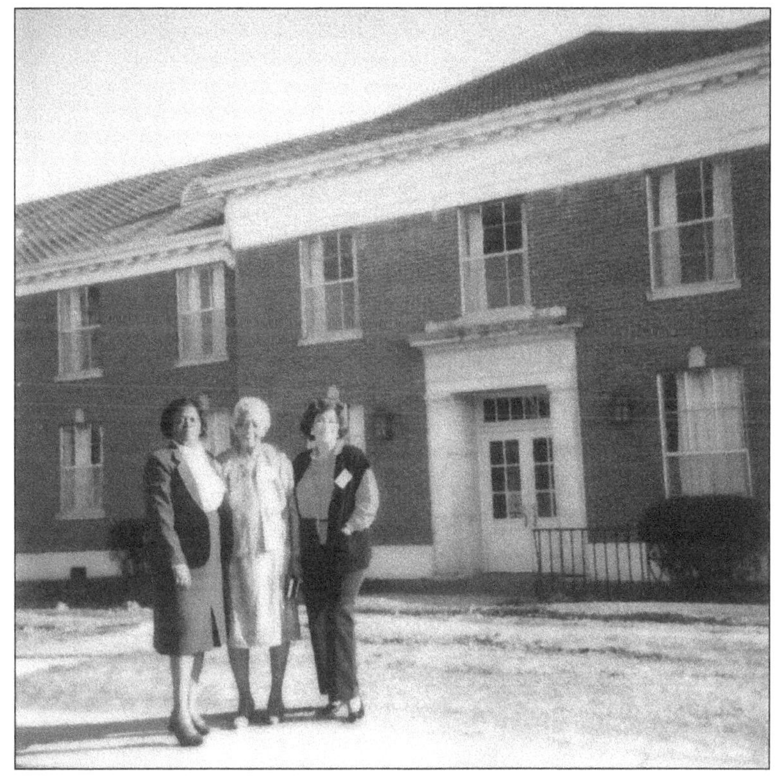

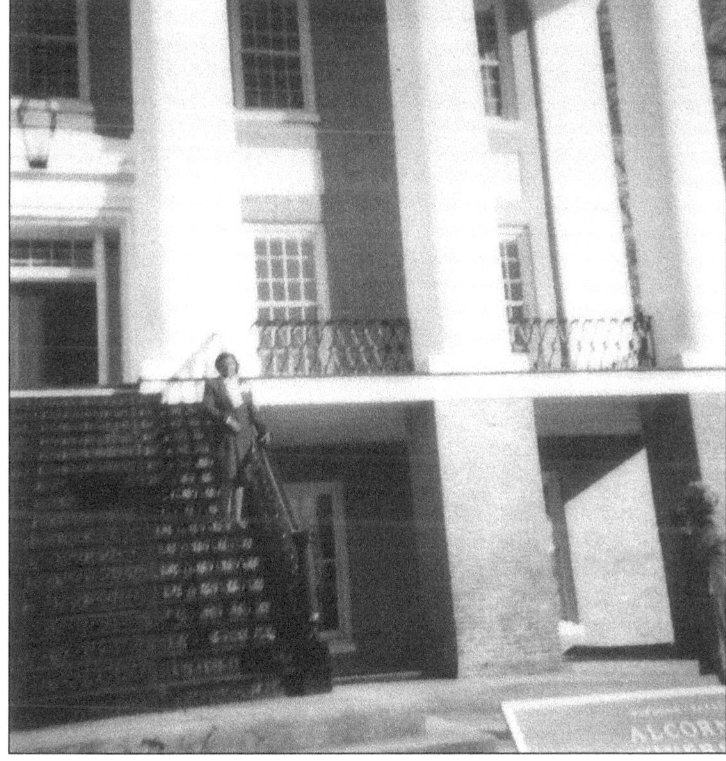

Lorine Minor visits Alcorn and has her picture taken on the steps of the chapel. She returns to the campus as often as possible to attend various functions.

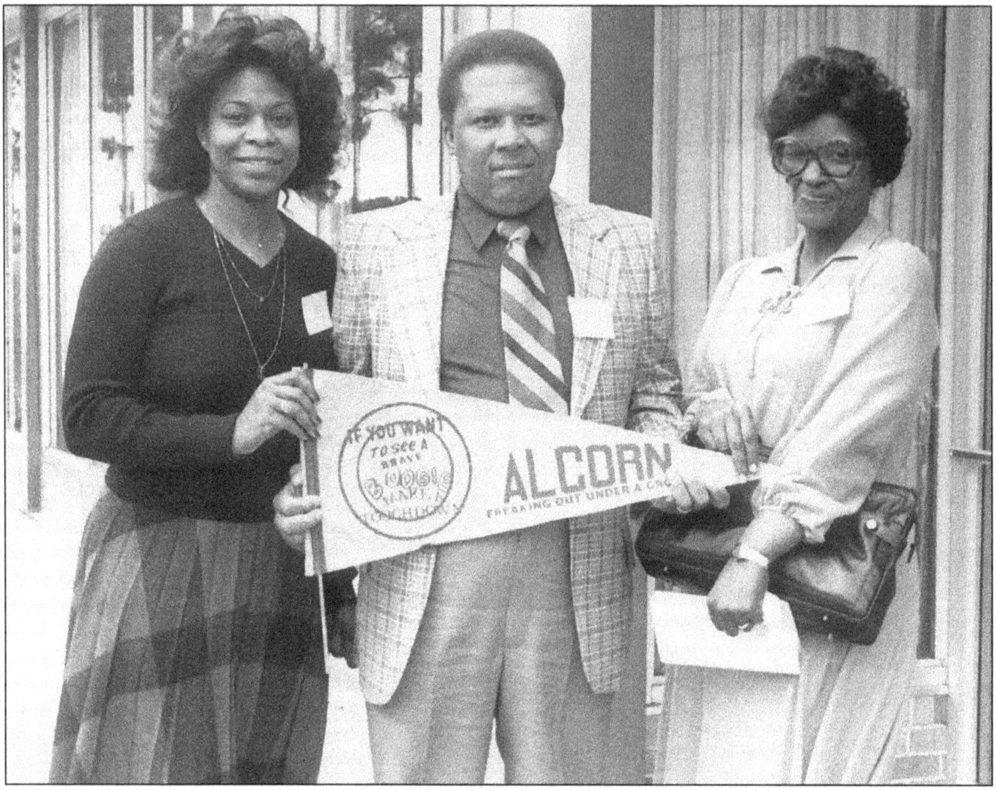

Alcornites hold a banner that reads, "If you want to see a Brave boogie, make a touchdown." Go Belinda! Belinda (left) is joined by two Alcornites, including a former Miss Alcorn, Vera Bryant.

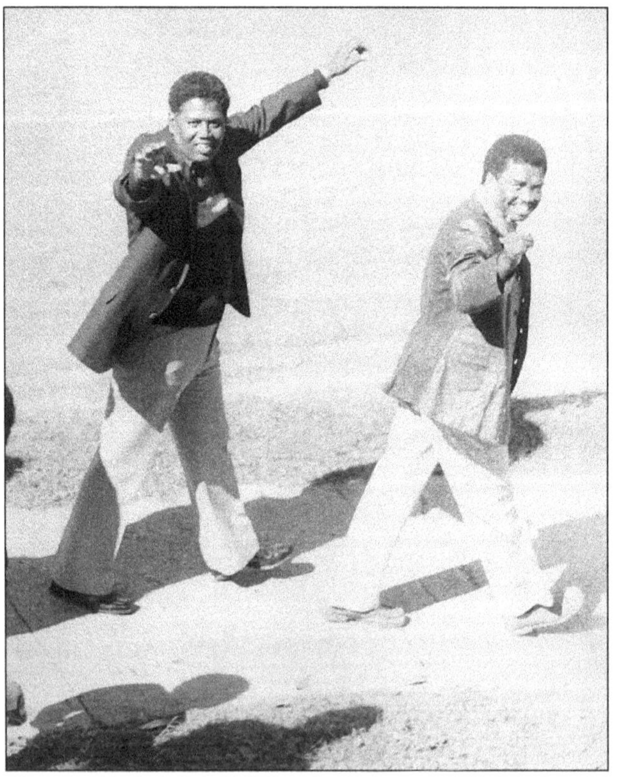

Luther Alexander and Arthur Peyton give the signs of victory. Go Braves Go! The Braves just beat rival Jackson State University and fans celebrate the victory.

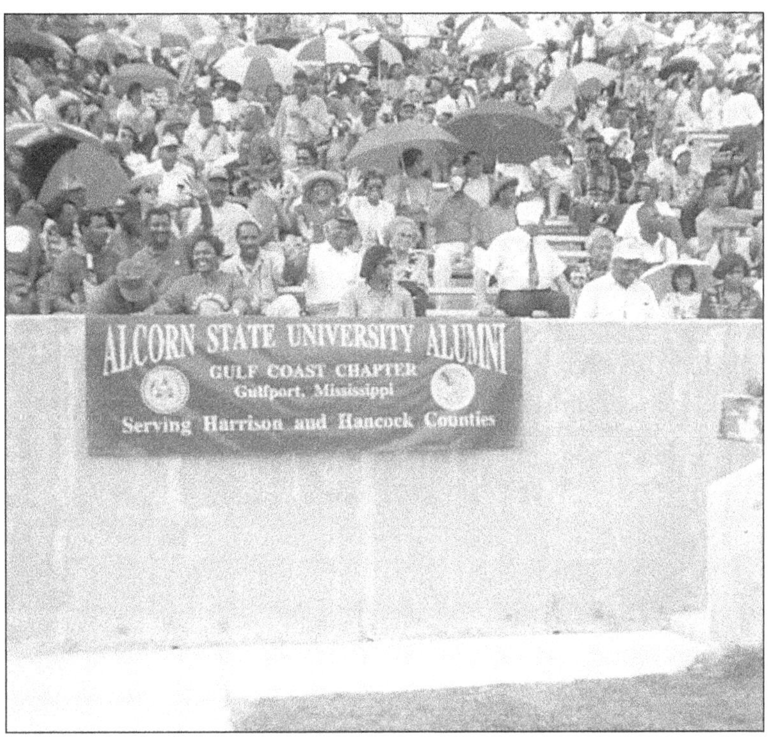

The Gulf Coast chapter of Alcorn Alumni serves Harrison and Hancock Counties, as their banner points out.

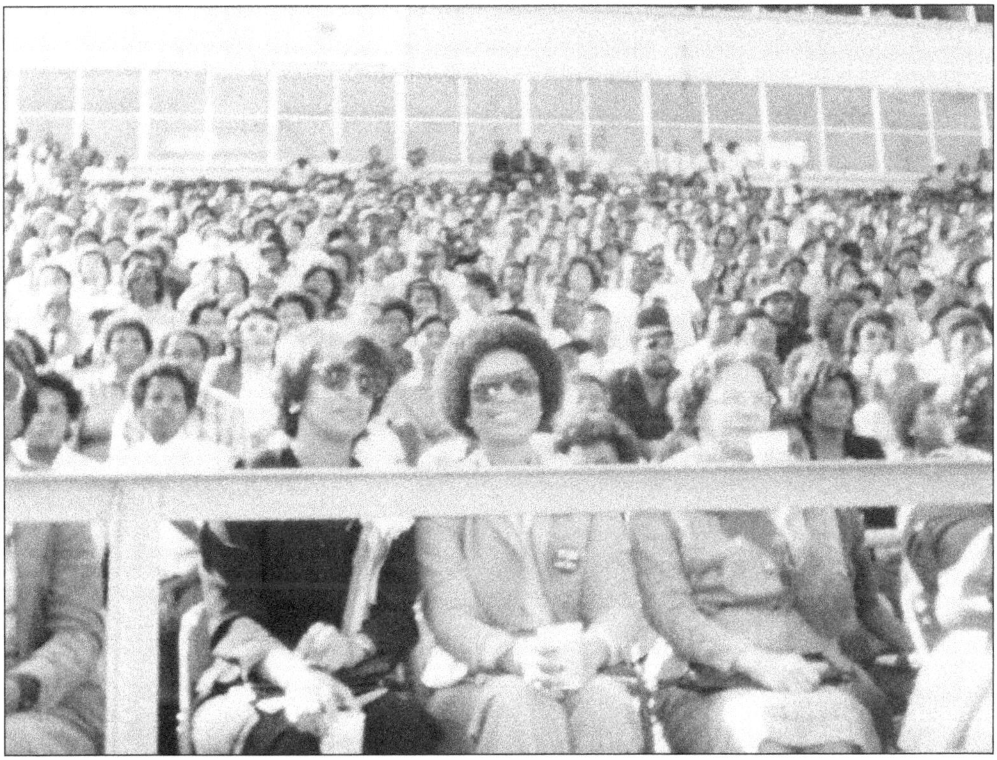

Homecoming brings friends and loved ones back to the university. Here, they watch a football game in high anticipation of an Alcorn win.

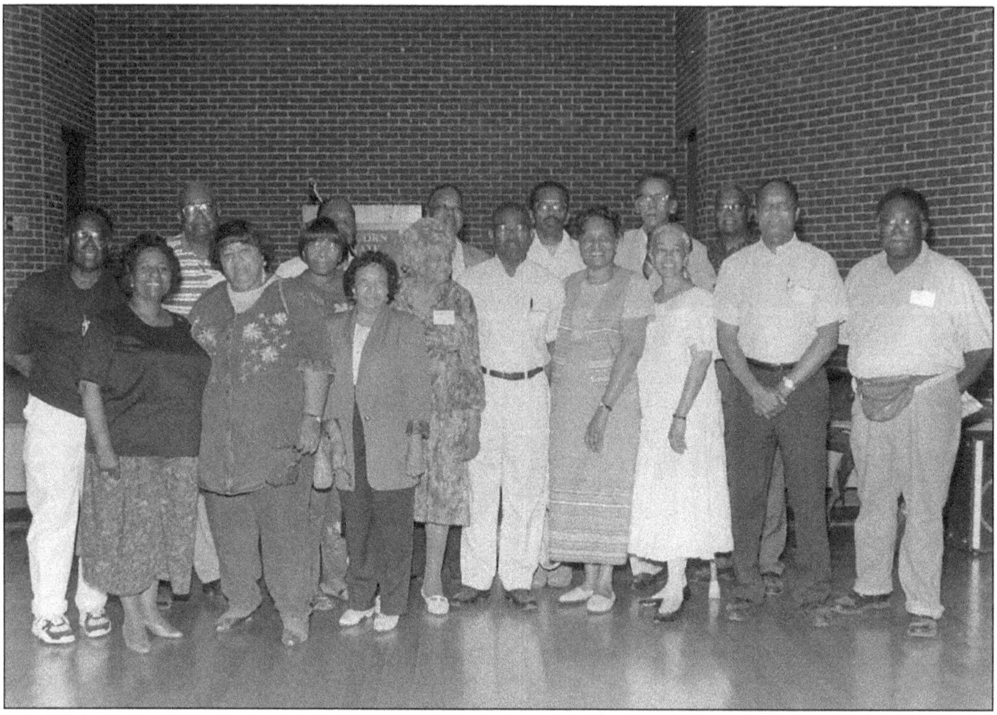

Their 40th class reunion was a memorable occasion for the Alcorn Class of 1956.

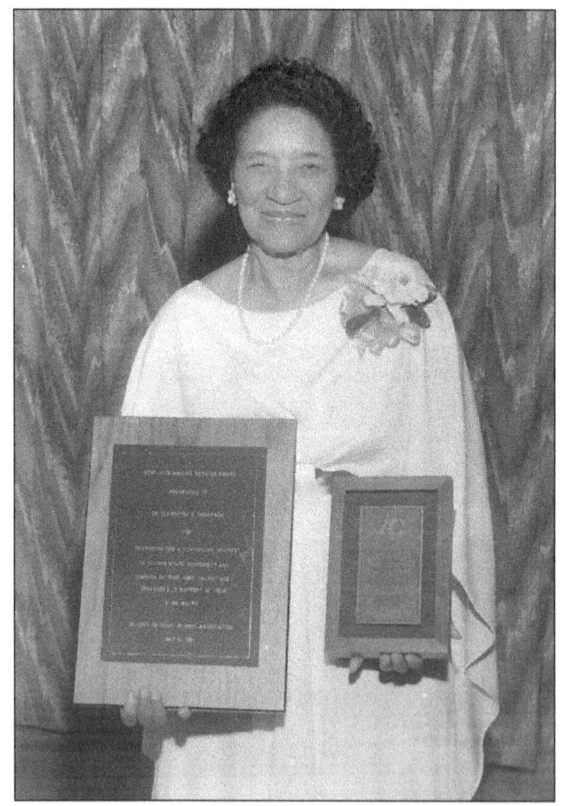

Longtime educator Dr. Cleopatra Thompson, a 1932 graduate of Alcorn, holds two awards. Over the years, she received many accolades and acknowledgments for her service to the community and to the state.

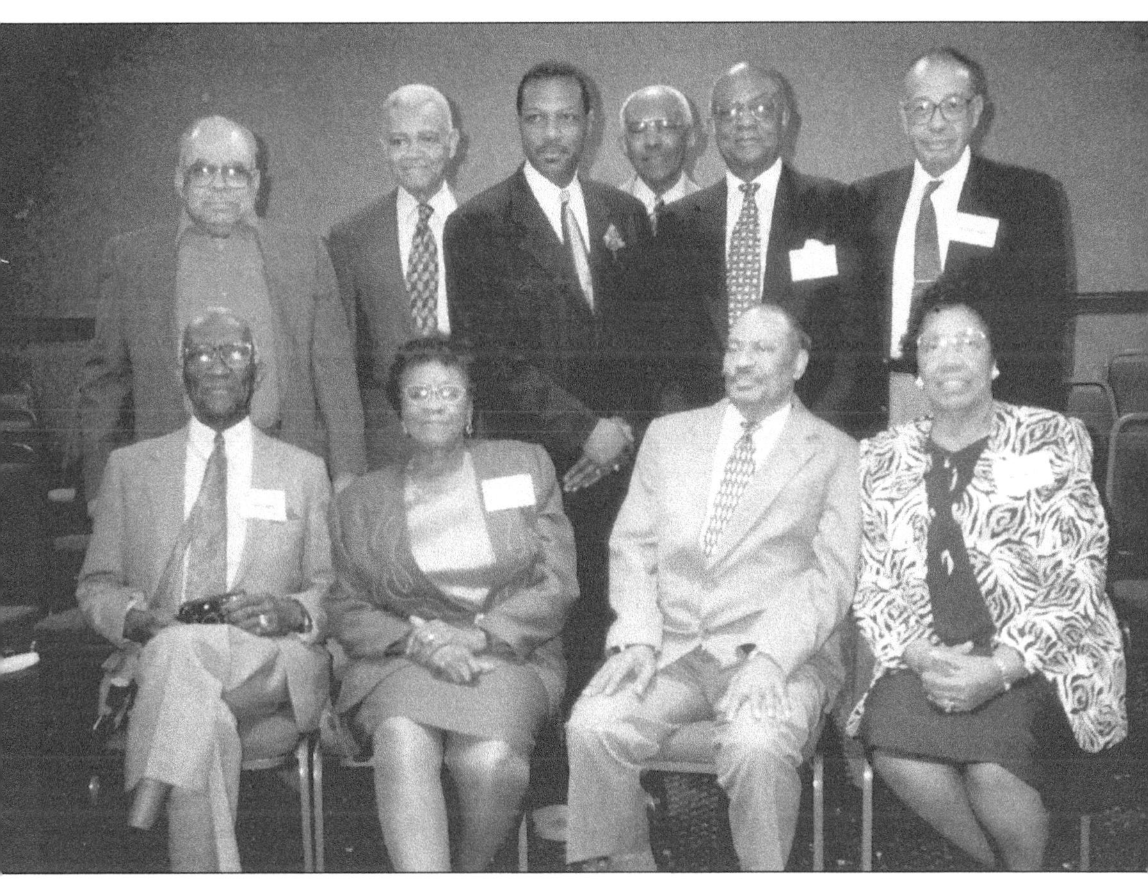

The Class of 1942 held their class meeting at a recent mid-winter conference. Here, they are accompanied by Alcorn's current president, Dr. Clinton Bristow Jr. (standing, third from left), who took over as the president in 1996.

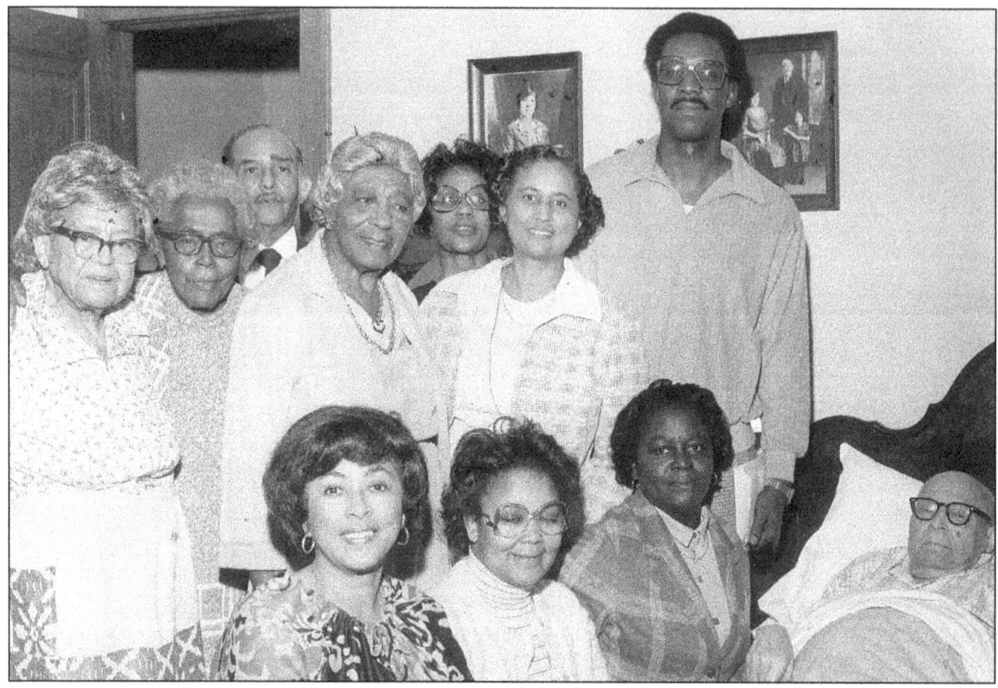

The Calumet chapter is on the move. Pictured, from left to right, are (front row) Sammie Kales, Betty Eichelberger, Lorine Minor, and Dr. Dudley Turner; (back row) Norma Hayle, Jannie Chatters, Lucius Patton, unidentified, unidentified, unidentified, and Preston Lee (president at the time).

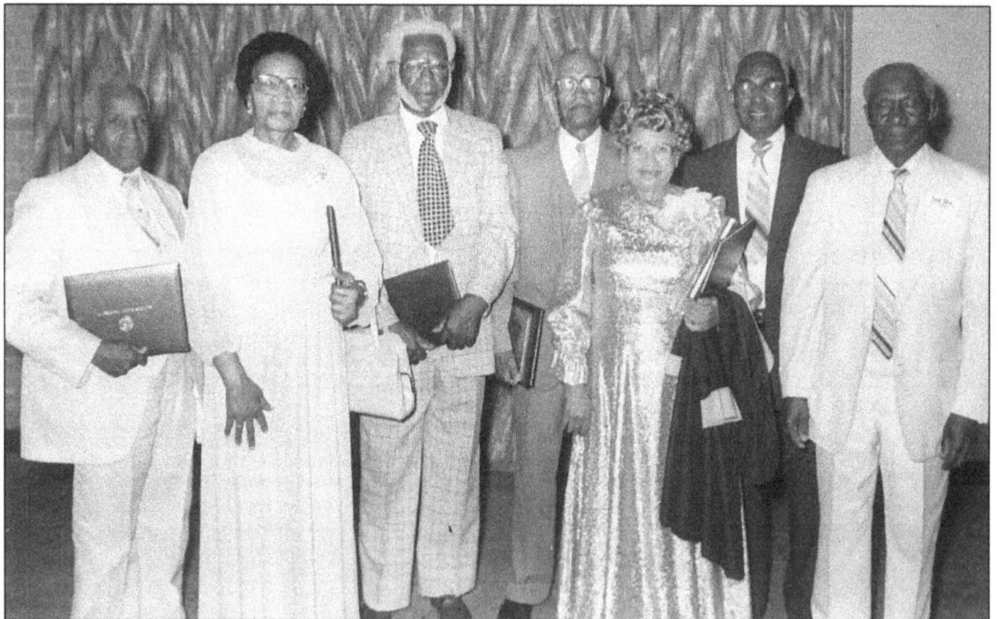

Members of a Golden Class pose for a picture after receiving their 50th-year golden diploma. Alumni receive golden diplomas after 50 years and are a part of the commencement exercise during the applicable year. They march and take an active role in the weekend of activities.

Lutille Stepney (right) and John Bates (left), husband of Gladys Noel Bates, Miss Alcorn 1956, attended the National Education Association Convention in 1960. Gladys Noel Bates was a national pioneer for teacher salaries.

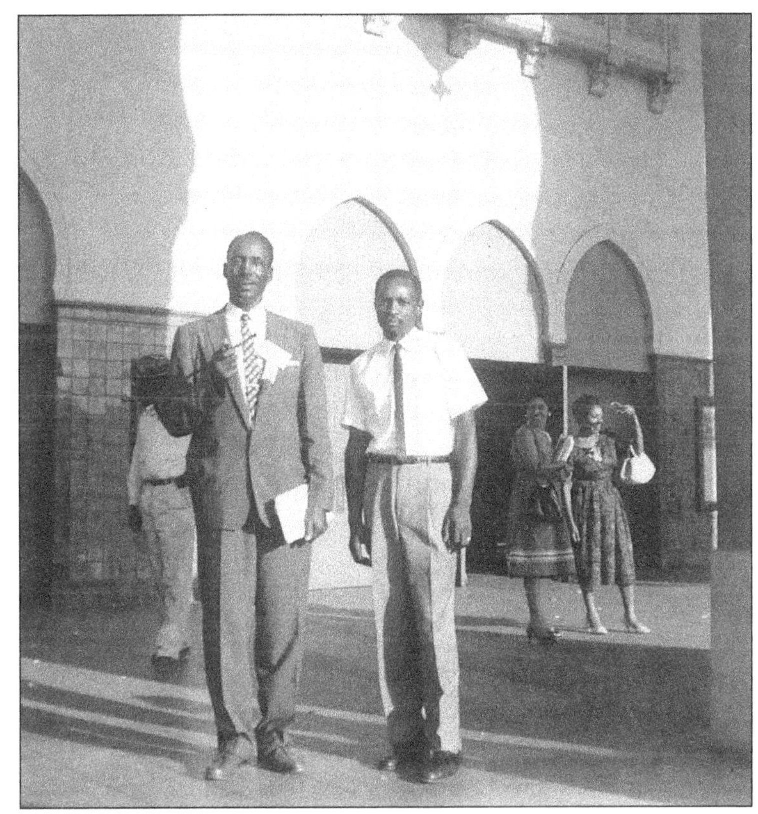

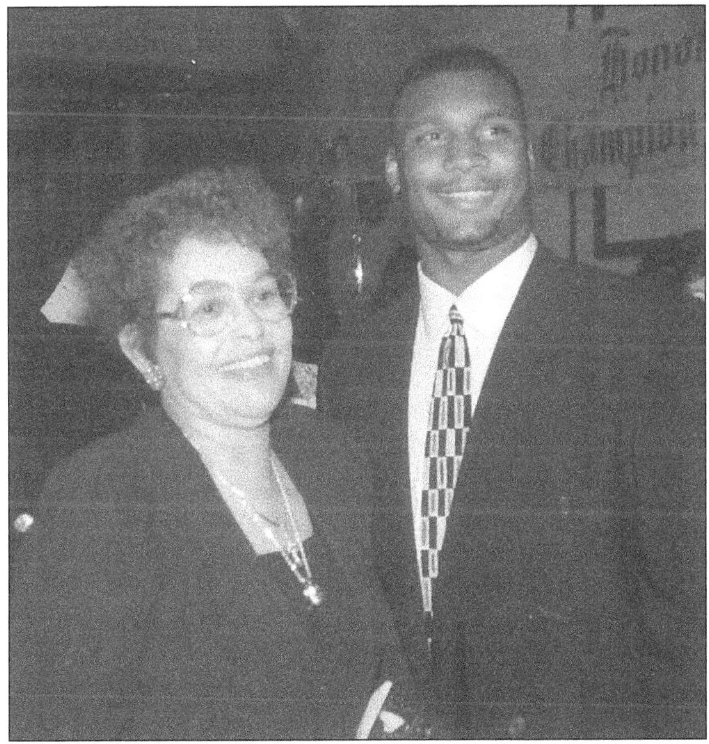

Verna Spinks, the wife of the legendary Jack Spinks, poses with Steve McNair, who was one of the greatest in Alcorn football history. He was a finalist for the Heisman Trophy in 1993, the highest honor ever achieved by an athlete in the Southwest Athletic Conference.

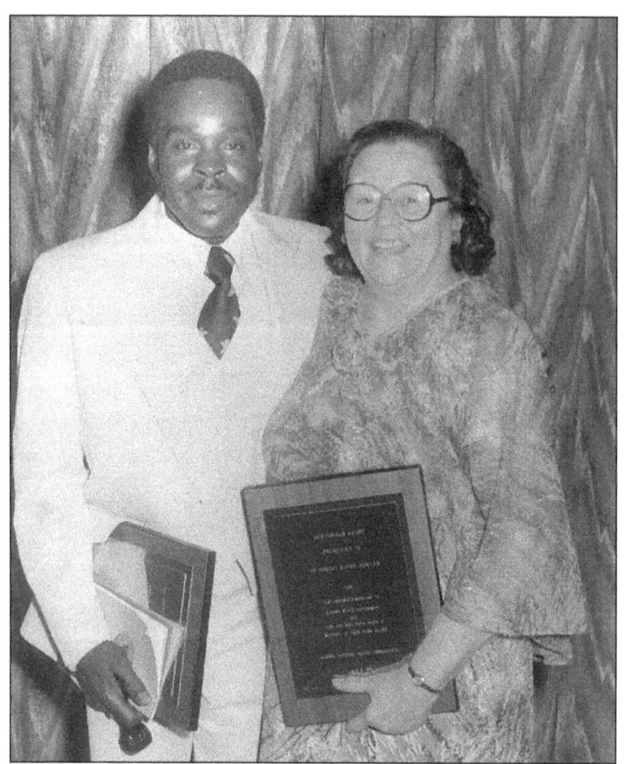

Coach Willie McGowan and Mrs. Lula Kelly O'Neal, Miss Alcorn 1937–1938, accept alumni awards at a special function in McComb, Mississippi.

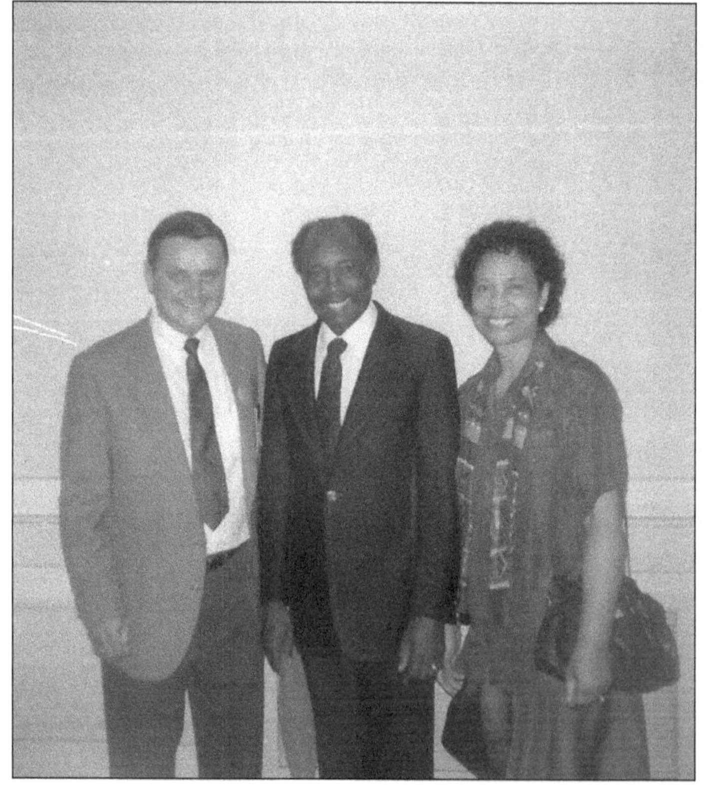

Lutille Stepney Day was proclaimed in Gulfport in honor of Stepney for his long years of inspiring students to excel in athletics. He was honored by the mayor at the time, Ken Combs, and by the city council. He is accompanied here by the mayor and his wife, Annie Ruth Stepney, whom he affectionately refers to as "Baby," Miss Alcorn 1950–1951.

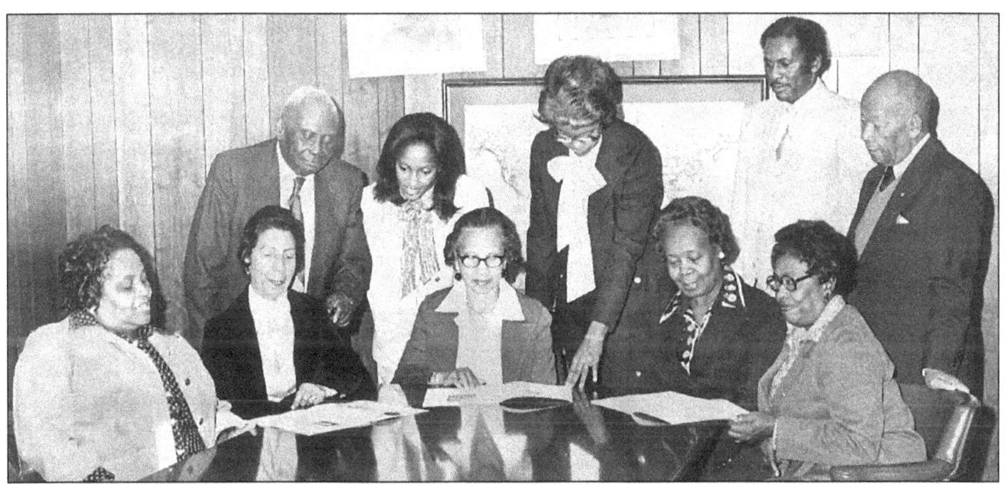

The Warren County Alcorn Alumni chapter plans for the 1980 Mid-winter Conference. From left to right are (seated) Ruth Dunlap, Janice Gardner, Melissa Demby, R.M. Perry, and Rebecca Vaughan; (standing) W.S. Demby ("Mr. Alcorn"), Connie Stirgus, unidentified, Jim E. Stirgus (local president at the time), and G.C. Garner.

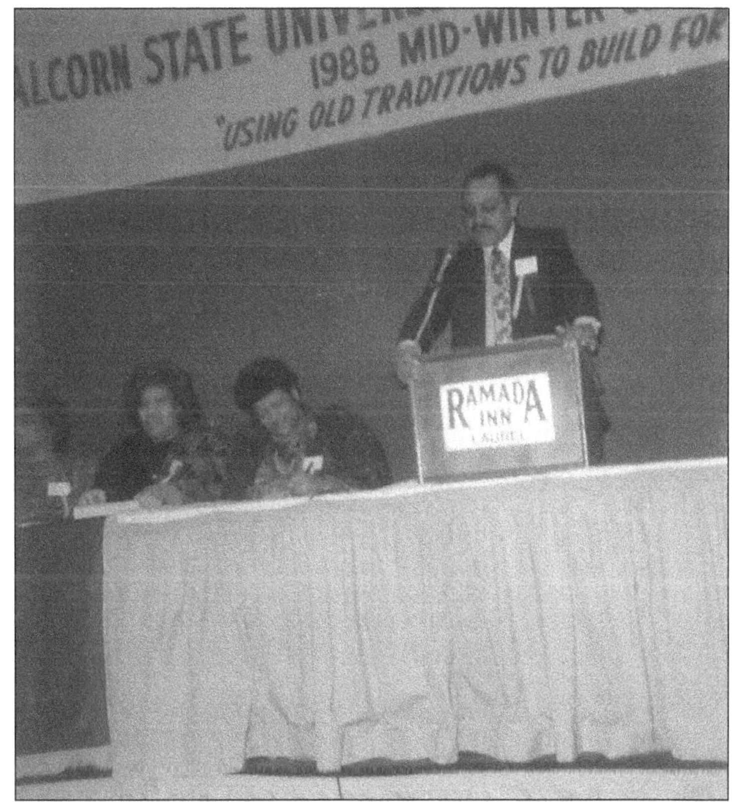

Matt Thomas, 1986–1990 president of the National Alumni Association, addresses alumni at the 1988 Mid-winter Conference. Thomas graduated from Alcorn in 1964 and served as chairman of the board of directors of the Alcorn State University Foundation for many years. He was Alcornite of the Year in 1991 and is an accountant, comptroller, and businessman.

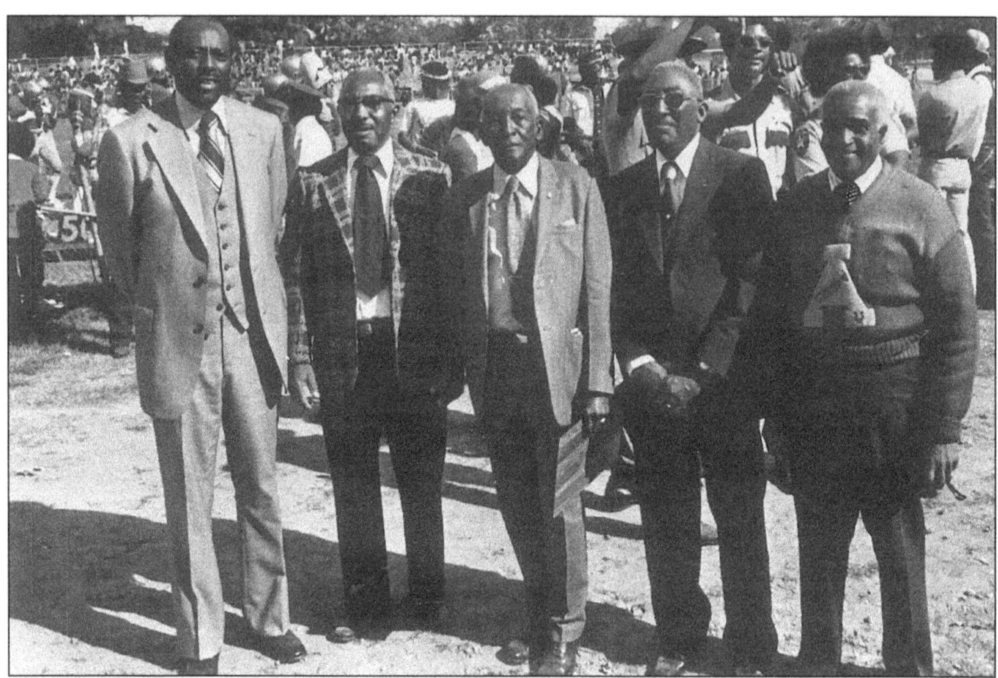

Dr. Walter Washington, president, and other great Alcornite men pose during a football game on campus.

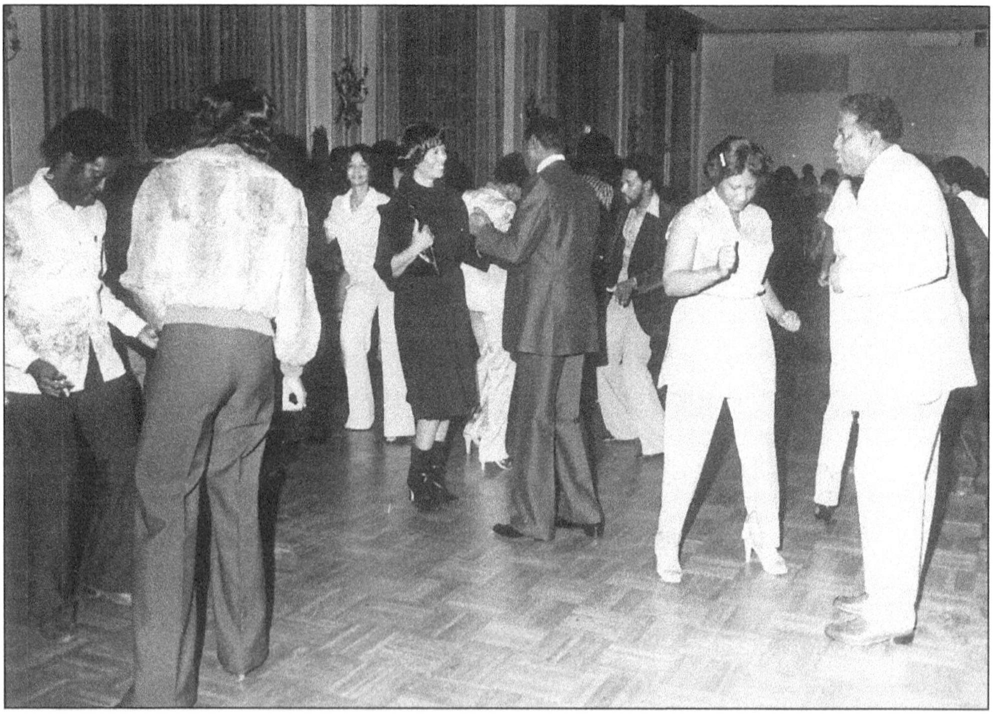

Alcornites take care of business but like to have fun as well. On the far right, Luther Alexander and his wife, Floyd (a Delta Devil—a graduate of Mississippi State University) dance to the music along with the Stepneys and others.

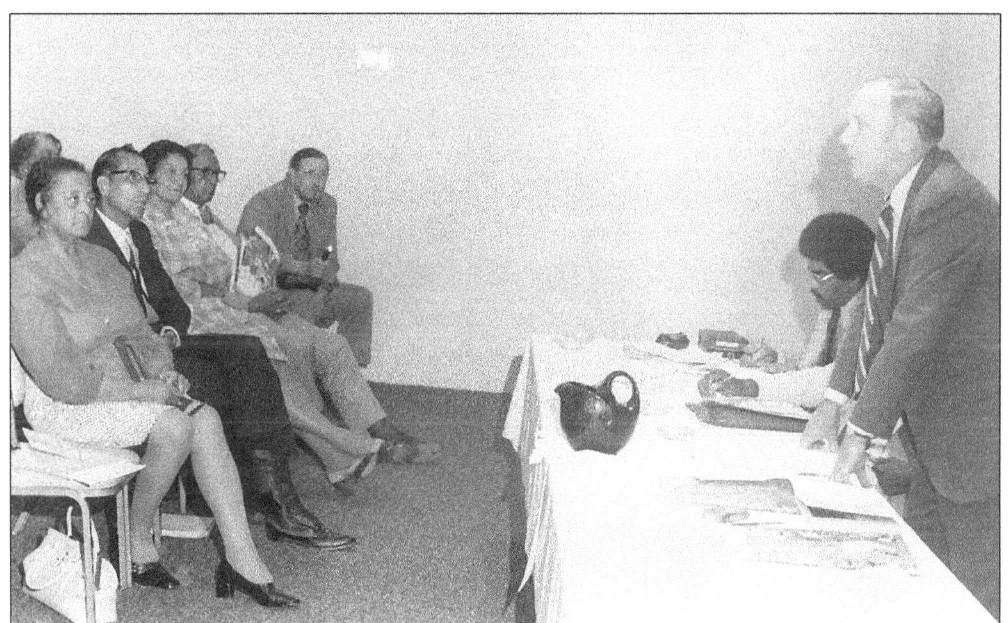

Alumni listen attentively as a foundation proposal is presented at a mid-winter conference.

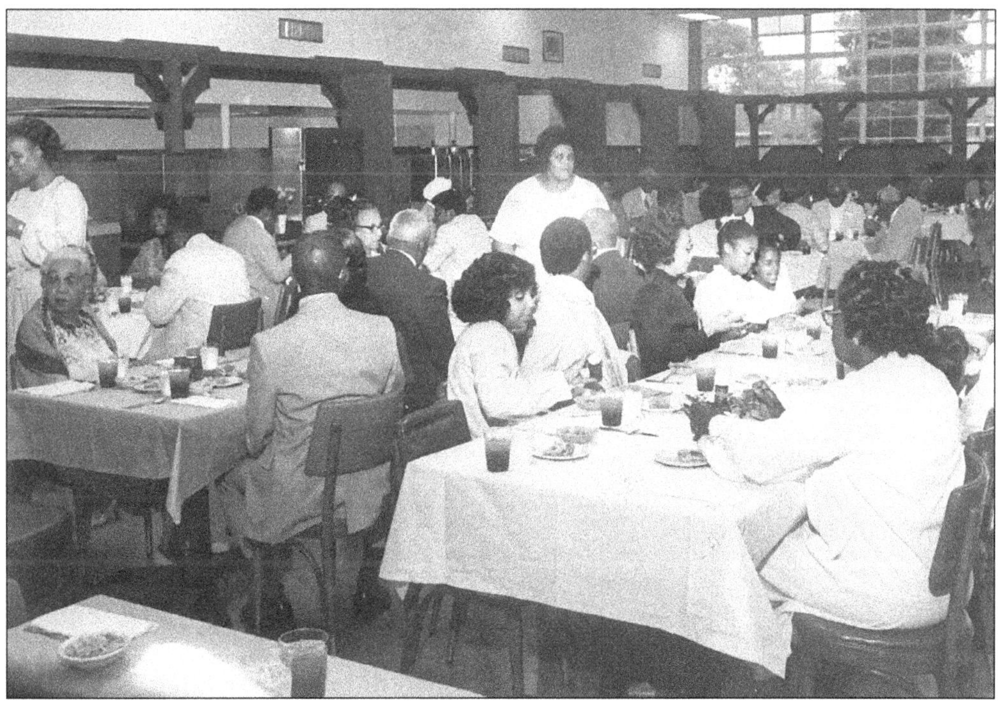

Alcornites gather for awards night in the William H. Bell Dining Hall on the Alcorn campus during an alumni weekend. Awards are given in various areas of service to the alumni, the university, and the community.

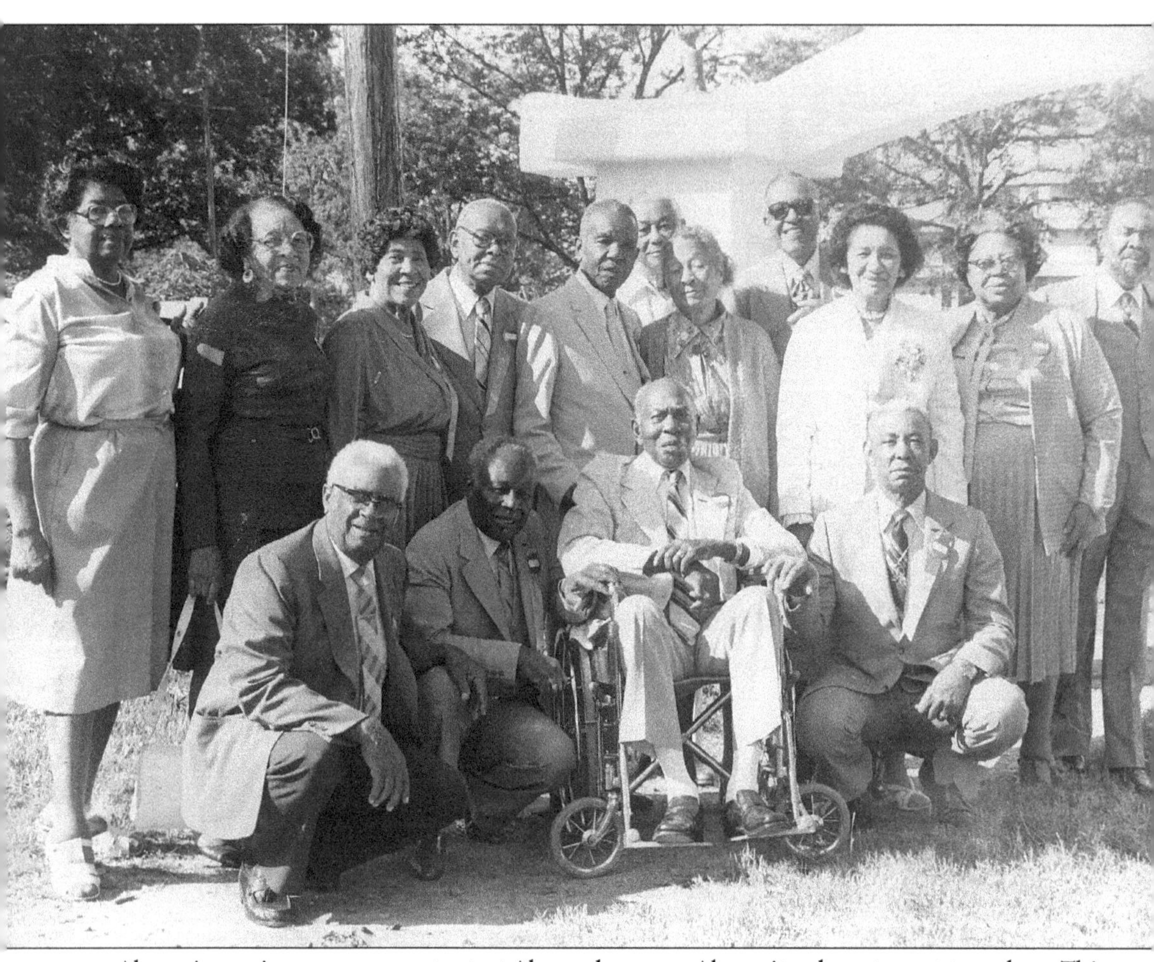

Alumni reunions are a constant at Alcorn because Alcornites love to get together. This photograph was taken after an alumni reunion meeting that is held on the Friday evening prior to graduation every year. This group represents a specific reunion class.

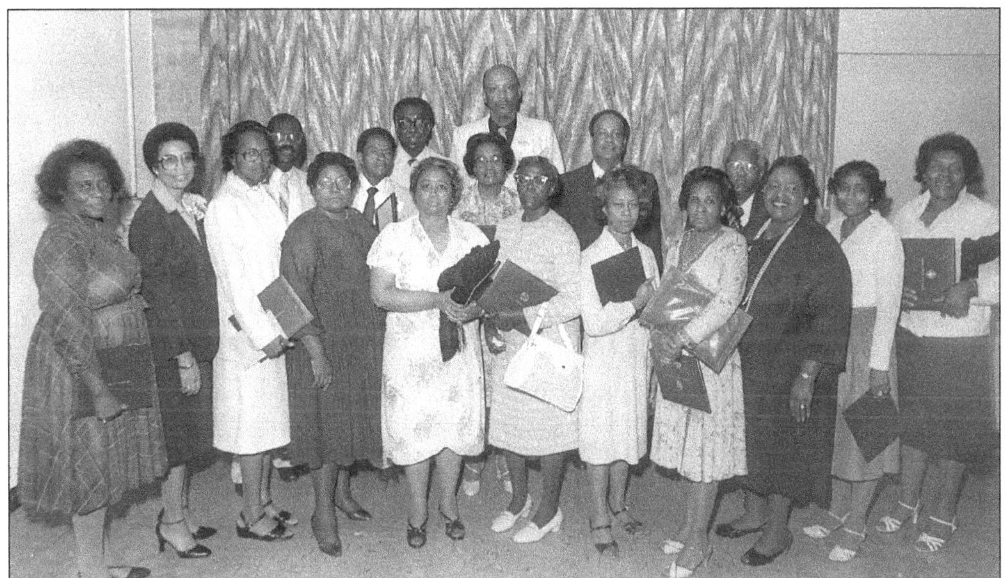

Alumni never lose their connection to their alma mater, and they are continuously involved in university functions. Several members in this picture hold their golden diplomas, which is received by alumni after the 50th anniversary of their graduation from Alcorn.

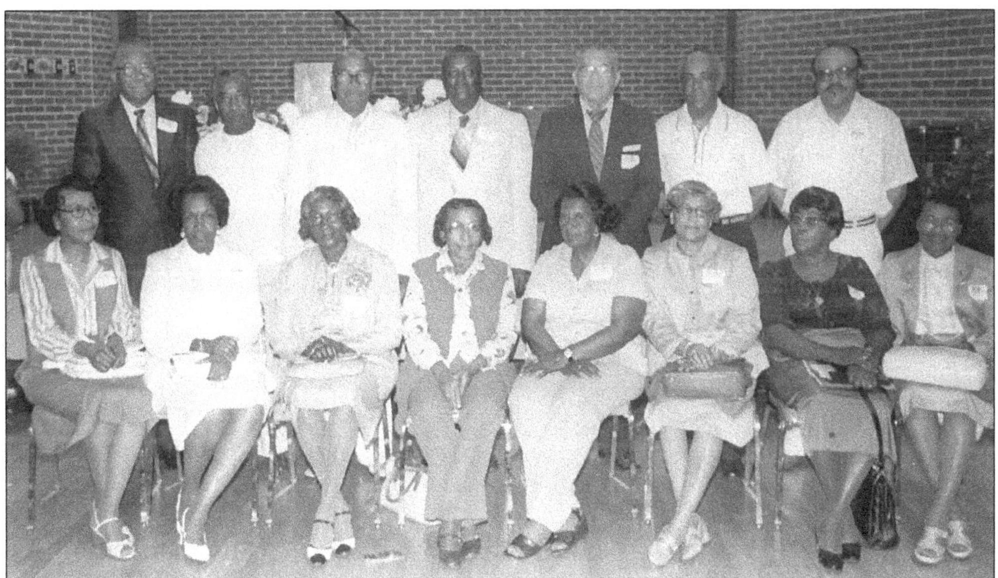

Alcornites take every opportunity to pose together when they meet on campus for various reasons. This photograph represents a reunion group that gathered following a reunion meeting held during alumni weekend each year.

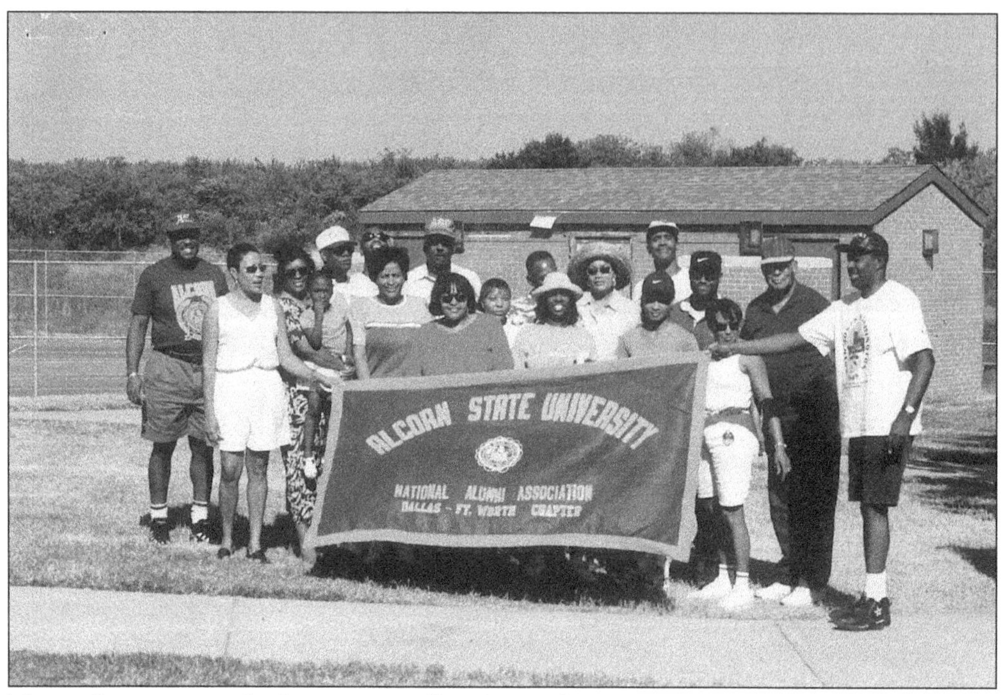

The Dallas-Fort Worth chapter proudly salutes Alcorn State University.

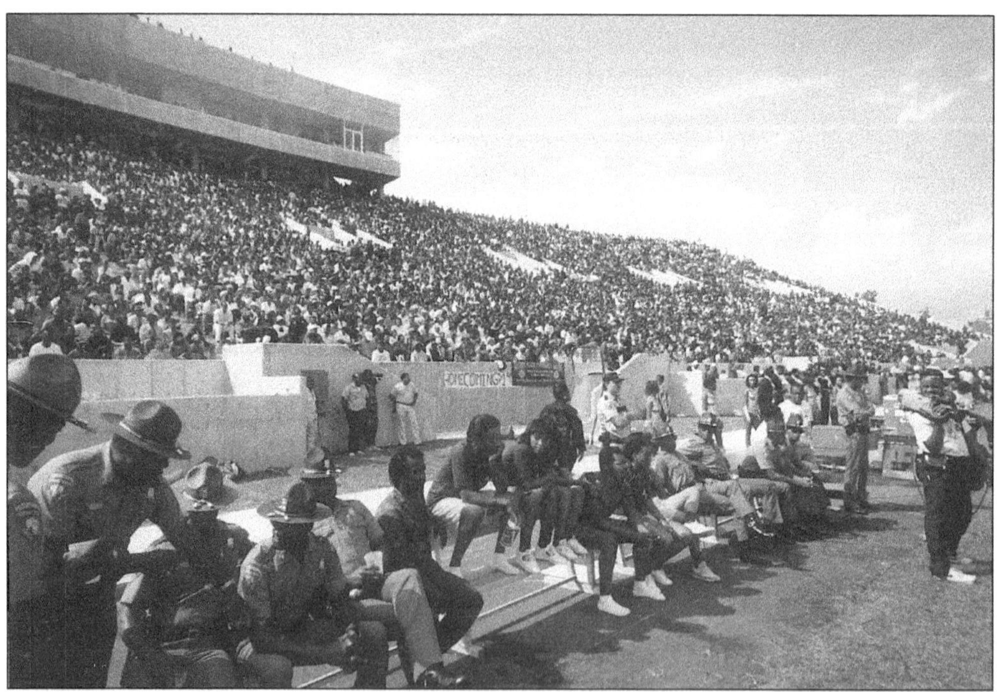

Alcornites are pictured at a homecoming game at Alcorn State University. This is one of the first football games to be held in the new Jack Spinks Stadium, and the stadium appears to be full.

Five

Alcornites in Love and Matrimony

Many students found themselves on the "love train" while at Alcorn; however, they did not forget that studying and graduating were priorities on the campus. Some married while students, others waited until after graduation. This chapter includes some of the Alcorn graduates who fell in love and married. Special recognition goes to Odessa Graves (Class of 1936) and Andrew Graves (Class of 1934), not pictured, for their loyal and dedicated service to our alma mater. They married, spent a wholesome life together, and were later tragically killed in a train wreck near their home in Scott County.

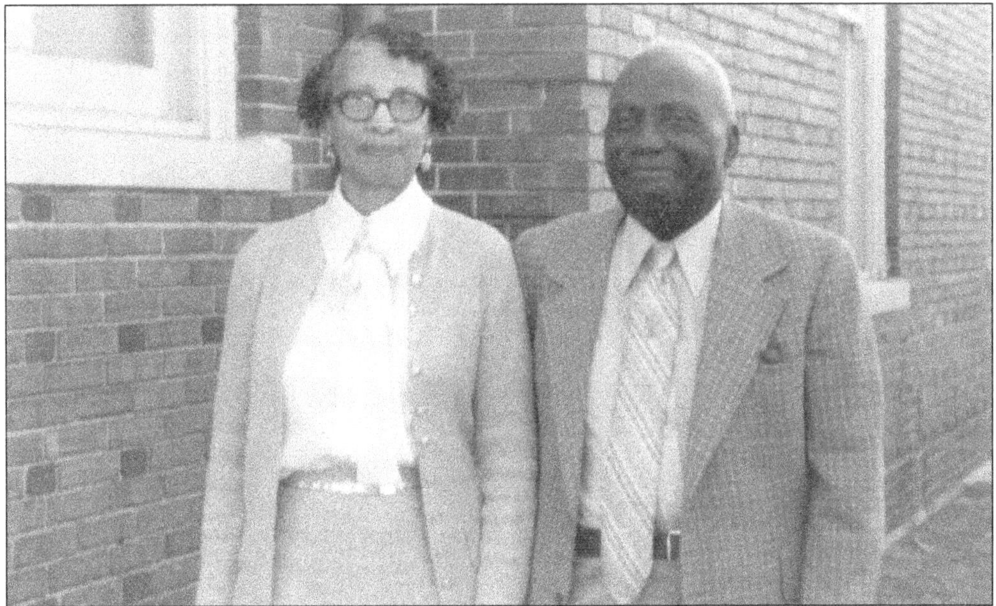

Melissa Demby, Class of 1956, and William S. Demby, Class of 1927, married on March 27, 1931.

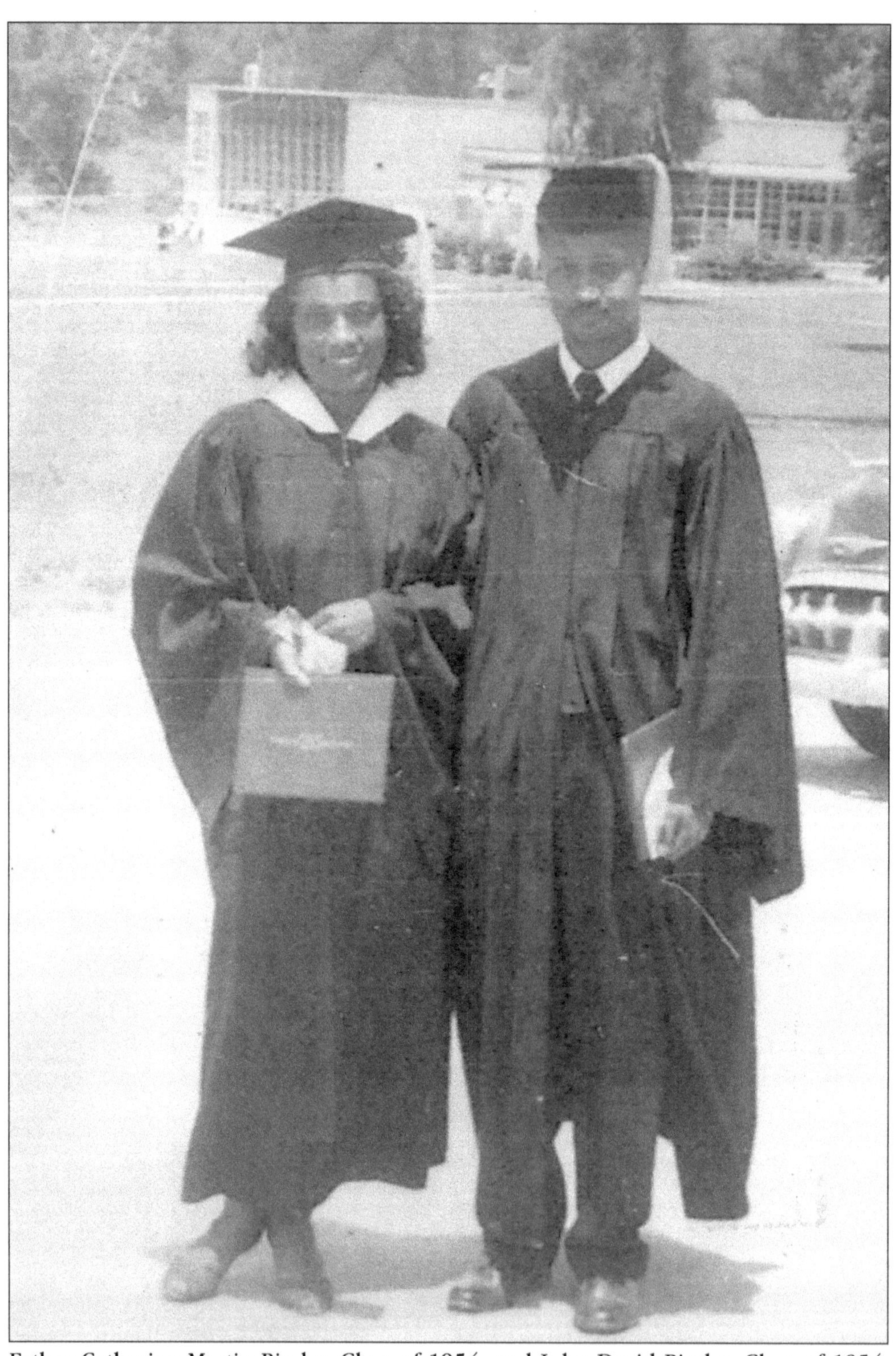

Esther Catherine Martin Rigsby, Class of 1954, and John David Rigsby, Class of 1954, married in December 1954.

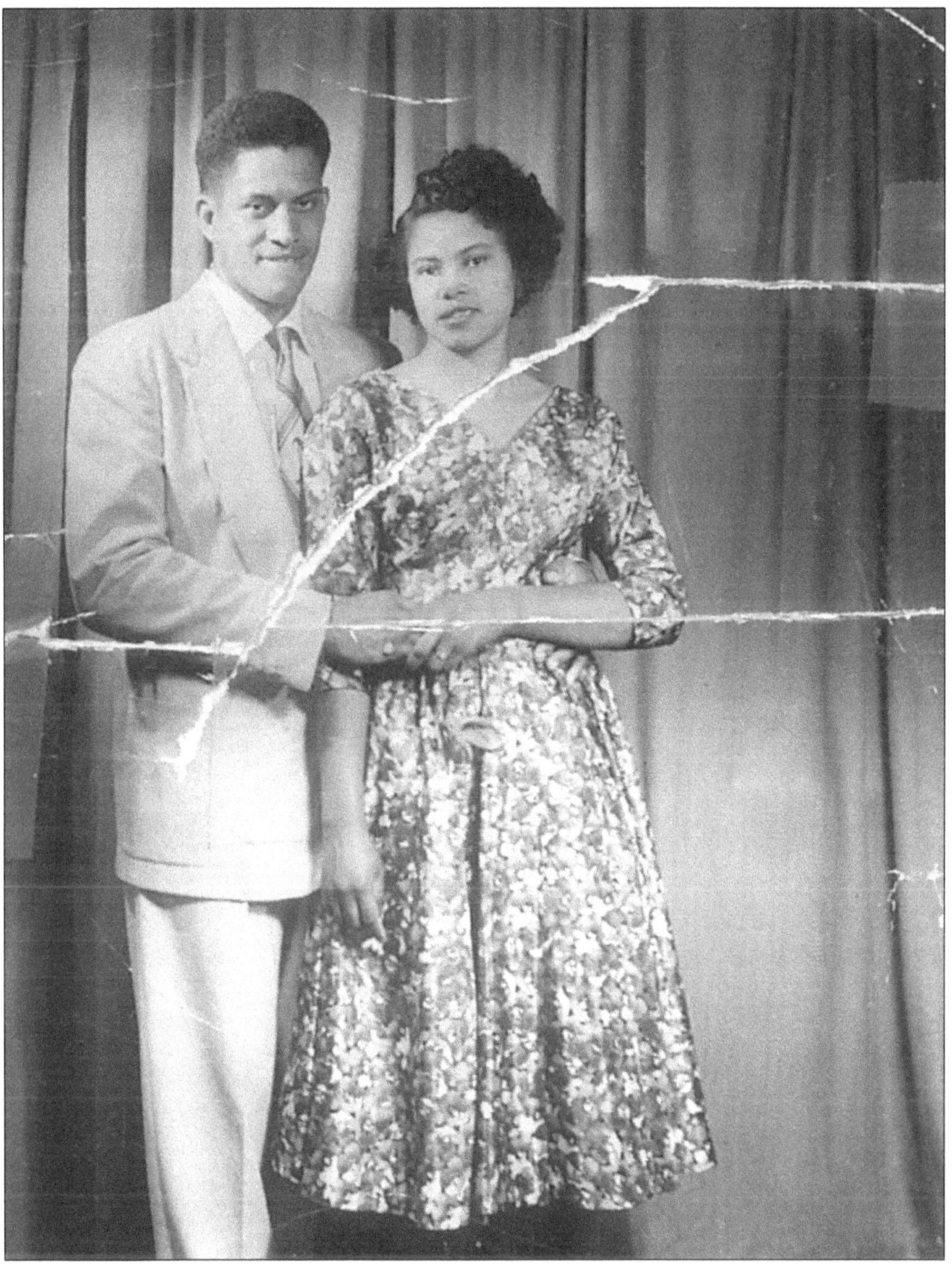

Clynell Moses, Class of 1958, and O.W. Moses, Class of 1954, were married on September 2, 1954.

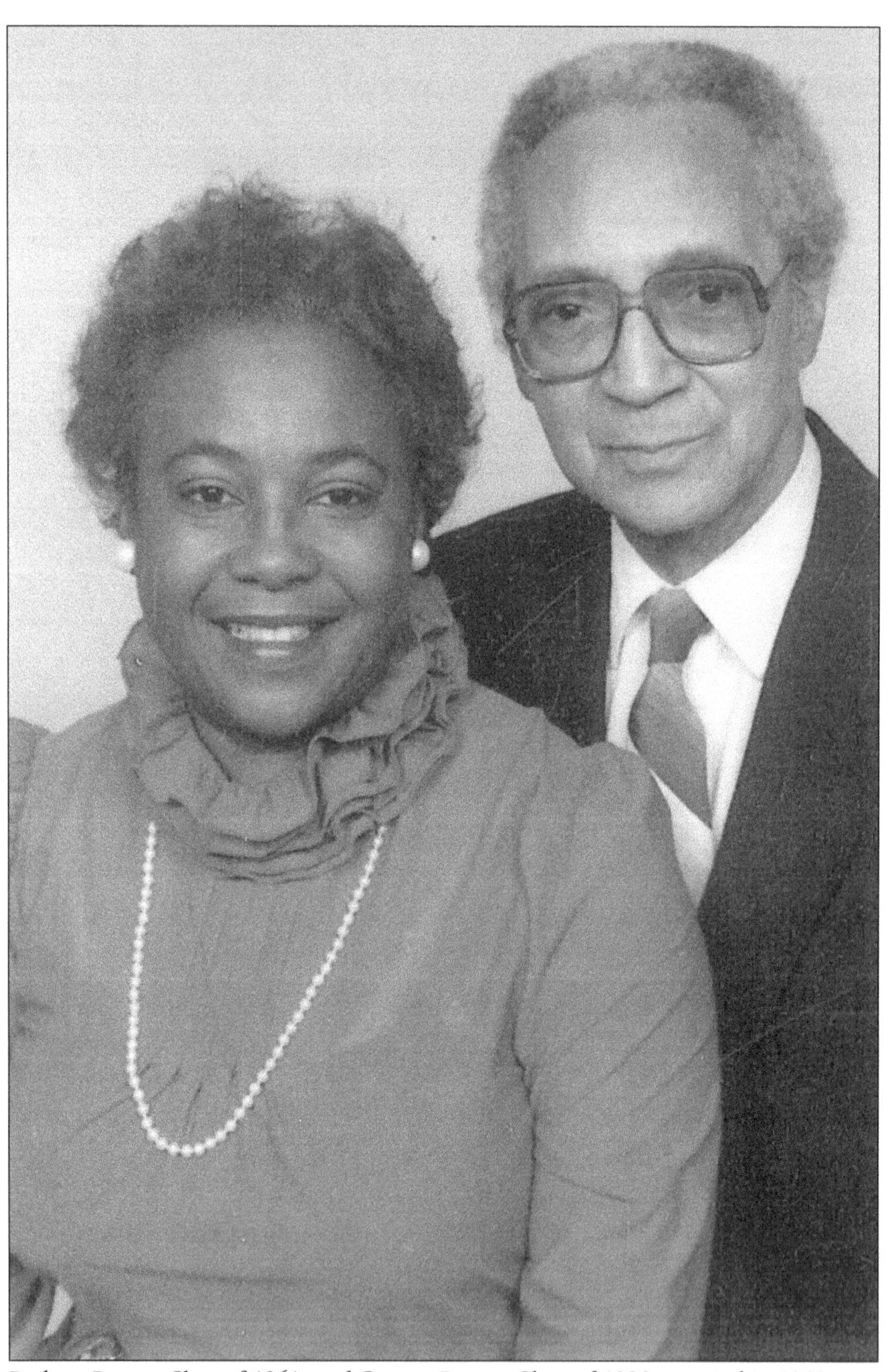

Barbara Bacon, Class of 1961, and George Bacon, Class of 1938, married in 1950.

Annie Ruth Stepney, Class of 1951, and Lutille Stepney, Class of 1953, married and have been parents to many students who have attended Alcorn. Dr. Robert Bowles (right), National Alumni President, poses with the couple.

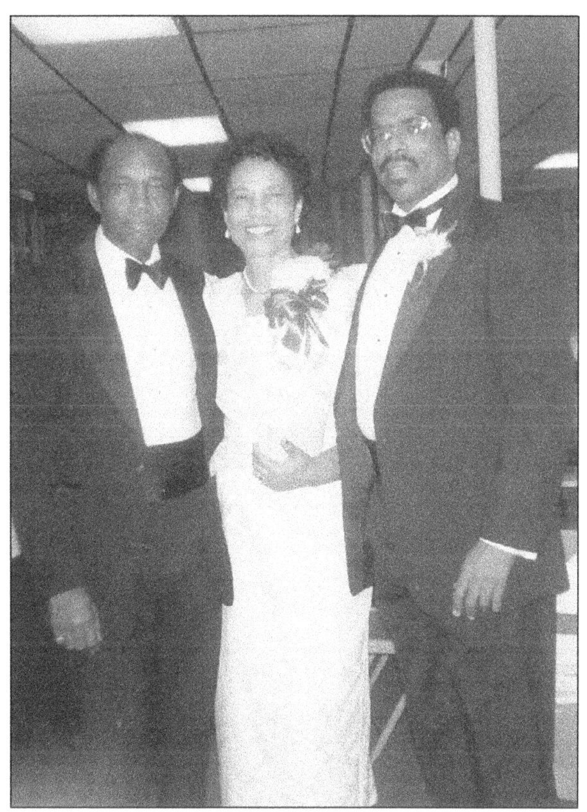

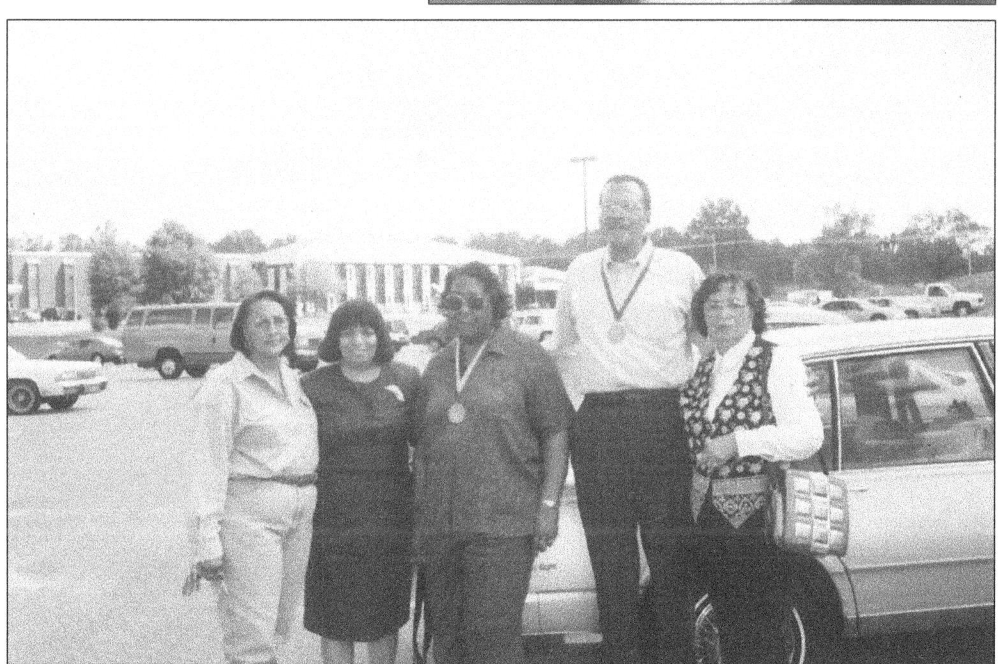

Lillie Ruth Beasley Garner, Class of 1952, and Lee "Chick" Garner, Class of 1952 (third and fourth from the left) married in 1953. Their cousins Carlee Ducksworth (left), Josephine Posey (second from left), and Mattie Thomas (right) are featured with them.

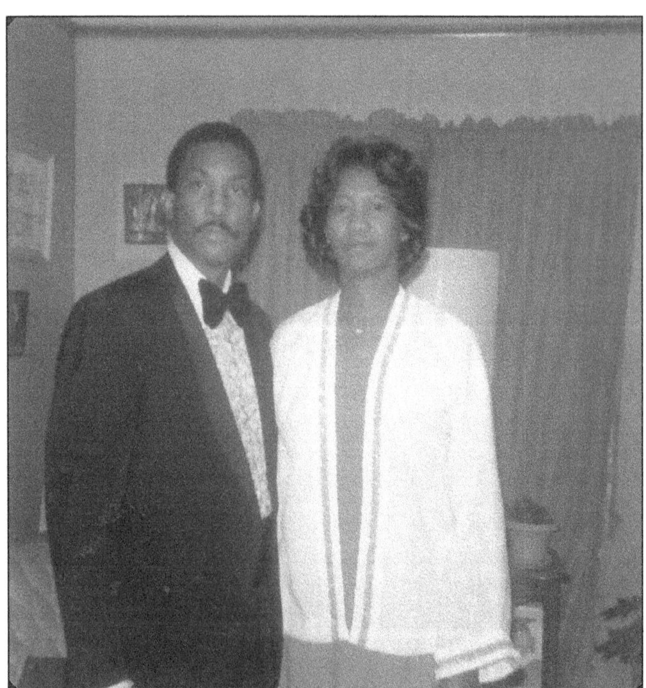

Annie Pearl Smith Taylor, Class of 1951, and James Oscar Taylor, Class of 1950, married on August 7, 1952. Annie is from Lorman, Mississippi, and James is from Winona, Mississippi.

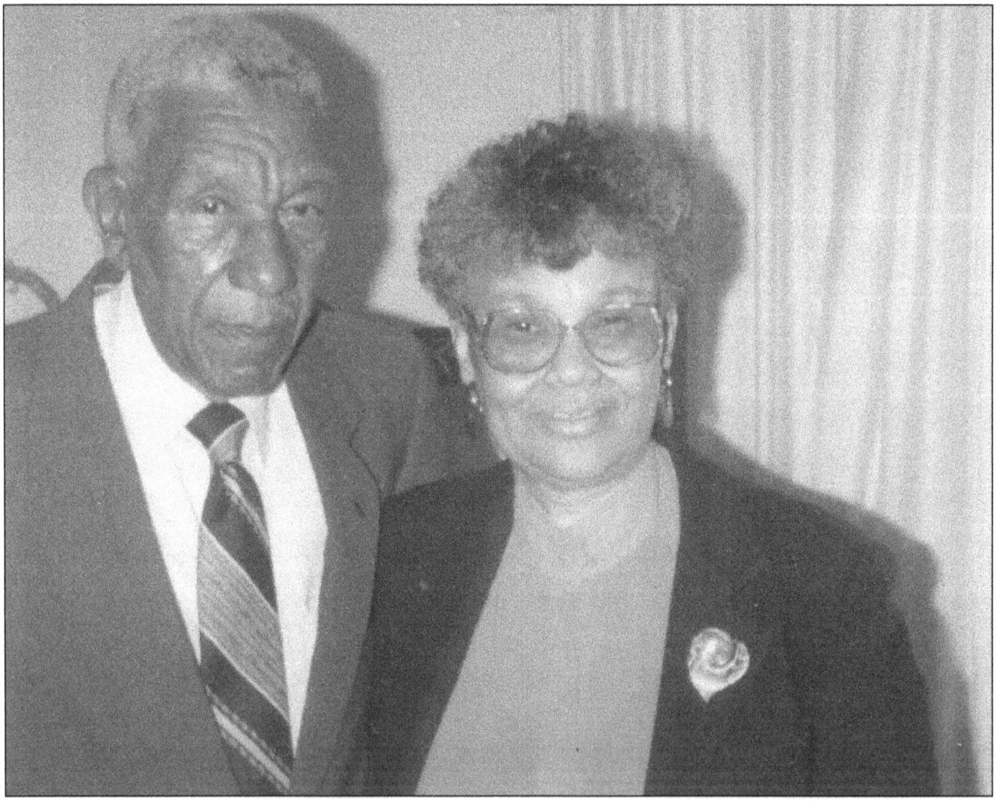

Evelyn R. Palmer, Class of 1945, and Charles W. Palmer, Class of 1948, married on November 19, 1942.

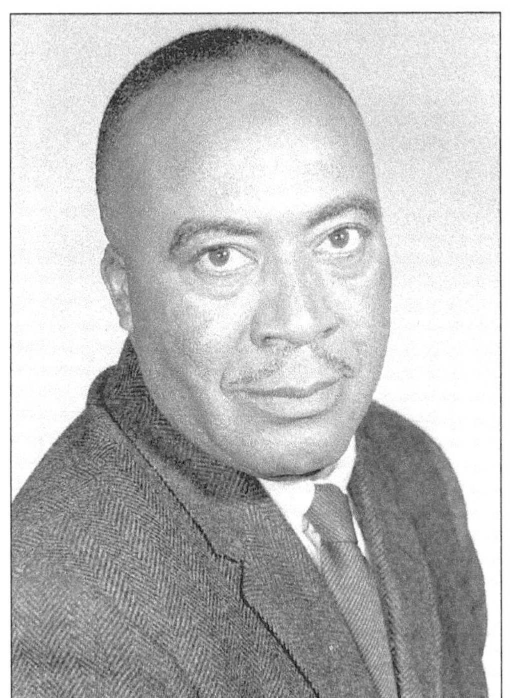
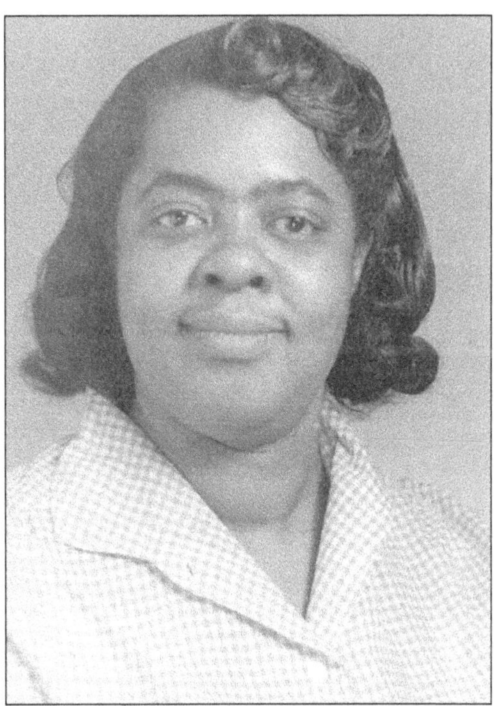
Charles Clark, Class of 1950, married Hazel Clark, Class of 1959, on June 12, 1946.

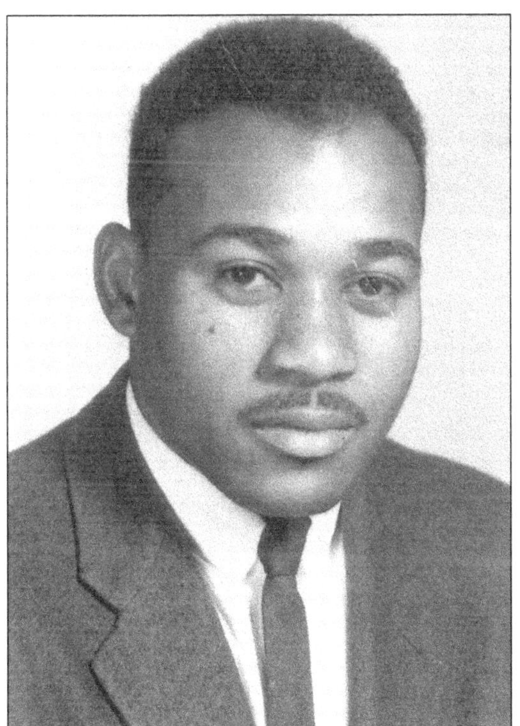
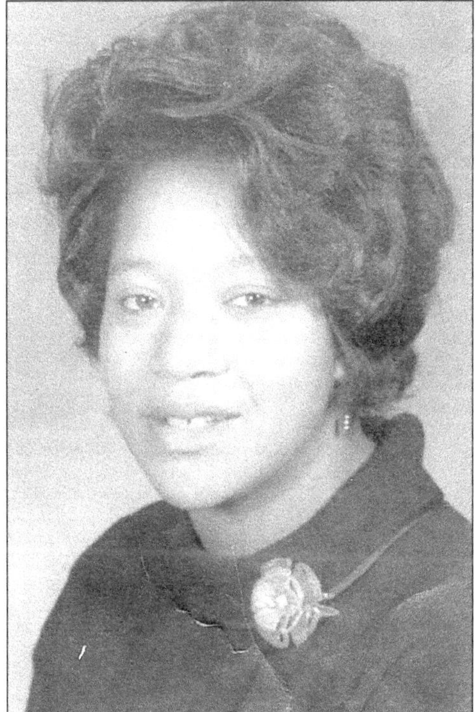
Robert L Smith, Class of 1961, married Georgia Montgomery Smith, Class of 1966, in 1961.

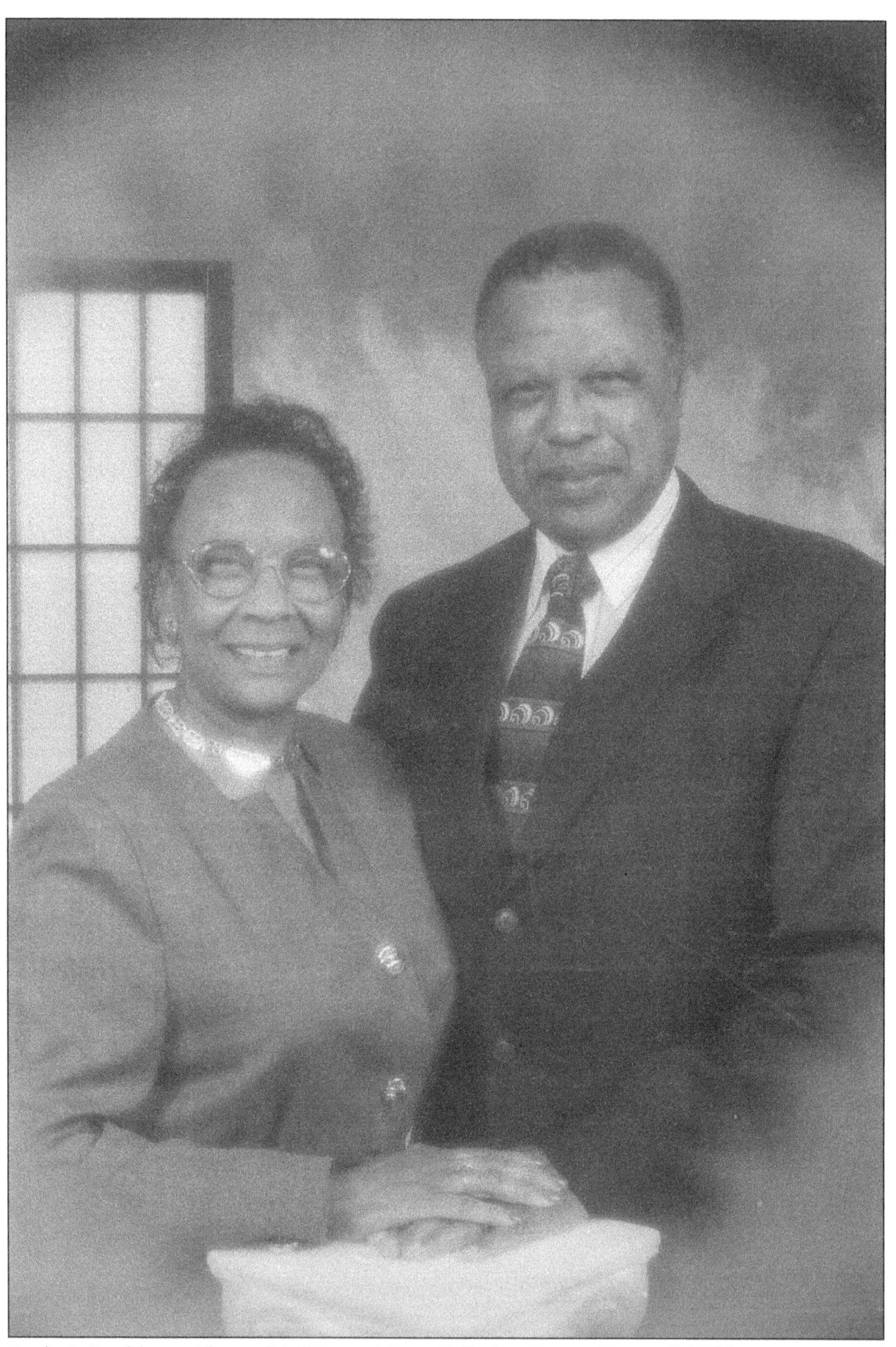

Ruth S. Lockhart, Class of 1958, and Jewell C. Lockhart, Class of 1956, were married on June 8, 1958.

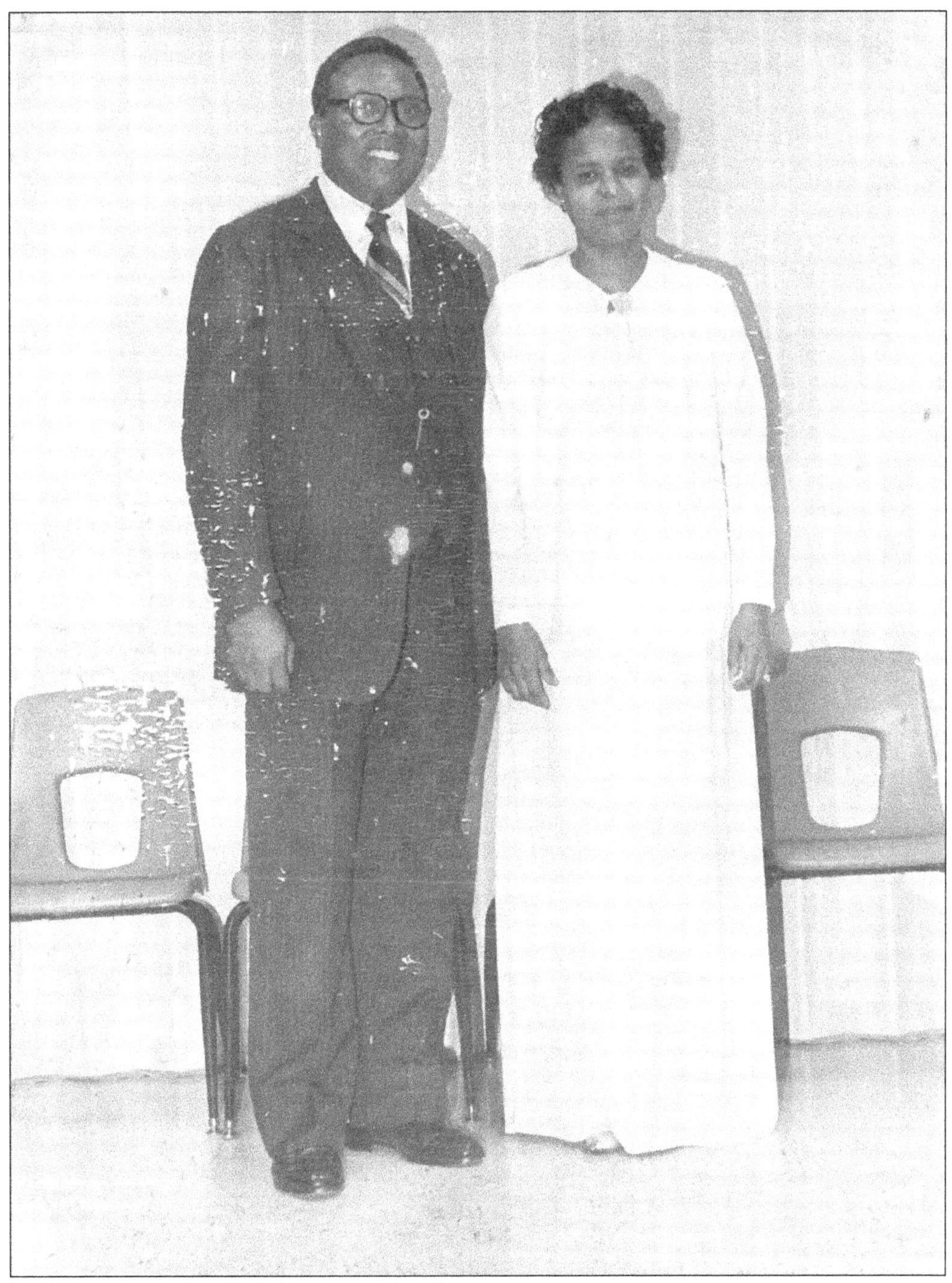

Alpha Lockhart Morris, Class of 1952, and Jesse A. Morris, Class of 1950, married on December 25, 1952.

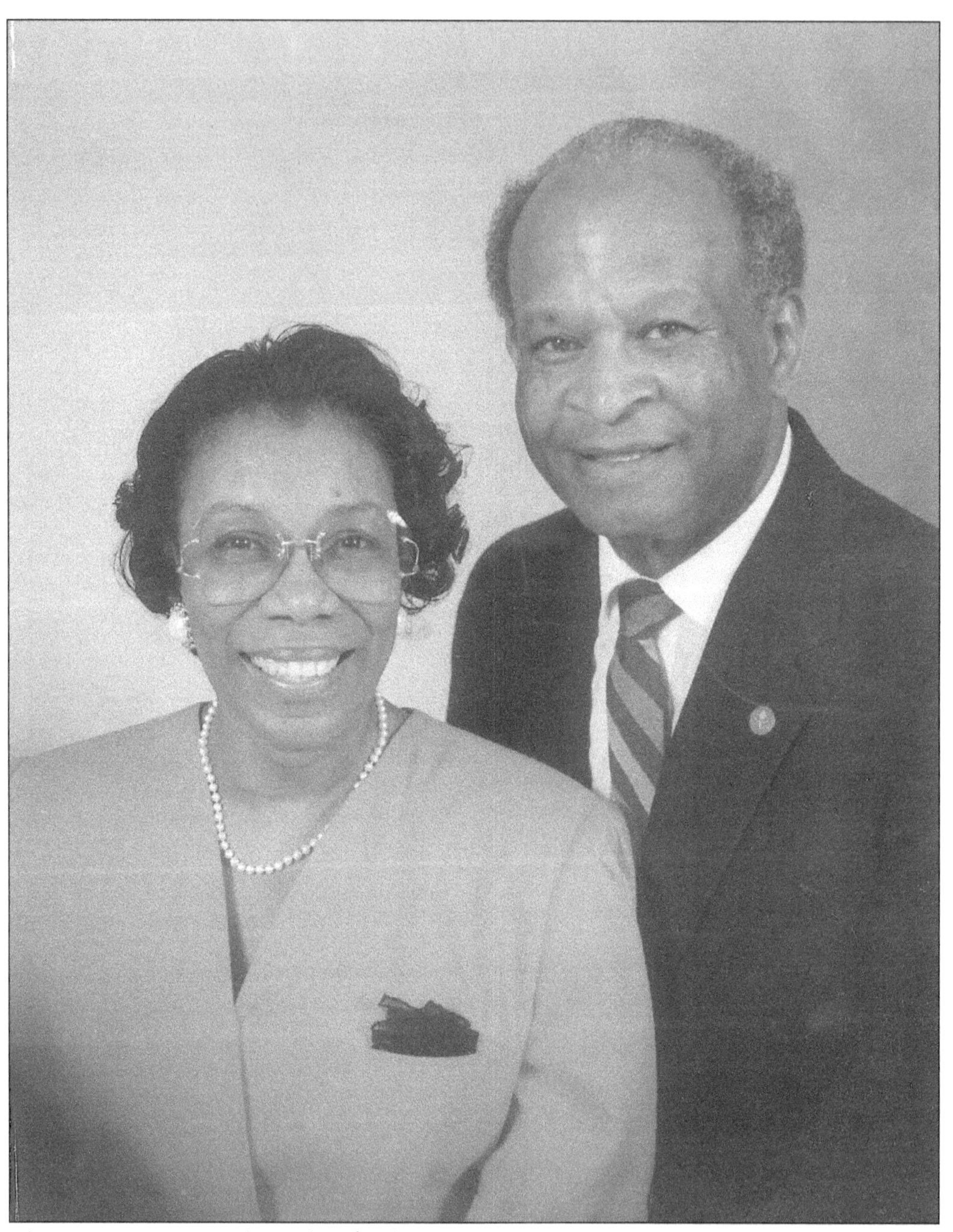

Christine Simmons, Class of 1961, from Winter Park, Florida, and Kenneth Simmons, Class of 1956, from Canton, Mississippi, married on December 30, 1956.

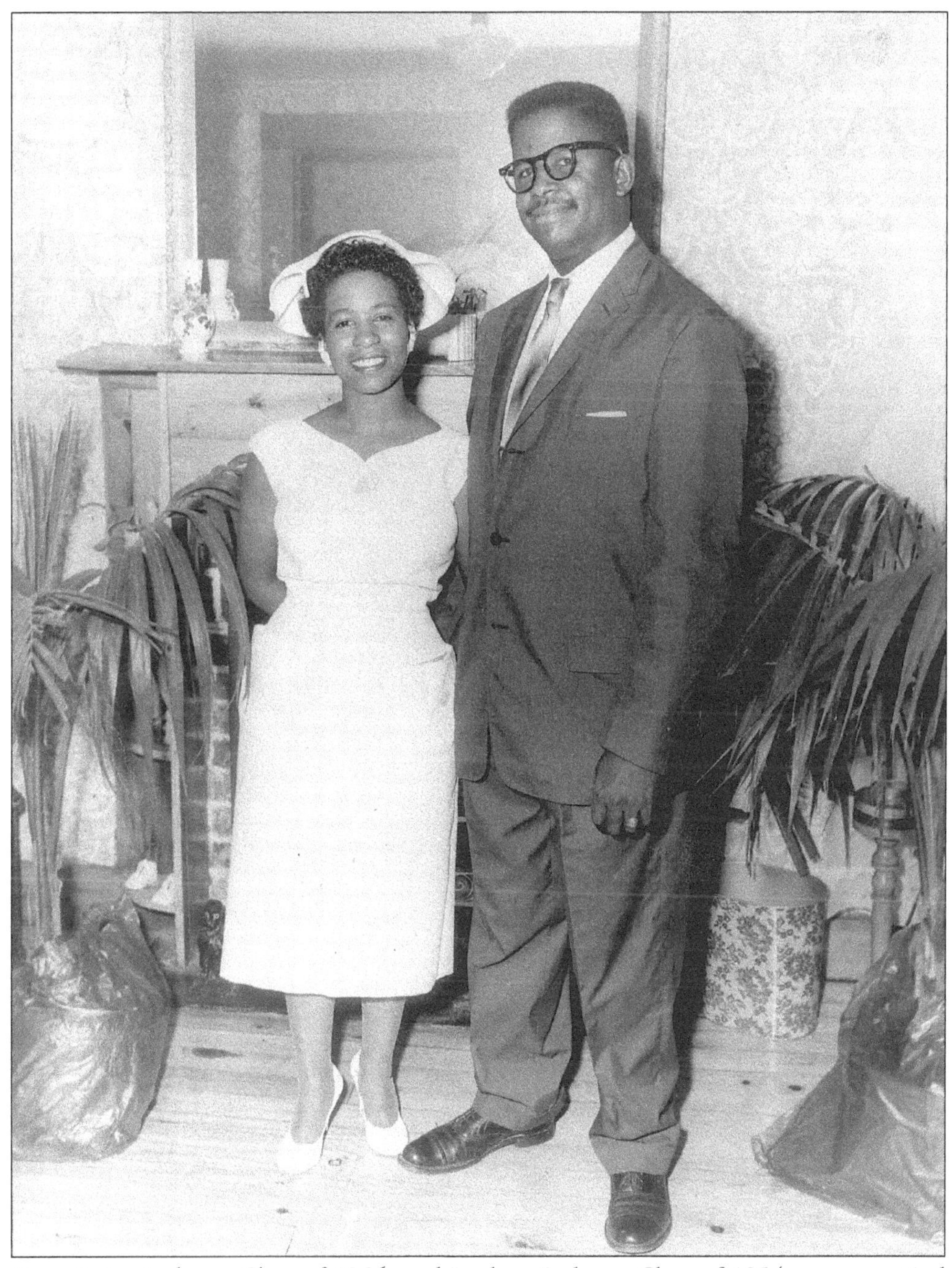

Mary Goins Jackson, Class of 1956, and Laplose Jackson, Class of 1954, were married on May 27, 1958.

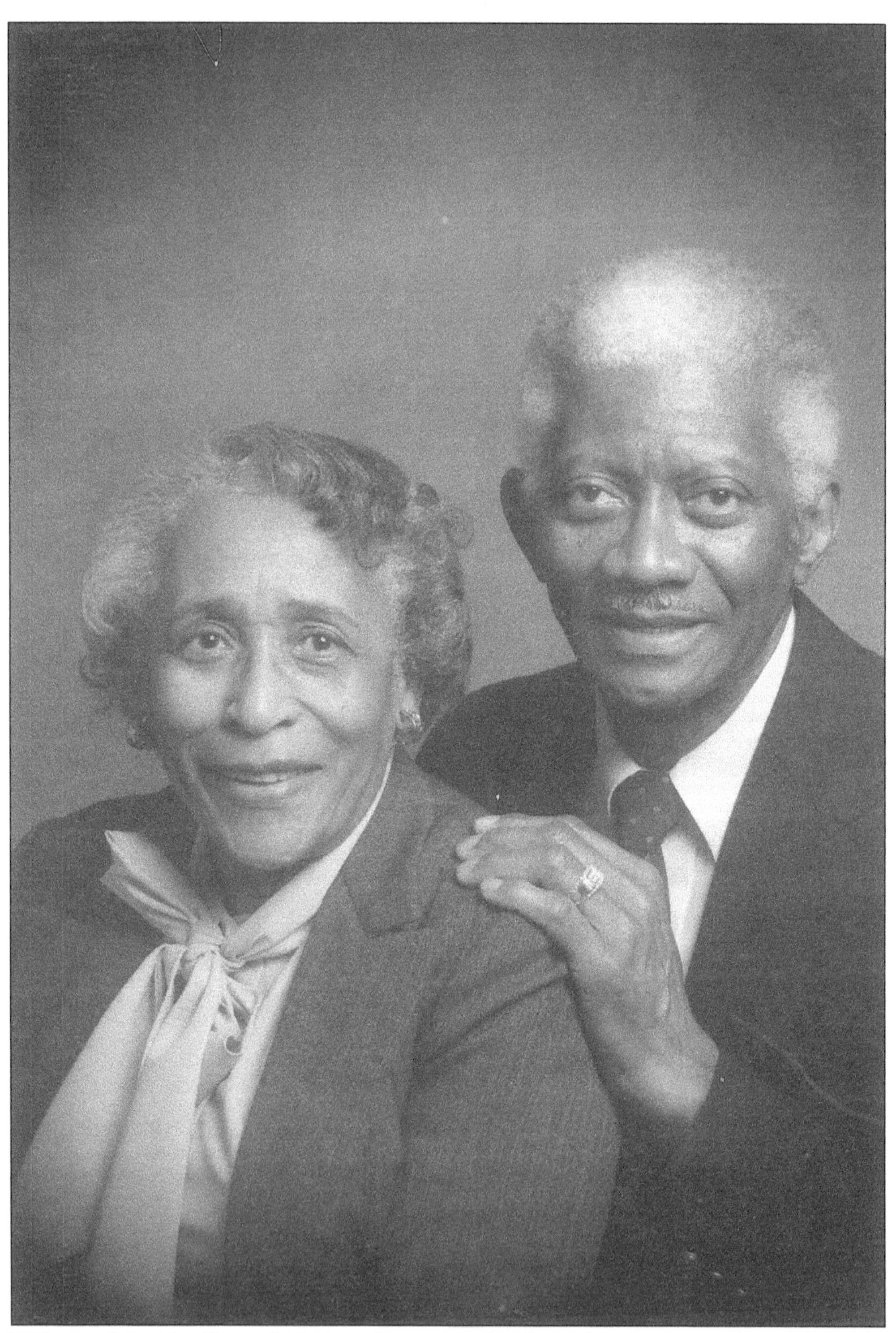

Willa Pearl Smith, Class of 1940, and H.R. Smith, Class of 1940, married in 1943.

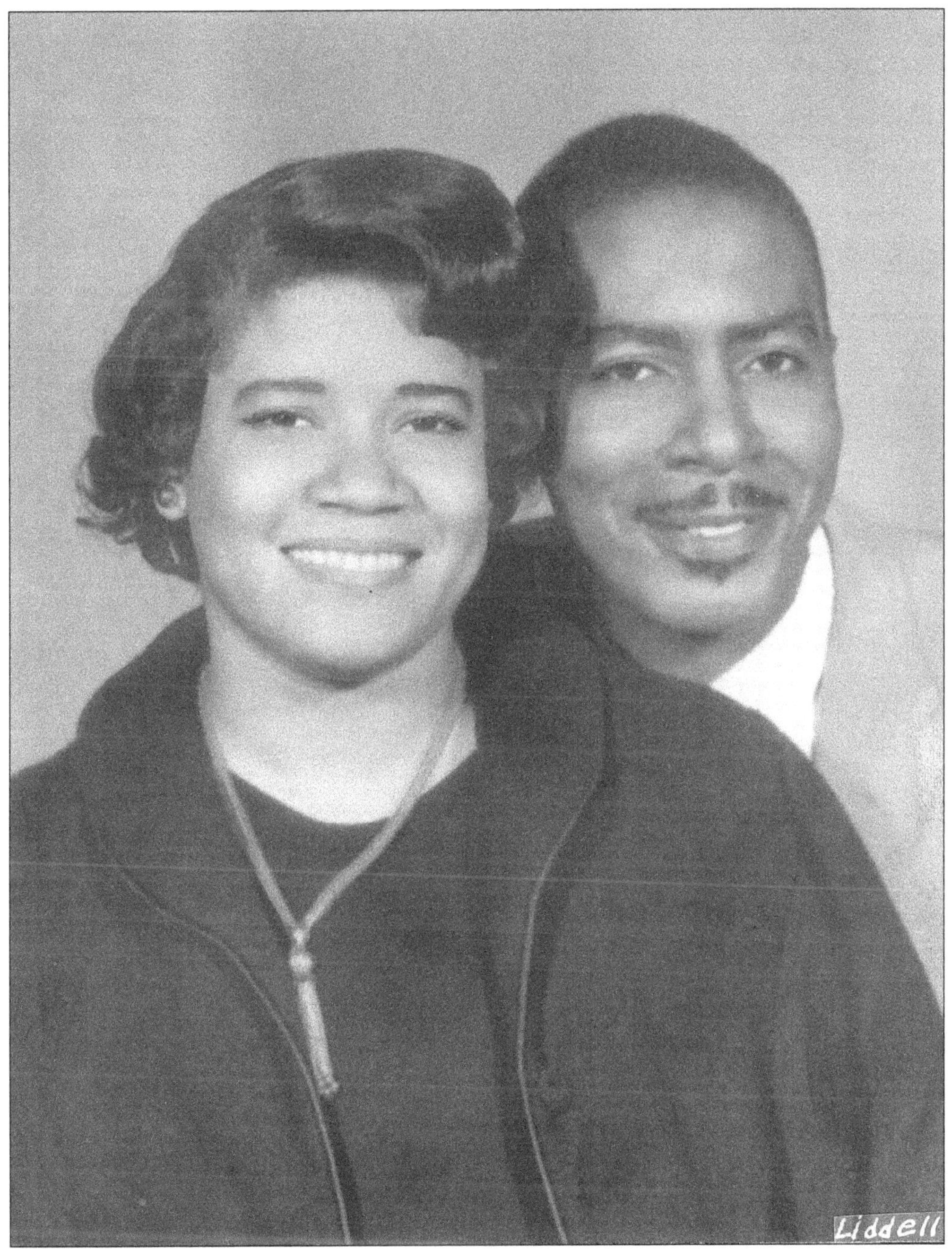

Henrienne Dunbar Heidelberg, Class of 1956, from Lorman, Mississippi, and Julius C. Heidelberg, Class of 1957, from Laurel, Mississippi, married on August 27, 1956.

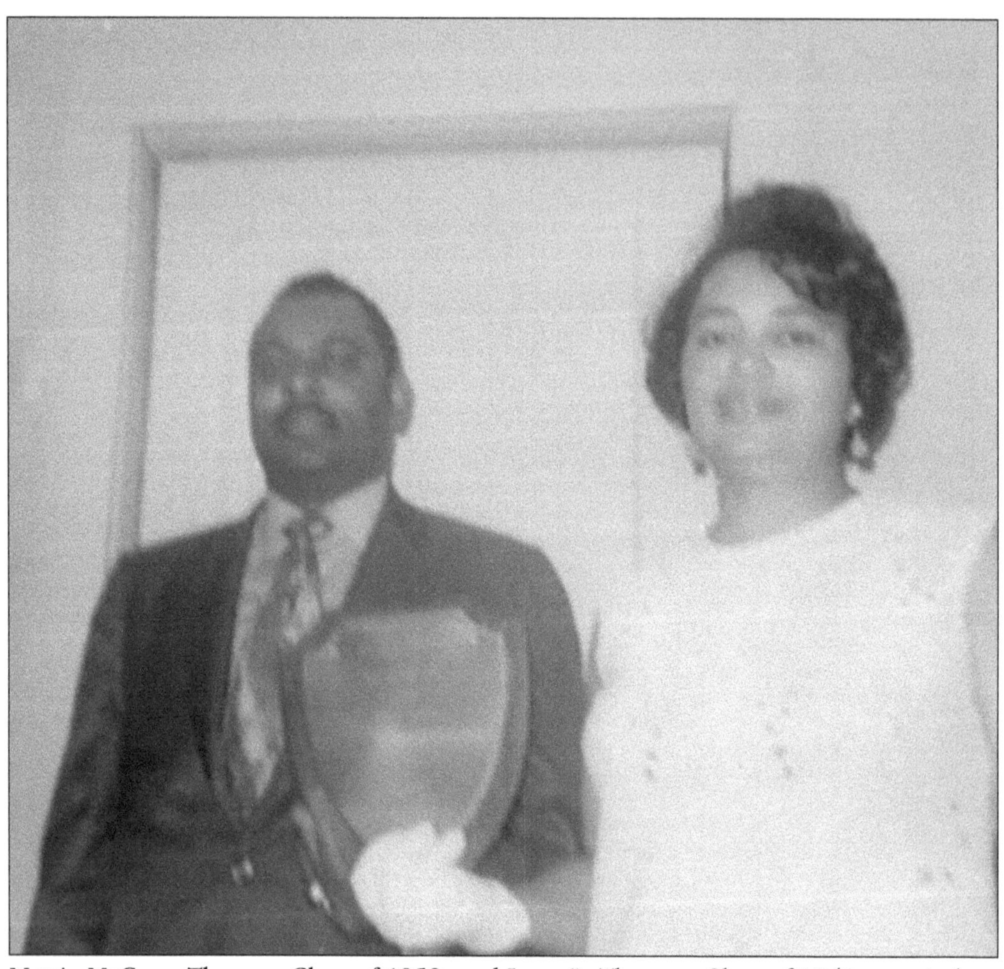

Mattie McCann Thomas, Class of 1952, and Isaac L. Thomas, Class of 1942, married on December 21, 1952.

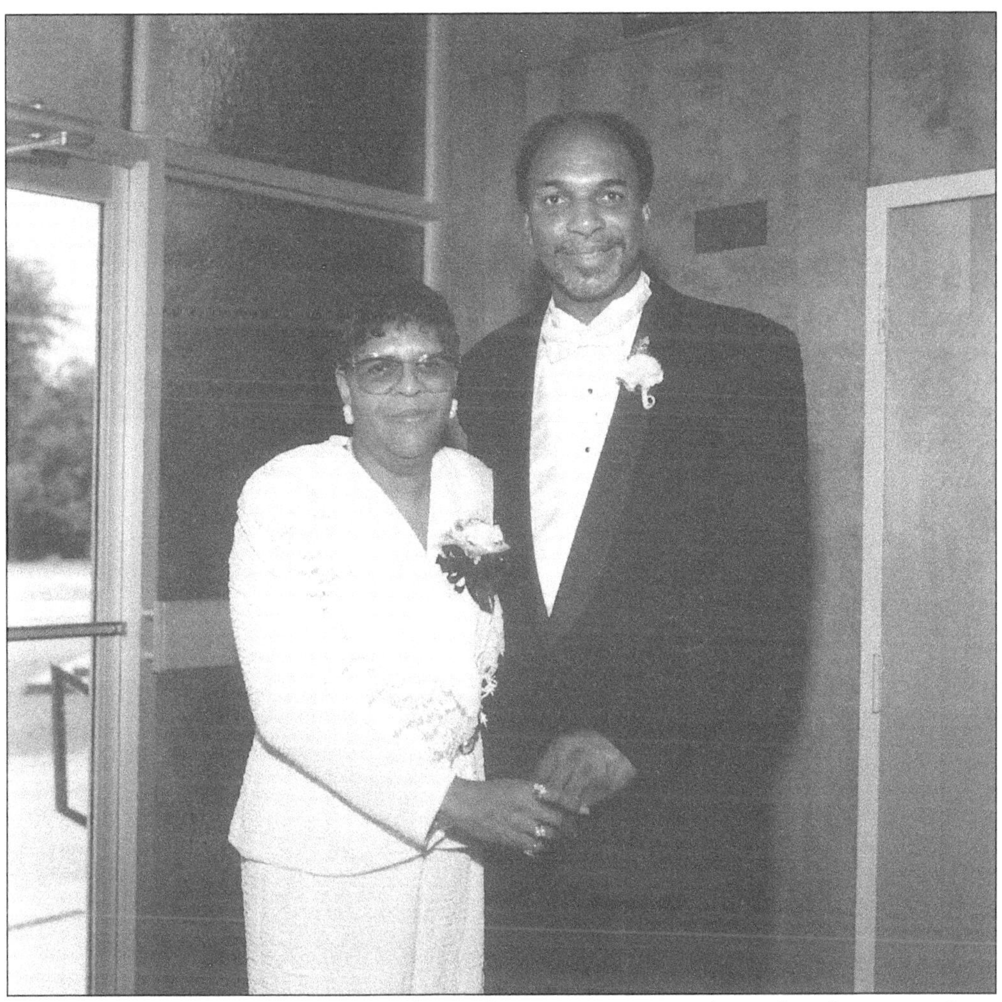

Mildred Diggs Bogan, Class of 1961, and Vernon Bogan, Class of 1962, married on December 23, 1961.

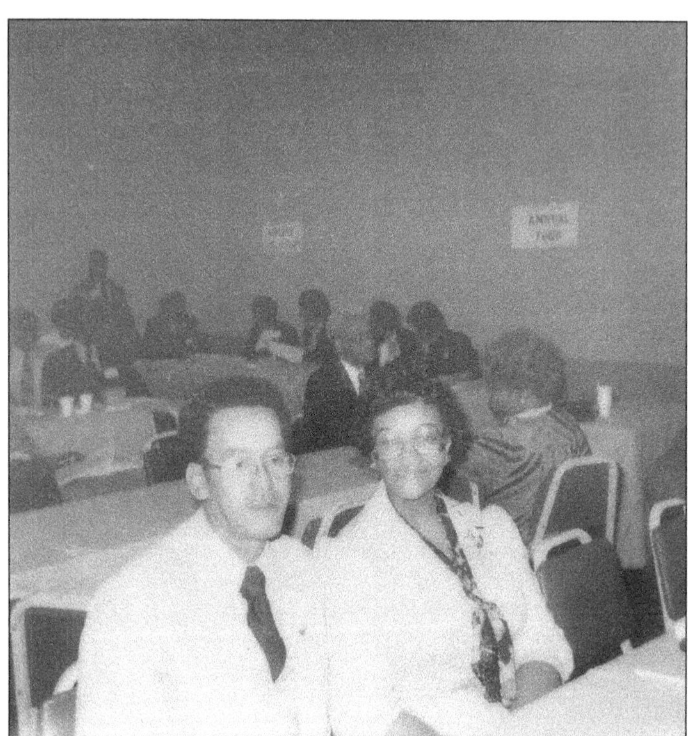

Vera Hendricks Bryant, Class of 1957, and Melvin Bryant, Class of 1956, married on June 7, 1959.

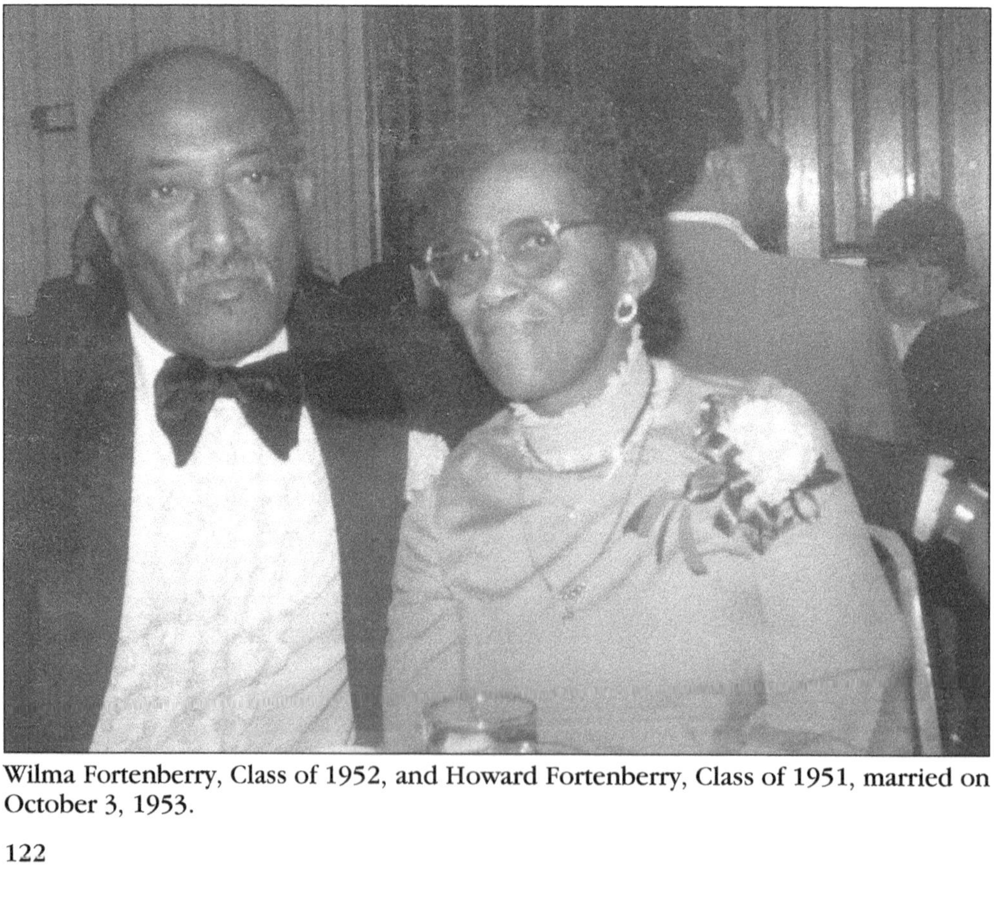

Wilma Fortenberry, Class of 1952, and Howard Fortenberry, Class of 1951, married on October 3, 1953.

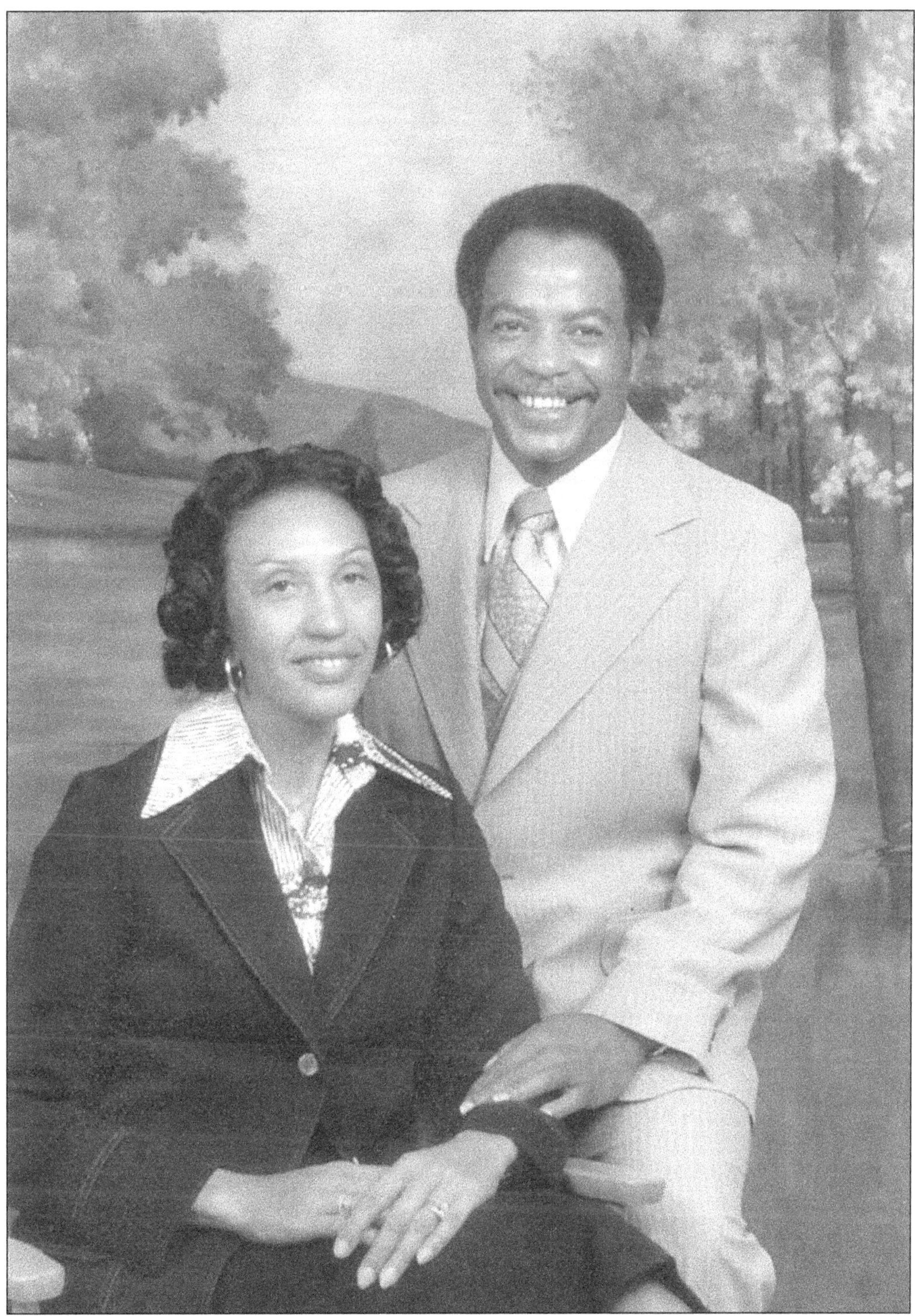

Madeline Hudson Robinson, Class of 1959, and Johnny Robinson, Class of 1959, married on April 4, 1958.

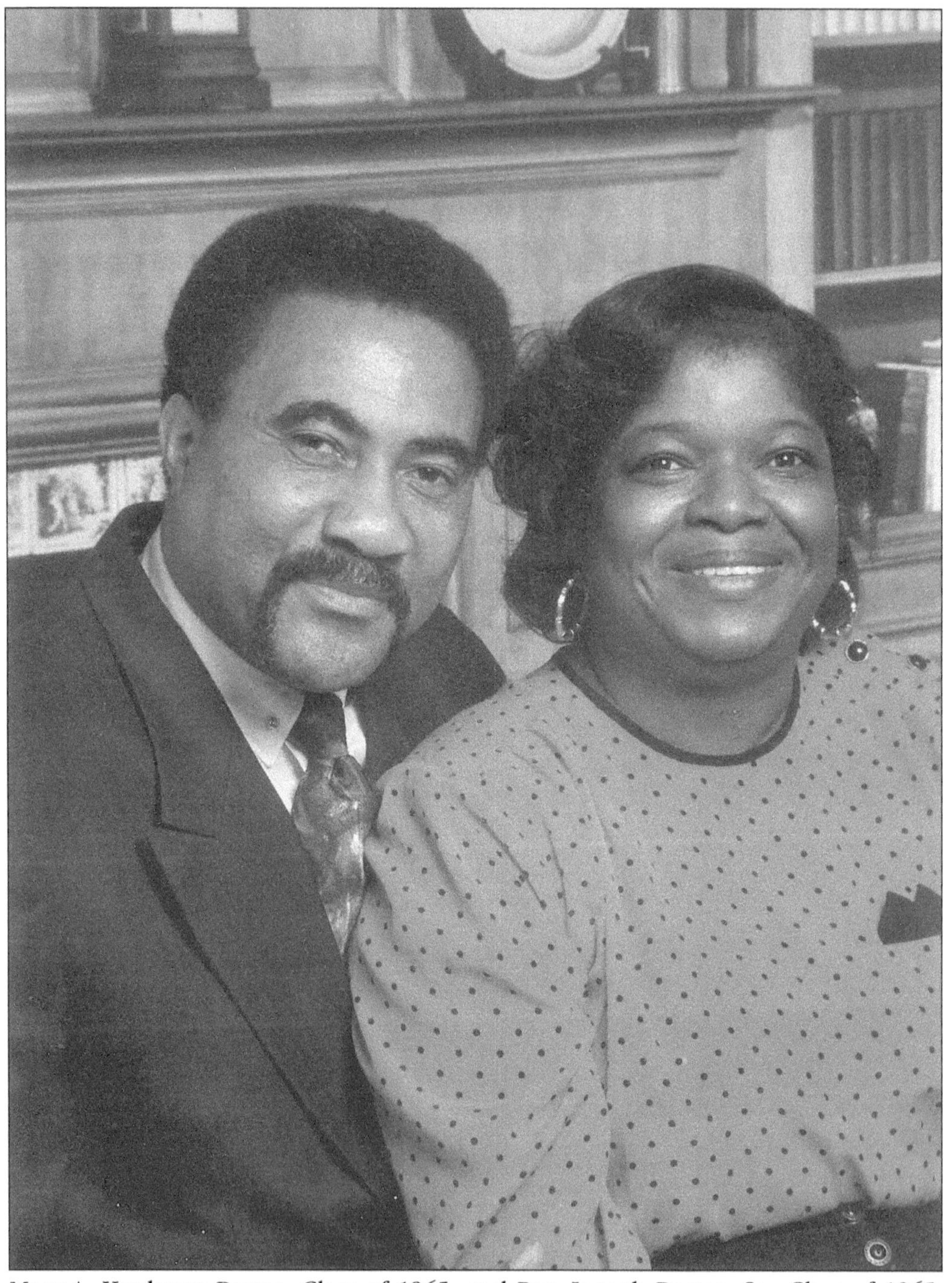

Mary A. Hardaway Bartee, Class of 1965, and Rev. Joseph Bartee, Sr., Class of 1965, married on September 12, 1965.

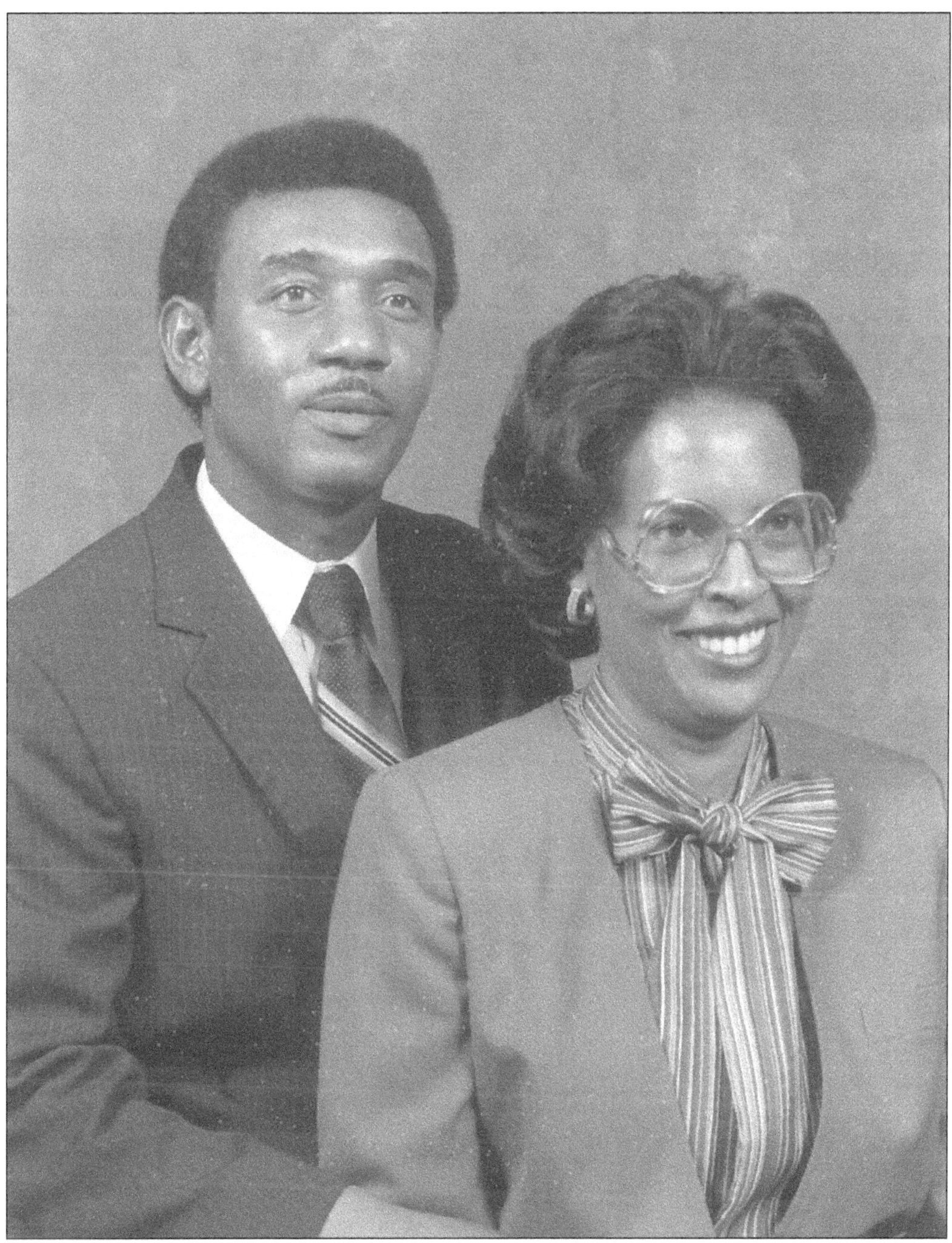

Lillie Hoskins, Class of 1964, and Willie Hoskins, Class of 1963, were married in August 1962.

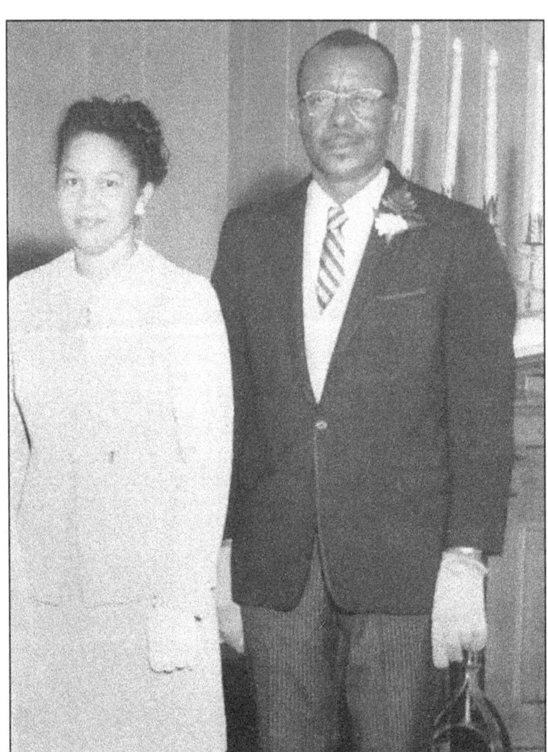

Lelia M. Johnson Ware, Class of 1950, and Floyd S. Ware Sr., Class of 1951, married in 1948.

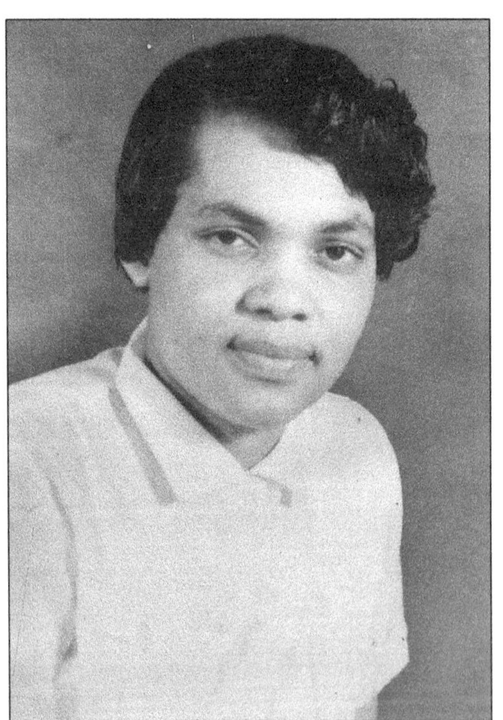

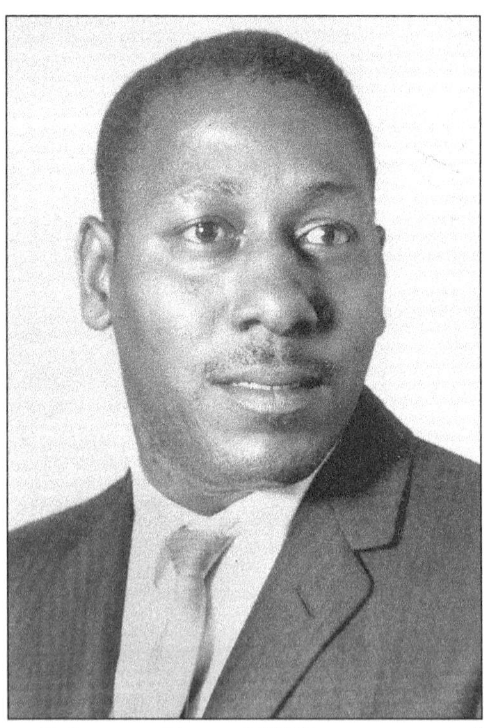

Bernadine Coleman, Class of 1956, and Henry Coleman, Class of 1957, were married in 1958.

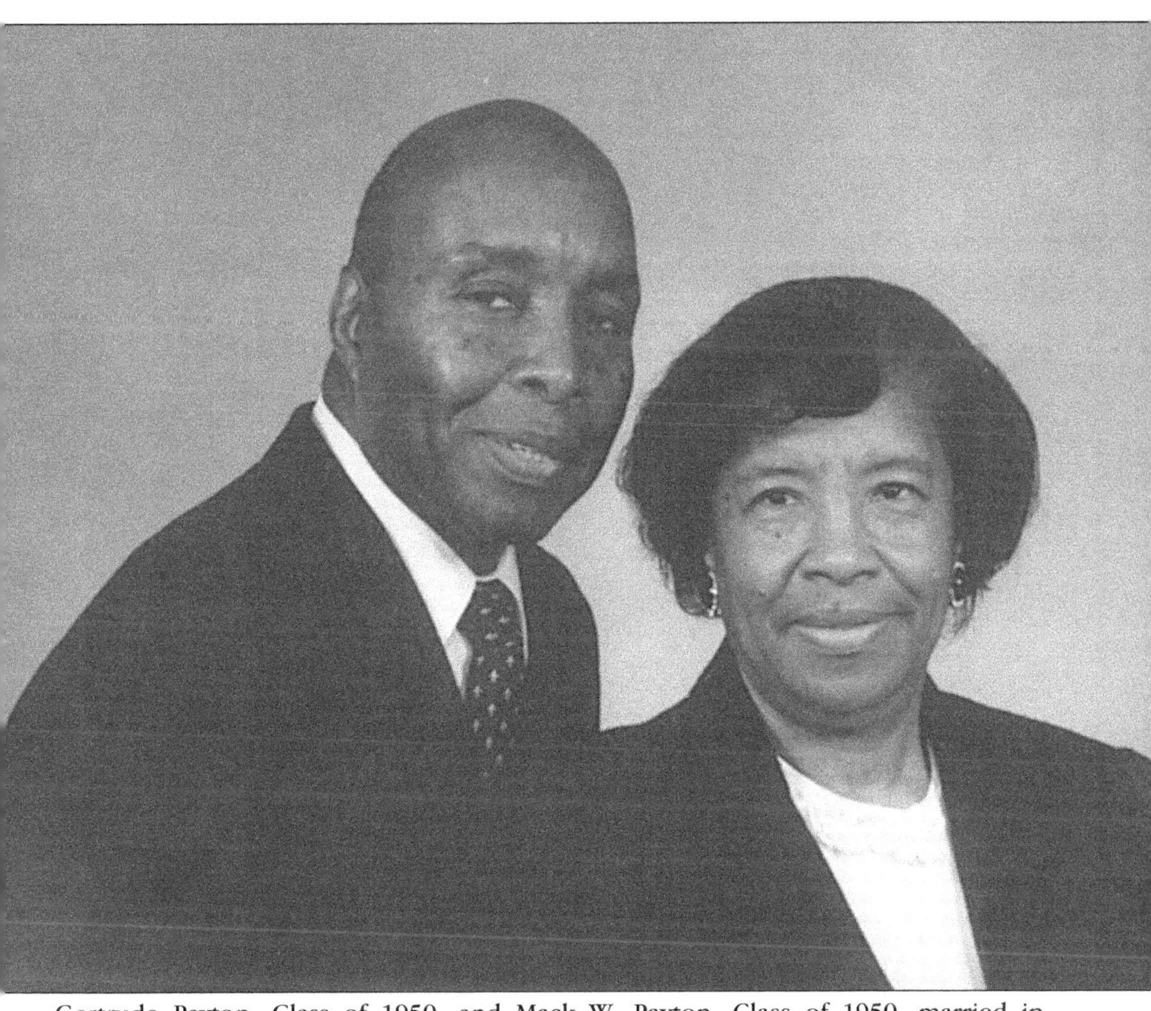

Gertrude Payton, Class of 1950, and Mack W. Payton, Class of 1950, married in September 1947.

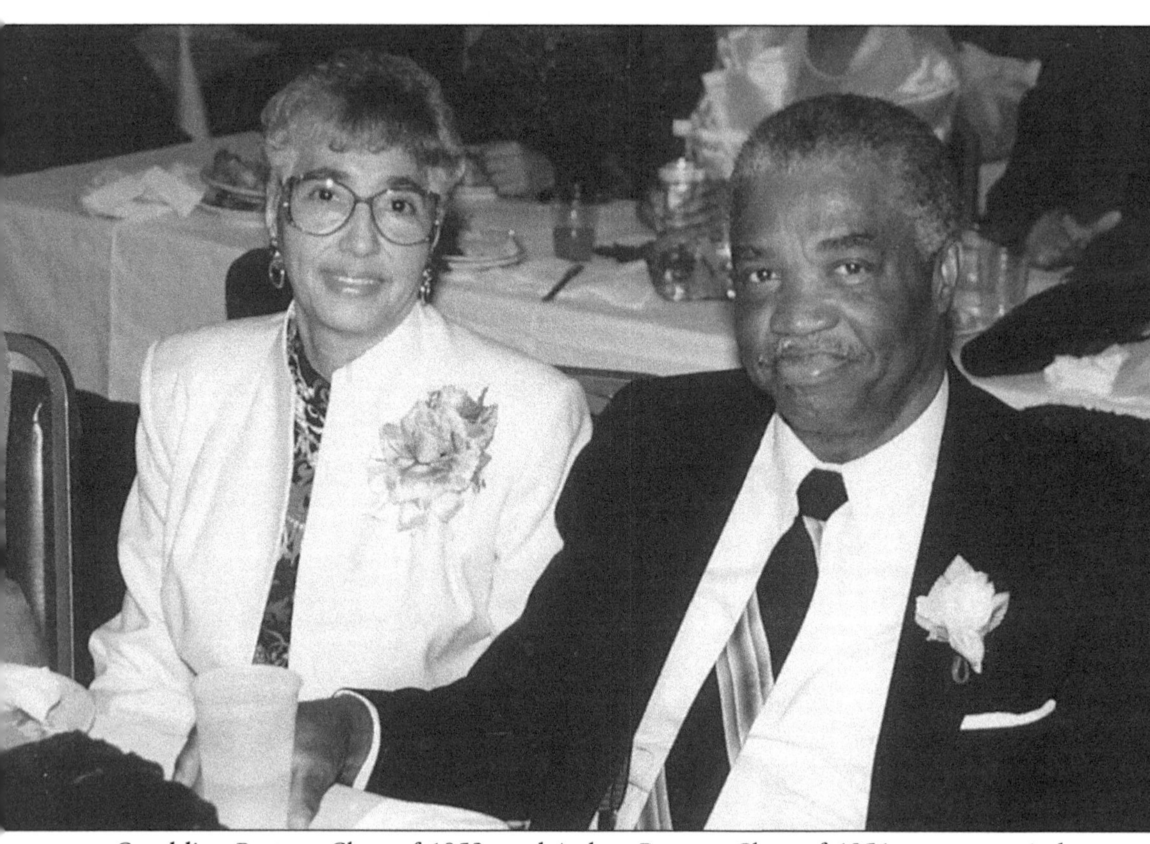

Geraldine Peyton, Class of 1953, and Arthur Peyton, Class of 1951, were married on April 29, 1951.

www.ingramcontent.com/pod-product-compliance
Lightning Source LLC
LaVergne TN
LVHW060624110826
845147LV00015B/928

* 9 7 8 0 7 3 8 5 0 5 9 1 6 *